BEYOND DOUBT

SECULAR STUDIES
General Editor: Phil Zuckerman

Beyond Doubt

The Secularization of Society

Isabella Kasselstrand,
Phil Zuckerman, *and*
Ryan T. Cragun

NEW YORK UNIVERSITY PRESS
New York

NEW YORK UNIVERSITY PRESS
New York
www.nyupress.org

References to Internet websites (URLs) were accurate at the time of writing. Neither the author nor New York University Press is responsible for URLs that may have expired or changed since the manuscript was prepared.

Please contact the Library of Congress for Cataloging-in-Publication data.
ISBN: 9781479814251 (hardback)
ISBN: 9781479814282 (paperback)
ISBN: 9781479814305 (library ebook)
ISBN: 9781479814299 (consumer ebook)

New York University Press books are printed on acid-free paper, and their binding materials are chosen for strength and durability. We strive to use environmentally responsible suppliers and materials to the greatest extent possible in publishing our books.

Manufactured in the United States of America

10 9 8 7 6 5 4 3 2 1

Also available as an ebook

CONTENTS

Introduction

Setting the Stage

"I just got off the phone with God."

It was around thirty years ago, and one of the authors—Phil—was in graduate school at the University of Oregon, working towards his PhD in sociology, with an emphasis on the sociological study of religion. One spring day, while walking across the grassy quad in front of the building that housed the sociology department, he ran into Professor Marion Goldman, one of his mentors, and casually asked her how things were going. It was then that she made the notable comment about her phone conversation with The Almighty.

"You were talking to God?" Phil asked bemusedly.

"Yes," she replied. "That is to say, I just got off the phone with Rodney Stark."

Her meaning was clear: Professor Rodney Stark was *huge*. For sociologists of religion back in the 1990s, he was a truly formidable figure, being one of the most prolific and prominent scholars in the discipline. Rodney Stark's books and articles were widely read, widely discussed, and widely assigned to both undergraduates and graduates. His academic stature was—as Phil's mentor quipped—veritably godlike.

A long-time professor at the University of Washington before moving to Baylor University in 2004, Professor Stark is the author or co-author of over 140 scholarly articles and over 30 books, including *The Future of Religion* (1985), *The Churching of America* (1992), *The Rise of Christianity* (1996) and *Acts of Faith* (2000)—the first two won the Distinguished Book Award from the Society for the Scientific Study of Religion. His influence on the sociological study of religion has been immense; he's written about a lot of topics of significance over the years, including religious conversion, sects and cults, rational choice theory, the history of Christianity, Mormonism, monotheism, religion and deviance, and so on.

One of his most prominent arguments to emerge within this lengthy and productive career—an argument that he developed both theoretically and empirically in various writings spanning decades, and which came to be supported by a range of prominent scholars churning out a vast body of publications—concerns the matter of secularization.

Secularization Theory's Origins

Towards the end of the nineteenth century, as sociology was coming into its own as a discipline, many leading intellectuals observed—and wrote extensively about—the significance of religion as a social phenomenon.[1] But they also sensed that religion's influence and even presence in society was on the wane.[2] For example, Auguste Comte (1798–1857) predicted that as societies progressed and matured, they would lose their superstitious beliefs and religious frames of reference and instead become characterized by more scientific, positivistic worldviews. Jean Marie Guyau (1854–1888), in his unambiguously-titled 1886 treatise *The Non-Religion of the Future,* predicted the imminent "dissolution" of religion, the inevitable fading of religious faith, and the ultimate ascendancy of scientific views over religious dogma. Max Weber (1864–1920) wrote of the growing "disenchantment" or "demagicalization" of the world as rationality becomes increasingly dominant in bureaucratic, industrialized society.[3] Emile Durkheim (1858–1917) alluded to the dying out of "old gods,"[4] and described religion's significance in the modern world as "continually diminishing."[5]

As the twentieth century unfolded, most social scientists agreed that religion was, in fact, on the decline; the secularization of society was almost unanimously taken for granted by those paying attention. In the words of leading American sociologist C. Wright Mills, writing in 1959: "the forces of modernization [have] swept across the globe and secularization . . . loosened the dominance of the sacred. In due course, the sacred shall disappear altogether except, possibly, in the private realm."[6] Or as Bryan Wilson pronounced in his 1966 book *Religion in Secular Society,* religion's weakened influence in society "is simply taken as fact,"[7] and as modern societies advance, the result is "the decline of religious values . . . and the impact of religious institutions in public life."[8] Various other like-minded scholars further observed, described, and discussed the secularization of society in numerous well-known books, such as Harvey Cox's (1965) *The Secular City*, Peter Berger's (1967) *The Sacred Canopy*, David Martin's (1978) *A General Theory of Secularization*, and Philip Hammond's (1985) *The Sacred in a Secular Age*, in which it was stated as a sociological given that religion was fading in contemporary society: "whereas legitimate authority once depended on religious sanctions; whereas social control once relied heavily on religiously defined rewards and punishments; whereas social policies . . . at one time needed supernatural endorsement . . . and whereas revealed faith once specified the boundaries of true learning—now, all these functions have been superseded . . . Religion has lost its presidency over other institutions."[9]

Beginning in the late 1980s, Rodney Stark stepped into this taken-for-granted discussion of secularization and—well, frankly—called bullshit. For Stark, secularization had actually *not* occurred. He argued that despite all the prognosticating of so many sociologists over the decades, religion was as strong as ever—maybe even stronger. In his view, better theorizing and clear-eyed analysis of existing data revealed that secularization theory had, in fact, been "falsified."[10] As he declared in 1996, "the so-called secularization thesis is simply wrong."[11] Since secularization hadn't occurred, it was a worthless concept; the very term itself, Stark urged, ought to be scrapped altogether.[12] In his unequivocally-titled article "Secularization, R.I.P.," published in the 1999 volume of the journal *Sociology of Religion*, Stark declared that the entire secularization thesis—the very premise that religion has weakened, diminished, or faded over time—ought to be carried to "the graveyard of failed theories."[13]

Contra Secularization

To be sure, Stark was not alone in his unflinching rejection of secularization theory. There were others, over the years, who also criticized the large body of work attesting to a presumed weakening or fading of religion in society over time. For example, back in the early 1970s, Andrew Greeley had argued that "there is no real reason to believe that the supernatural is any more absent or remote from the horizons of everyday life of most people today than it was six thousand years ago."[14] Furthermore, according to Greeley, humans' basic, inherent religious needs "have not changed very noticeably since the late Ice Age."[15] Offering a similar take, Robert Bellah characterized his sociological view as being "as contrary to so-called secularization theory as is humanly possible"; Bellah dismissed the presumed decline or diminishing of religion in modern society as an unsubstantiated "myth," and insisted that religion consistently remains at the "center of our cultural preoccupations."[16] In the 1980s, Jeffrey Hadden argued that there was no convincing evidence that religiosity had declined, and those social scientists who saw secularization occurring only did so because it fit their personal ideological views.[17] In the early 1990s, Stephen Warner confirmed that secularization theory "does not seem to work."[18] And none other than the eminent Peter Berger—who decades earlier had written a classic articulation of secularization theory—joined the secularization denial bandwagon, claiming that secularization theory "has been falsified with a vengeance,"[19] "is essentially mistaken" and that "the world is as furiously religious as it ever was."[20] In the early 2000s, Philip Gorski and Ates Altinordu argued that it was time to move past the basic assumptions of secularization theory, given that religion was "surging" and "flourishing" throughout most of the world,[21] while co-authors Kevin Christiano, William Swatos, and Peter Kivisto[22] mockingly characterized secularization theory as a "religion" in and of itself—that is—an idea or belief not grounded in empirical fact, but held to be true by data-denying believers who ideologically cling to some notion of the world despite evidence to the contrary.

Professor Stark's work bolstered these voices critical of secularization; he took their skeptical notions and ran with them—or rather—sprinted.

In Stark's extensive theorizing, secularization does not occur—and, in fact, *cannot* occur—because religion addresses certain fundamental human needs that are always in demand. It works like this: the special ingredient that makes religion "religion," is supernatural assumptions; as Stark and his co-author, William Sims Bainbridge, assert, "a religion lacking supernatural assumptions is no religion at all."[23] The supernatural beliefs people hold—such as belief in gods, transmigrating souls, miracles, heavens, hells, etc.—are uniquely potent because, in Stark's view, they provide strongly desired ideological compensation to people who will always seek existential answers and comfort in the face of mortality. "Only the gods," Stark and Bainbridge write, "can assure us that

X — understand that is limited to 1 life

suffering in this life will be compensated in the next [and] . . . only the gods can offer a next life."[24]

Thus, religions are defined as "human organizations primarily engaged in providing general compensators based on supernatural assumptions."[25] And here's the thing: this human desire for such religious compensation is, according to Stark and his like-minded colleagues, pretty much universal and constant. As such, secularization never gets very far; it is self-limiting,[26] with instances of apparent religious decline always giving way to religious revival and innovation.[27] And so, according to Stark, while some aspects of religion may sporadically decrease here and there, in this or that part of a given society, "a countervailing intensification of religion goes on in other parts."[28] Thus, even if the specific manifestations of religion may shift or decline now and then, "the amount of religion remains relatively constant."[29]

Likening the religious landscape in society to an economic marketplace,[30] Stark and his various co-authors, such as Roger Finke and Laurence Iannaccone, argued that if religion happens to seem weak or muted in a given society, it is simply because the existing "firms" in that society—that is, the religious organizations—are not doing a good enough job meeting the human demand for supernatural compensators. And that demand doesn't change much, but rather, is "very stable over time."[31] Thus, if religious organizations grow lazy—usually because they are supported by the government or because they hold a monopoly on the religious marketplace without much in the way of competition from other religions—then it is possible for religiosity to become temporarily anemic. But all it takes is a little savvy marketing on the part of religious organizations—often spurred on by competition from others—and religiosity will be readily rekindled, keeping religion strong, stable, constant, and pervasive in society.[32]

Given the above perspective, Stark insisted that any claim that religion has diminished over time—secularization's main premise—is not based on a proper understanding of religious dynamics and "isn't supported by the data."[33] In fact, he argued that not only has religion not weakened over time, but it has actually *strengthened*. In some of his writings, Stark argued that people are *more* religious today than they were in the past and, thus, the commonly-held notion that people were more faithful or pious in earlier centuries is a "myth."[34] He and his co-author

Roger Finke maintained that—thanks to innovative marketing strategies by various religious groups—religiosity has *increased* over the course of American history, not declined.[35] Even in Europe, that part of the world most often held up as proof of secularization, Stark claimed that religion has not faded over the centuries, insisting that "there has been no demonstrable long-term decline in European religious participation."[36] Nor has secularization occurred in Asia; Stark maintained that even in Japan, religiosity has shown no signs of declining, characterizing Japanese people as "deeply and very *actively* religious."[37]

In sum, for Stark and his co-authors, since the demand for religion remains relatively stable and constant over time, secularization theory is based on nothing more than "wishful thinking."[38] Indeed, "even the weakest version of secularization," he declared, "fails to find support."[39] As of 2015, Stark has remained intransigent; he proclaimed in his book *The Triumph of Faith* that "the world is . . . much *more* intensely religious than ever before,"[40] and all views to the contrary amount to nothing more than "unfounded nonsense."[41]

As leading sociologist Christian Smith has confidently concluded, "the modern prophets of secularization have largely been proven wrong."[42]

The Situation Today

Secularization theory as unfounded nonsense? Secularization theorists proven wrong?

Really?

It has now been nearly fifty years since Andrew Greeley, Robert Bellah, and a handful of others first argued against the classical secularization paradigm, asserting that religion is as strong and widespread as ever. And it has been some thirty years since Stark and his colleagues broadened and bolstered such assertions by condemning secularization as a failed theory that ought to be summarily laid to rest.

Well, were they correct? Is the secularization of society nothing but a myth? Is the world as religious as ever? Is there no empirical support for the decline of religiosity over time?

No, no, no, and no.

First off, although Stark and his colleagues certainly offered some important critiques of this or that aspect of classical secularization theory, they were ultimately wrong in their central insistence that the demand for religion always remains constant and stable; religiosity *can*—and often *does*—diminish significantly in society. Secondly, far from being a falsified myth, the secularization of many societies is readily observable by numerous objective measures, and the last half century has provided irrefutable examples of both the demonstrable possibility and unambiguous reality of secularization. Third, much of the world is markedly less religious today than it was in the past: religious beliefs, religious practices, and the number of people simply identifying as religious have all plummeted—sometimes dramatically—in many societies. And finally, there exists a plethora of rigorous research and empirical data evidencing the decline of religion in numerous countries over time.

Admittedly, religion has not disappeared. Older predictions that religion would vanish from the face of the earth were clearly half-baked. Much of the world today is still quite religious, and many countries—such as Ethiopia, Bangladesh, and the Philippines—are extremely religious. Furthermore, a minority of societies, such as Latvia, Ukraine, and Moldova, have seen an increase in religiosity over the past several decades. But none of these facts counter the basic, underlying reality that numerous societies around the world today—from Sweden and Scotland to Japan and South Korea, and from Chile and Uruguay to Canada and the United States—are markedly less religious than they were in previous decades. Although not in the exact way or to the extreme degree that certain thinkers of the nineteenth century predicted, much of the world has, nonetheless, secularized.

Consider this assorted spate of journalistic reports from the previous decade. In 2015, *The New York Times* proclaimed, "The Rise of Young Americans Who Don't Believe in God,"[43] *USA Today* declared, "Christians Drop, 'Nones' Soar in New Religion Portrait,"[44] and *The Washington Post* announced, "Nominal Christians Are Becoming More Secular, and That's Creating a Startling Change for the U.S."[45] In 2016, *National Geographic* ran a cover story declaring: "The World's Newest Religion? No Religion," in which it was documented that while "there have long been predictions that religion would fade from relevancy as the world modernizes . . . all the recent surveys are finding that it's happening startlingly fast. France will have a majority secular population soon. So will the Netherlands and New Zealand. The United Kingdom and Australia will soon lose Christian majorities. Religion is rapidly becoming less important than it's ever been, even to people who live in countries where faith has affected everything from rulers to borders to architecture."[46] In the words of a *Religion News Service* headline, "A Majority of People in Scotland Have No Religion."[47] In 2017, *U.S. News and World Report* proclaimed, "Americans are Becoming Less Religious,"[48] *CNN* declared, "Australians Ditch Religion at Rapid Rate,"[49] *Al Jazeera* reported on "Why Young South Koreans Are Turning Away from Religion,"[50] and *The Independent* announced, "Record Number of British People Say They Have No Religion."[51] In 2018, *Scientific American* proclaimed, "The Number of Americans with No Religious Affiliation Is Rising," charting the significant growth of secularity in the United States, and noting that the number of Americans who do not identify with a religion has risen from 36.6 million in 2007 up to 55.8 million a decade later.[52] *The Guardian* ran this bold headline: "Christianity as Default Is Gone: The Rise of a Non-Christian Europe,"[53] reporting that a majority of young adults in many countries in Europe do not self-identify as religious, do not attend religious services, and do not pray. *American Quarterly* reported that Chile "has become increasingly secular."[54] In 2019, *CNN* proclaimed, "There Are Now as Many Americans Who Claim No Religion as There Are Evangelicals and Catholics,"[55] *The Atlantic* declared that in the late twentieth century "America Lost Its Religion,"[56] *FiveThirtyEight* announced, "Millennials Are Leaving Religion and Not Coming Back,"[57] the *CBC* announced "Canada Set to Lose 9,000 Churches,"[58] and according to *The Guardian*, "Faith in Religion Is Dwindling,"[59] while *BBC* asked "Are Arabs Turning Their Backs on Religion?"[60]

And so on.

The above headlines—while far from comprehensive—constitute an illustrative indication of what has been happening to religion in many nations around the world: it has been declining. To be sure, such secularization isn't merely something that journalists are pronouncing; social scientists are documenting it, as well. For example, the scholarly work of Callum Brown,[61] Darren Sherkat,[62] Steve Bruce,[63] David Voas,[64] Ariela Keysar,[65] Mark Chaves,[66] Sarah Wilkins-Laflamme,[67] as well as the authors of this book,[68] all document the current reality of secularization. Indeed, both sociological works and the newspaper articles cited above are based on rich and robust sources of empirical data. And it is this data that we will present throughout the chapters ahead—all attesting to the secularization of many societies around the world.

Defining Religion

In order to develop the main thesis of this book—that religion has diminished significantly in many societies, and thus secularization has, in fact, occurred—we need to define our terms.

Let's start with religion, a notoriously difficult phenomenon to define.[69] Rather than delve into and wade through the long and tortured discussions and debates about how best to define religion—something already undertaken by many others elsewhere[70]—we're just going to directly lay it out. We define religion as *the amalgamation of ideas, rituals, practices, symbols, identities, and institutions that humans collectively construct based upon their shared belief in the supernatural*. As is apparent, we agree with Stark that some element of supernatural assumption is central to the religious enterprise; whether it is a belief in the existence of a god or gods, or in transmigrating souls, or angels and demons, or ancestral spirits, or other realms of existence beyond this known universe, or past lives, or future lives—faith in that which cannot be empirically proven, but is taken for granted by believers as real and true, is the distinguishing hallmark of religious life. There are certainly many other important aspects of religion, such as cultural aspects, emotional aspects, and—as we have included in our definition—ritual aspects and institutional aspects. But all of these revolve around a set of established supernatural beliefs. Hence, religion.

In order to operationalize our definition—that is—in order to break down religion into identifiable components that are observable and measurable, we focus on the three interrelated Bs of religious life, namely: belief, behavior, and belonging.[71] By *belief*, we mean the cognitive acceptance of supernatural assumptions as true, faith in supernatural tenets, and ideological assent concerning supernatural claims and assertions. Belief is not something that can be seen or observed but can only be ascertained and measured based on what people say, write, or otherwise share and express. *Behavior*, on the other hand, can be readily observed. Behavior refers to all the things people actually *do* in relation to established religious beliefs: attending religious services, performing rituals, celebrating holidays, praying and genuflecting, body modifying, feasting or fasting, singing, studying scriptures, and so forth. Inversely, religious behavior can also include what people do not do: eating pork, consuming alcohol, having pre- or extra-marital sex, etc. And finally, *belonging* refers to the matter of membership, affiliation, or self-identification with a religious congregation, denomination, or tradition.

Of course, not everyone is religious to the same degree in all three dimensions. For one given individual, belief might be the central core of her religiosity, while for another, it might be mainly about performing certain behaviors, and while for still yet another, it could almost solely be about identifying with a given religious group, tradition, or heritage. For someone else, two out of the three Bs might be significant, while for yet someone else, all three are vital. Nor does every religion emphasize all three Bs equally: for some religious traditions, belief is supreme; for yet others, ritual takes pride of place; while for still other religions, membership is key. That is, the significance, importance, or meaningfulness of belief, behavior, or belonging shift and change—both for individuals as well as for various religions. But whatever the configuration or matrix of the three Bs, it is to their weakening, diminishing, or lessening within a society, over time, that we are to look for as evidence of secularization. In the following chapter, we'll discuss the varied levels of secularization in societies—micro, meso, and macro.

Defining Secularization

Just as the attempt to define religion has generated extensive discussion and debate, so too has the attempt to define secularization.[72] Indeed, one of the more memorable criticisms of secularization theory, as put forward by Jeffrey Hadden back in the 1980s,[73] has been its history of looseness of terms, fuzzy wording, and lack of coherent definitions. Consider some of the well-known and at times disparate definitions of secularization below.

Milton Yinger, back in the 1950s, defined secularization as the process "in which traditional religious symbols and forms have lost force and appeal."[74] According to Bryan Wilson, secularization is "the process whereby religious thinking, practice and institutions lose social significance,"[75] yet elsewhere, Wilson defined secularization as "a process of transfer of property, power, activities, and both manifest and latent functions, from institutions with a supernaturalist frame of reference to (often new) institutions operating according to empirical, rational, pragmatic criteria."[76] Peter Berger defined secularization as both "the process by which sectors in society and culture are removed from the domination of religious institutions and symbols," as well as a situation in which "an increasing number of individuals . . . look upon the world and their own lives without the benefit of religious interpretations."[77] In one instance, José Casanova defined secularization as "actual or alleged empirical-historical patterns of transformation and differentiation of the institutional spheres of 'the religious' (ecclesiastical institutions and churches) and 'the secular' (state, economy, science, art, entertainment, health and welfare, etc.) from early modern to contemporary societies,"[78] but he has also offered a more complex, three-part definition, which renders secularization as 1) "the decline of religious beliefs and practices in modern societies," 2) "the privatization of religion," and 3) "the differentiation of the secular spheres (state, economy, science), usually understood as 'emancipation' from religious institutions and norms."[79] Mark Chaves has more succinctly defined secularization as "the declining scope of religious authority."[80] Karel Dobbelaere defined secularization as "a process by which the overarching and transcendent religious system of old is reduced in modern functionally differentiated societies to a sub-system alongside other sub-systems, losing in this process its overarching claims over them."[81] And yet for Steve Bruce, secularization entails a combination of the following: "the decay of religious institutions . . . the displacement, in matters of behavior, of religious rules . . . by demands that accord with strictly technical criteria . . . the sequestration by political powers of the property and facilities of religious agencies . . . the replacement of a specifically religious consciousness . . . by an empirical, rational, instrumental orientation . . . the shift from religious to secular control of a variety of social activities . . . the decline in the proportion of their time, energy, and resources that people devote to supernatural concerns."[82]

We could present many more definitions—but hopefully, you get the idea: lots of scholars have defined secularization in lots of ways. While we have neither the space nor inclination to present, sift through, interpret, analyze, and/or synthesize all the various definitions of secularization that have been put forth over the decades, it is enough to observe that—whether terse or verbose, complex or cogent—what most definitions of secularization have in common is that they seek to describe or capture some sort of change or transformation over time in the way religion exists in society—a change that entails some type of differentiation, weakening, diminishment, decline, and/or loss. Whether we are talking about religion being increasingly separated, sequestered, or cut off from other sectors or institutions of society—such as government or education—or whether we are describing religion as holding less authority, symbolic sway, or hegemonic might, or whether we are observing fewer people seeing the world in religious terms or engaging in religious activities, the bottom line is an observable trajectory whereby religion becomes less of a dominant or all-pervasive power in society and there is a demonstrable decreasing of religiousness among the population. Of course, these processes play themselves out on many different levels—and in many different ways—depending on the contours and contents of the religious landscape of a given society, and the unique historical developments thereof.

We will provide a formal definition of secularization in chapter 1, but in general we understand secularization to include 1) the process of religion losing its overarching, hegemonic significance as a result of its being increasingly differentiated and sequestered from other institutional sectors of society and 2) the concomitant processes whereby religiosity weakens, lessens, diminishes, or fades in society. At the micro level, secularization is best understood, articulated, and measured in relation to the three Bs. That is, secularization entails a social process in which fewer people, over time, *believe* in supernatural claims, fewer people engage in religious *behaviors*, and fewer people *belong* to or identify with a religion.

Secularization as Differentiation and Decline

In our analysis of secularization, we accept and affirm that religion has become increasingly differentiated and significantly separated from other dominant institutions in most societies over the course of the past two centuries. This aspect of secularization has been widely discussed and historically documented;[83] it is easily the least controversial component of secularization theory, generating little if any debate.[84] Thus, in this book, we are primarily concerned with the more controversial claim of secularization: religiosity giving way to secularity. Our emphasis is therefore on the extent to which people in given societies are less religious than those of previous generations. We argue that since a statistically significant and substantively meaningful percentage of people living in nations all over the world are less religious than those of previous generations—in terms of belief, behavior, and belonging—secularization has occurred.

What follows are some brief illustrations of declining belief, behavior, and belonging. Later chapters will approach this issue more systematically. We'll start with *belief*:

- In 1967, 77 percent of British adults said that they believed in God;[85] in 1993, that had fallen down to 64 percent;[86] in 2012, it had declined to 37 percent;[87] in 2015 it was down to 32 percent.[88] Simultaneously, 10 percent of British adults described themselves as "confident atheists" back in 1998, and that rose to 18 percent in 2008, and then again up to 26 percent in 2018.[89] Clearly, these percentages indicate a stark fading of belief in God in Britain over several decades.
- In 1947, 71 percent of Japanese adults said that they held religious beliefs; that dropped down to 56 percent in 1965, 33.6 percent in 1979, 29.1 percent in 1984, 26.1 percent in 1994, 20.3 percent in 1995, and while there was a slight uptick to 22.9 percent in 2005, the overall trajectory since 1947 of the percentage of Japanese people who held religious beliefs has been one of decline.[90]
- In 1976, nearly 40 percent of Americans believed that the Bible was the actual word of God to be taken literally, while only 13 percent believed that it was a collection of fables, history, and morals written by men; by 2017, only 24 percent of Americans believed that the Bible was the actual word of God to be taken literally, while 26 percent believed that it was a collection of fables, history, and morals written by men[91]—a clear trend over several decades indicating a decline of the percentage of Americans holding supernatural beliefs regarding the Bible.

Now let's consider a few examples of secularization in the realm of behavior:

- In 1950, 44 percent of Australians attended religious services on a regular basis, but by 2016, only 16 percent of Australians were regular church attenders.[92]
- In 1970, 80 percent of babies in Sweden were baptized and 80 percent of teenagers went through the Lutheran ritual of confirmation, but by 2021, 35 percent of babies in Sweden were baptized and 20 percent of teenagers went through confirmation.[93]
- In the early 1990s in Spain, only 20 percent of weddings were performed as civil ceremonies while 80 percent were religious ceremonies held in church, but by 2018, this had completely reversed, with 80 percent of weddings being performed as civil ceremonies and only 20 percent being religious ceremonies held in church.[94]

All of the above indicate a clear decline in the number of people engaging in religious behaviors over time in three different societies.

Finally, consider these examples of secularization in the realm of *belonging:*

- In 2001 29.6 percent of New Zealanders identified with no religion; in 2018, 48.2 percent identified with no religion.[95]
- In 2007, 78 percent of Americans identified as being Christian, while 16 percent did not identify as being affiliated with any religion, but in 2019, 65 percent of Americans identified as Christian and 26 percent as religiously unaffiliated;[96] additionally, while 73 percent of Americans were members of a church, synagogue, or mosque back in 1940, only 47 percent are members today—the first time in the nation's history when less than half of the population were members of a religious congregation.[97]
- In 2013, 10 percent of Libyans and 13 percent of Tunisians said that they had no religion, but six years later, in 2019, those percentages claiming no religion had increased to 25 percent of Libyans and 30 percent of Tunisians.[98]

As we can see, in the past two decades, the percentage of people belonging to or identifying with a religion has decreased significantly in

New Zealand, the United States, Libya, and Tunisia. Of course, we could present many more examples such as the ones above, illustrating many other instances of various societies experiencing differing manifestations of secularization. In the pages ahead, we will approach this topic more systematically, presenting data from numerous countries all over the world, as we show the ways in which religious belief, behavior, and belonging have all been trending downward.

Considerations and Caveats

The scholarly debate over secularization has been going on for quite a while now. Some highlights from this ongoing discussion include *Religion and Modernization: Sociologists and Historians Debate the Secularization Thesis*, edited by Steve Bruce back in 1992, as well as *The Secularization Debate*, edited by William Swatos and Daniel Olson in 2000, not to mention important journal articles and book chapters seeking to navigate the debate, such as David Yamane's "Secularization on Trial" from 1997 and Philip Gorski's "Historicizing the Secularization Debate" from 2003. While there have been some extremely important contributions detailing various aspects of secularization and religious decline in recent years,[99] aside from Steve Bruce's book *Secularization: In Defence of an Unfashionable Theory* from 2011, there has been no book-length, in-depth defense of secularization—especially one that goes beyond the confines of Europe and the United States. And given the abundant data and burgeoning global evidence showing, unambiguously, that secularization has been occurring, it is high time that the prominent, decades-old claims of Rodney Stark and his colleagues be strongly refuted.

Hence, this book.

But before we proceed, some important considerations and caveats.

First, some scholars have argued that what we are seeing is not actually a decline of religion, per se, but rather, a *change* in the way religion is expressed.[100] While there is no question that religiosity morphs, mutates, transforms, and changes, over time—with certain beliefs, rituals, and identities abandoned that are subsequently replaced with newly emerging ones—what the current evidence shows, as we will present in chapter three, is that the more common pattern in modern societies is one of change *and* decline. So for example, while it is true that when a society begins to secularize, fewer people believe in God, but may instead believe in some sort of higher power (in which case this one indicator of religious faith has not necessarily declined, but merely changed), the reality is that, in societies that are further down the path of secularization, *both* may and often do decline: belief in God *and* in a higher power.[101] In such cases, religious change is not a contradiction to, but rather a key element in, secularization processes.

Second, we acknowledge that many indicators of secularization—such as those presented above in terms of belief, behavior, and belonging—are limited snapshots. They don't tell the whole picture of religious life. Or of secular life. And sometimes, such snapshot survey results are based upon problematically worded questions. For instance, survey results about belief in God among a given population are far from perfect; different surveys word questions differently, so that one might ask, "Do you believe in God?" while another might ask, "Do you believe in God or a Universal Spirit?"—the latter being a compounded question that allows people to say "yes" to two very different yet undifferentiated options. Fortunately, some of the data we now have allow us to look at changes of religiosity within the same countries on questions that have been asked the same way every time, over the years. This helps.

Another issue is that, in many countries, there is a stigma attached to not believing in God,[102] so that many people will be hesitant to admit as much, rendering significant undercounts of atheism and agnosticism. Furthermore, statistics about declining church attendance rates may be misleading; while people in a given society may no longer attend church as much as previous generations, they might be engaging in new, novel, non-traditional forms of religious behavior, thereby rendering such a measure of secularization as nothing more than an indication of religious change, not decline, an issue we address in subsequent chapters.

While acknowledging the shortcomings above, we must stress that they are shortcomings of social science in general, not of secularization theory, specifically. That is, survey research is always fraught with problems of incompleteness and ambiguity; it has always been the case that surveys can only tell us so much. That's the nature of the beast. Our only option, then, is to soldier on, making do with the best data available. That is exactly what we do in the pages ahead, drawing from a plethora of data on a wide range of nations from a wide range of geographic regions, cultures, and societies at various levels of development. And when it comes to assessing changing levels of religiosity and secularity, we have better data—and more of it available—than ever before. And, when possible, we augment and enrich the findings of quantitative research with relevant qualitative findings.[103]

Third, it is important to stress that there are actually two separate kinds of claims contained within secularization theory: 1) a descriptive claim and 2) various explanatory claims. The descriptive claim includes assertions that religion has weakened, faded, or diminished in a given society, while the explanatory claims entail attempts to explain this weakening, fading, or diminishing. Thus, one can agree with the claim that religiosity has declined, and simultaneously disagree with the explanations put forth in attempting to account for that decline. In the chapters ahead, we will be mindful of both claims of secularization theory—the descriptive and the explanatory—doing our best to defend the assertion that religion has weakened and diminished in many societies, and also providing what we think are the best accounts and explanations for this phenomenon.

Fourth, secularization should always be conceived of as occurring on a spectrum, and always be characterized as a matter of degree. We do not believe that there are any societies that are totally and completely religious in all aspects of belief, behavior, or belonging, nor do we believe that there are any societies that are completely secular in all three aspects. Rather, it is best to conceptualize such extremes as hypothetical ends on an imagined spectrum, with secularization merely indicating a noticeable shift from the more religious end to the more secular end. Secularization does not require the complete disappearance of religious beliefs, or the total absence of religious behaviors, or the full erasure of religious belonging. Instead, it is sufficient to describe it as a weakening, lessening, diminishing, or fading of these in a given society over time. That's all.

Finally, as we explain in the next chapter, secularization is not inevitable—it is merely *possible*. We do not believe that there are any ironclad laws of history, or unavoidable and inescapable outcomes in social life. We don't believe that in all societies, at all times, any specific social trends or historical occurrences will always and in every instance result in the same social or historical outcome. More to the point: we don't believe that religion is somehow—inevitably—fated to die. Various manifestations of something we might call religion have been a part of every human society for which we have record, and various aspects of religious life will undoubtedly continue to exist well into the future. But to repeat, we believe that secularization is *possible*. And we are convinced—unlike Stark and his colleagues—that religion can decline in society, sometimes dramatically. In fact, it already has.

Book Plan

We start, in chapter 1, with the theory. We present and discuss attempts to explain secularization, from classical understandings to more current versions. We also lay out our understanding of secularization and provide a formal, testable theory of secularization.

Next, we get decidedly empirical. In chapter 2, we present evidence attesting to secularization from over 100 societies around the world, specifically focusing on the three Bs. This is followed by a closer look at secularizing societies in chapter 3, where a selection of countries serves to offer case studies of secularization, examining measures of religion in depth.

In chapter 4, we discuss the matter of the presumed naturalness and universality of religion; many have posited that religious needs are innate to the human condition and that religious needs are universal. We debunk these notions directly, showing that secularity is just as "natural" to the human condition as religiosity and that religious needs are not universal, but can be much stronger or much weaker at different times in history and in different societies.

In chapter 5, we will see what secular life actually looks like, presenting significant components of "lived secularity." That is, we explore the way nonreligious people live their lives—raising children, engaging in life-cycle rituals, organizing community, and so on.

As mentioned earlier, while secularization has occurred in many parts of the world, it hasn't occurred everywhere. Thus, in chapter 6, we will look at presumed exceptions to secularization: various societies that have not experienced much in the way of religious decline, and in some instances, have experienced an increase in religiosity. We will explain these cases, drawing from our understanding of secularization theory to account for religion's persistence and even resurgence.

Our conclusion will summarize the main arguments of the book—the most important empirical findings and theoretical considerations—before offering some predictions about the future of religion and secularization.

1

Secularization Theory

In the 1850s, Catholic German immigrants in St. Louis, Missouri, pooled their resources together in order to erect a church. In 1889, St. Liborius Church was successfully completed: a large, Gothic-style house of worship with high ceilings, pointed arches, and plenty of space for many, many pews. A century later, in 1992, St. Liborius Church closed down due to a lack of members. Today, it has been repurposed into a thriving skateboard park, renamed "Sk8 Liborius."[1] What happened to St. Liborius Church is not some isolated incident. It is emblematic of a much wider trend: in the United States, somewhere between 6,000 and 10,000 churches close down every year, either to be repurposed as apartments, laundries, laser-tag arenas, or skateparks, or to simply be demolished.[2]

There are many additional, related signs of religion's weakening in the USA: the number of Americans who are priests or nuns is now at an all-time low: in 1965, there were nearly 180,000 nuns in the US, but that has fallen down to only around 50,000 today, with the number of priests declining from around 58,000 to 38,000 over the same time period.[3] As for belief in God: 64 percent of Americans born between 1927 and 1945 believe that God is the all-knowing, all-powerful, and just creator and ruler of the universe, but only 31 percent of Americans born between 1982 and 2002 believe as much.[4]

Something is clearly going on.

Obviously, that something is the subject of this book: secularization.

In this chapter, we provide a summary of secularization theory that includes the most important nuances and recent contributions, as well as clearly stated definitions and propositions. We also examine the most prominent critiques and challenges to the theory.

At the outset, it is worth noting that secularization is both a theory and a process. Distinguishing between theory and process is important, as one is the explanation (the theory) while the other is empirical (the process). The theory of secularization is an explanation of how and why religiosity and religious authority[5] decline over time as a result of modernization, differentiation, and rationalization, as will be detailed below. However, secularization is also a process.[6] In the 2001 Census in the United Kingdom, around 16 percent of the population identified as having no religion (i.e., "nones") and 71.6 percent identified as Christian. In the 2011 Census, the percentage of the population who identified as Christian had declined to 59.5 percent and the percentage identifying as having no religion had increased to 25.7 percent of the population. We thus can observe declining religiosity over time, illustrating the process of secularization. It is of course possible that society could secularize over time but that the theory could be wrong. We don't believe that the theory of secularization is wrong, but distinguishing between theory and process is important for this reason. In this chapter, we focus primarily on secularization theory. In much of the rest of the book we will provide evidence for secularization.

Philip Gorski has argued that any general theory of religious change, to be compelling, must accomplish three things: 1) explain how and why religious/nonreligious values and institutions change over time; 2) explain historical change in religiosity within particular societies; and 3) explain how those two processes are related.[7] In what follows, we do our best to illustrate how secularization theory meets all three requirements laid out by Gorski. It is a compelling theory of religious decline.

Secularization Simplified

Secularization theory can be summarized in a single phrase: "modernization creates problems for religion."[8] Of course, there is a lot more to the theory. Secularization theory asserts that, as people experience modern life, adopt modern sensibilities, and develop modern understandings of life and the universe, they will be less likely to adhere to religious or supernatural explanations, respect religious authority, identify as religious, and engage in religious behaviors.

Formal Definitions:

- *Secularization*: The process of shifting from beliefs, values, and behaviors rooted in the supernatural to beliefs, values, and behaviors rooted in the natural.

- *Modernization*: The transition from a traditional, rural, non-industrial society to a contemporary, urban, industrial (or post-industrial) society.
- *Core Proposition*: The more modernized a society and its institutions and individuals are, the greater the likelihood of secularization.

A concrete example may help illustrate the basic idea of secularization. Imagine you get in your car, try to start it, and nothing happens. What do you do? Do you look for a shaman to intervene with the gods on your behalf? Do you call your local Catholic priest to anoint your car with holy water? Do you request a visit by Mormon missionaries to bless your car? Do you sacrifice a chicken to appease the angry spirits that are keeping your car from working?

If all of the above options sound absurd and you thought to yourself, "Of course not. I'd take the car to a mechanic," you have some "modern sensibilities and understandings." What makes this example particularly fascinating is that many people don't know how either gas or electric cars work. But they do know that they don't run on chi, blessings, or karma. And, most importantly, they know that someone knows how cars work. Knowing that someone knows how cars work is a manifestation of modernization. And knowing that cars are not powered by some supernatural force is a manifestation of secularization. It is important to note here that there are many devoutly religious people who know how cars work; knowing that cars are not supernatural does not equate to someone being secular, and living in a modernized world or having some modern sensibilities does not automatically result in secularization. The example above is just a simple illustration of the underlying principle: modernization causes problems for religion.

There are at least two elements of modernization that contribute to secularization.[9] The first is differentiation, or the process of separating religion from other aspects of life.[10] That religion used to be integrated into most everything that people did may seem foreign now in the twenty-first century, but it was the case in millennia past. For instance, Mayans engaged in a variety of human, blood, and animal sacrifices, each of which was intended to appease various gods for various reasons.[11] Many of these sacrifices were tied to the leaders of states who used decapitation, for instance, to usher in a new ruler by cutting off the head of a different leader, ideally an opposing king. Appeasing the gods with sacrifices does seem archaic, but in 2011, Texas Governor Rick Perry designated April 22 through April 24 as official days of prayer for rain in the state.[12] Perry's attempt to appease a god through prayer is a softer, less jarring approach to accomplishing the same thing as human sacrifice—intervening with a god on behalf of the leadership of the state. In both instances, leaders drew upon religion for the purposes of governing.

It is decreasingly the case, in most developed countries, that government and religion are intertwined in ways like those in the above paragraph. There are some countries where religion and state are closely connected, like Iran and Saudi Arabia. But most countries today have a clear distinction between the two, even though there are many situations when the government steps in to regulate religion. Most telling of all is that we have a distinction between the very concepts of "religion" and "government," which was not always the case in centuries past.

Differentiation of religion from other aspects of society has also occurred. Many older colleges and universities were founded to train clergy and were often run by monastic orders. Harvard University was founded for this purpose with *Christo et Ecclesiae* (Christ and Church) as one of its early mottoes along with *In Christi Gloriam* (For the Glory of Christ) rather than its current motto, *Veritas* (Truth). Many older hospitals and charitable organizations were also founded and run by religions. Goodwill, which is an international nonprofit with no meaningful connection to religion anymore, was founded as part of the ministry of a Methodist pastor, Edgar J. Helms, in Boston, Massachusetts. Both Harvard and Goodwill, even though they were founded by religions or religious individuals, have secularized over time such that, today, Harvard is far more likely to be associated with scientific advances than with its Divinity School, and Goodwill is more likely to receive attention for providing jobs to unskilled workers[13] than for proselytizing to customers.

At the individual level, differentiation also occurs. Some theorists have, however, thought of differentiation at the individual level as a separate process with a different name: privatization.[14] The basic idea is that individuals separate out the elements of their life that involve religion from the elements of their life that do not (e.g., work, family, recreation, etc.). Thus, a devout Muslim may request a private space at her workplace to say her five daily prayers so as not to draw the attention of her

SECULARIZATION THEORY | 25

coworkers to her religiosity. Another example might be a workplace allowing an employee to decorate their desk with secular Christmas symbols (e.g., a small tree, snowflakes, or Santa Claus) but not explicitly Christian Christmas symbols (e.g., a manger scene). Or, it could simply be someone who "does religion" strictly on Sundays with their family at church, but the rest of their week is completely engaged with and occupied by secular activities and pursuits. There is no meaningful difference between differentiation at the individual level and privatization. Privatization is removing religious beliefs, values, or behaviors from public spheres where it is no longer considered socially acceptable—or even personally desirable—even though such behaviors can continue in private. Removing religious beliefs, values, or behaviors from one sphere— say, the workplace—but allowing them to continue at home is simply differentiation, just at the individual level.

In 2021, the European Union's Court of Justice decided that companies can ban employees from wearing a headscarf when it is deemed necessary to portray neutrality to customers.[15] The case was brought by two Muslim women who had started their jobs at a daycare and drugstore not wearing headscarves but, after parental leave, wanted to begin wearing them. The court decided that, in cases where employers felt obligated to project an image of religious neutrality, employers could prohibit employees from wearing headscarves. Such cases differentiate whether religious beliefs, values, or behaviors—in this case, behaviors that reflect religious beliefs and values—can take place in public or private. The court's decision does not prohibit the women from wearing headscarves in private or even in other contexts where their religious neutrality is not important. Court decisions like this one wrestle with the extent of differentiation that should exist for individuals based on the differentiation of religion at the societal and institutional level. There is clearly an interplay between these three levels of differentiation, with trends towards societal (macro) and institutional (meso) secularization influencing individual level differentiation, and vice versa.

Formally, then, we summarize the relationship between differentiation and secularization in the following proposition:

- *Definition*: Differentiation is the separation of religion from various aspects of societies, institutions, or individuals.

- *Proposition*: The greater the differentiation at the societal, institutional, or individual levels, the more likely secularization is to occur.

Some scholars have conflated secularization and differentiation, assuming that differentiation *is* secularization.[16] They are not the same. Two examples illustrate that differentiation is not secularization. Secularization had long been taking place in Norway before the Norwegian State Church was formally and completely separated from the state on January 1, 2017. While secularization has continued since the Norwegian State Church was separated from the secular government, the point here is that secularization is not differentiation; one can occur without the other. In contrast to the Norwegian State Church, when the USA was founded, a formal separation between the federal government and religion was included. That is an example of differentiation. However, the differentiation of the federal government and religion in the US did not immediately result in secularization. As we detail in this book, the US has most assuredly secularized since 1776, and the differentiation of religion from the federal government has likely facilitated that, but the point is that differentiation is not secularization or vice versa. Differentiation is a separate social process that can and often does lead to secularization.

Another aspect of modernization that contributes to secularization is rationalization. By rationalization we don't mean that individuals are more rational, which would be nice but isn't really in our nature.[17] Rationalization refers to the ordering of society based on technological efficiency, bureaucratic impersonality, and scientific and empirical evidence.[18] In other words, rationalization is not to suggest that all of humanity is becoming more rational but rather that the social structure that undergirds our societies moves away from a reliance on irrational ideas or the whims of some monarch or dictator as the basis of policy and toward ideas rooted in science, equality, and efficiency.

An example may help illustrate the idea: There is natural variation in fertility, with some women being able to get pregnant quite easily, other women being completely infertile, and a continuum of fertility in between. Likewise, some men are completely sterile while others are particularly fertile, with variation in between. While some people today may pray to a Catholic saint like Gianna Beretta Molla[19] to intervene with their god if they are struggling to get pregnant, in modernized societies, there is a more effective solution: fertility testing and fertility treatments. Modern science and healthcare can diagnose infertility and, in some cases, can treat it or can work around it, such as through in vitro fertilization. Note here, the level of analysis. We are not suggesting that religious individuals are irrational and secular individuals are rational. We are suggesting that there are more rational processes for treating infertility that have been shown to be effective, like modern healthcare. Rationalization happens throughout society, at macro, meso, and individual levels.

Formally, then, we posit the following relationship between rationalization and secularization:

- *Definition*: Rationalization is the ordering of society based on technological efficiency, bureaucratic impersonality, and scientific and empirical evidence.
- *Proposition*: The more rationalization that exists at societal, institutional, and individual levels, the greater the likelihood of secularization.

The above discussion raises another important clarification of secularization theory. Secularization does not take place at just the individual level or just at the societal level. Karel Dobbelaere made it clear that secularization takes place at three levels—at the macro or societal level, at the meso or organizational/institutional level, and at the micro or individual level.[20] Education provides a clear example of how this shift occurs at all three levels. In societies that are more religious, education was often the domain of religions, as was noted above with the example of Harvard University. However, secularization has changed education at all three levels. At a societal level, governments have assumed the responsibility for educating citizens by setting standards for what should be included in curricula, by accrediting educational institutions (or setting the standards for accreditation), and by providing the funds for education. Education is, at the societal level, a secular concern for a secular government. At a meso level, many educational institutions that were once religious have ended their affiliation with religious organizations, have siloed the religious elements of the institution into a school of theology or divinity, or require students to take some token courses in religion. But many other educational institutions were founded by the state and were always secular. At an individual level, the focus of education is now on secular knowledge, which is to say that the focus is not on training students to become clergy or theologians but rather to contribute to the modern, rationalized economy by providing them with knowledge and skills that will make them contributing members of secular societies. Secularization occurs at all three levels of society.

Figure 1.1 provides a very simple understanding of secularization, suggesting that differentiation and rationalization underlie this process. To be clear, we are arguing that differentiation and rationalization are the two elements of modernization that most directly contribute to secularization. Intriguingly, what is often left out of prior understandings of secularization is that both differentiation and rationalization have a common cause—economic stratification resulting from surplus. Once there is economic inequality in a society, specialization of roles begins to occur.[21] If farmers can produce more food than they and their family need, that frees up other people in a society to focus on other tasks. Thus, while farmers may specialize in growing food, merchants can specialize in the selling and distribution of food. Likewise, blacksmiths and carpenters can focus on creating the tools needed by both the farmers and merchants. Specialization of roles provides the starting point for differentiation. Without specialization, there would be no differentiation.

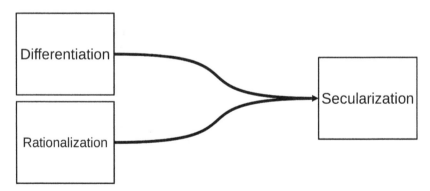

Figure 1.1: Simplified Model of Secularization.

Returning this discussion to religion, once a tribal chief rises to power and oversees the material needs of a tribe and a shaman assumes responsibility for the spiritual, religious, or supernatural needs of the same tribe, we observe the beginning of religious differentiation. The chief may depend on the shaman and the shaman may depend on the chief, but their roles are differentiated. We have the earliest forms of "church and state."

Specialization also leads to rationalization. Once people can dedicate time to their specialties, they can work to improve processes and experiment, leading to technological advancements. At the very heart of rationalization lies the concept of specialization—specialists are assumed to be more competent and capable of accomplishing tasks than are non-specialists. As the example above of the car that won't start illustrates, many people have no idea how to fix a broken car, but they know that someone does. Specialization leads to technological advancements which lead to rationalization—once there are alternative ways of accomplishing specific ends, we can weigh between the alternatives and choose the option that is more efficient, more effective, and/or more reliable. The origins of secularization, then, were seeded when humanity transitioned from hunters and gatherers to horticulture, pastoralism, and eventually agriculture.[22]

Finally, we want to reiterate the importance of having a clear understanding of our model of secularization theory. Modernization, including economic development and stratification, and the resulting rationalization and differentiation, are complex social processes. They are also best described as concepts, not variables. With each of these concepts, they must be operationalized in some fashion in order to make them measurable variables. Although differentiation exists at multiple levels, one way to operationalize it is by examining the extent of government restrictions in a society or how curtailed the freedoms are of citizens vis-à-vis religion. The ideal operationalization of rationalization might be something like examining people's preferences for modern, effective, and efficient solutions to problems (e.g., fertility treatments) over supernatural solutions (e.g., praying to a saint). However, such measures are not nearly as widespread as are measures of economic development that underlie rationalization, such as urbanization, GDP, and paid employment, which are measures that we use in subsequent chapters.

Variations on a Theme: Origins and Mechanisms

Classical Secularization Theory

Much of what is laid out above regarding rationalization and differentiation has its roots in the work of those who are now considered "classical" sociologists. That secularization would occur was proposed by Jean-Marie Guyau[23] and Auguste Comte[24] in the late nineteenth century. In 1883, Comte proposed, "From henceforth the belief in Monotheism, whether Christian or Mussulman, is left to its natural course of inherent decay."[25] Weber is largely responsible for connecting rationalization with secularization.[26] Weber famously argued in a 1917 lecture that rationalization would lead to the disenchantment of the world:

> The fate of our times is characterized by rationalization and intellectualization and, above all, by the "disenchantment of the world." Precisely the ultimate and most sublime values have retreated from public life either into the transcendental realm of mystic life or into the brotherliness of direct and personal human relations.
>
> Hence, it means that principally there are no mysterious incalculable forces that come into play, but rather that one can, in principle, master all things by calculation. This means that the world is disenchanted. One need no longer have recourse to magical means in order to master or implore the spirits, as did the savage, for whom such mysterious powers existed. Technical means and calculations perform the service. This above all is what intellectualization means.[27]

Guyau as well as Durkheim[28] argued for differentiation. Writing in 1893, Durkheim maintained that,

> If there is one truth that history teaches us beyond doubt, it is that religion tends to embrace a smaller and smaller portion of social life. Originally, it pervades everything, everything social is religious; the two words are synonymous. Then, little by little, political, economic, scientific functions free themselves from the religious function, constitute themselves apart and take on a more and more acknowledged temporal character. God, who was at first present in all human relations, progressively withdraws from them; he abandons the world to men and their disputes.[29]

Admittedly, some of these early scholars (particularly the Frenchmen Comte and Guyau) mistakenly believed that religion would disappear entirely. Additionally, there is a lack of clarity and often a fair bit of confusion in the work of these early scholars. Even so, the groundwork for understanding secularization was laid hundreds of years ago. Since it was first suggested, secularization has received lots of attention. In this section, we examine some of the proposed modifications that various scholars have introduced to secularization theory.

Religious Pluralism

One scholar who proposed a mechanism[30] that would contribute to secularization was Peter Berger, who is more famous for his co-authored book with Thomas Luckmann, *The Social Construction of Reality*.[31] We mention *The Social Construction of Reality* because it lies at the heart of Berger's arguments surrounding secularization. Berger and Luckmann illustrated that religion, like all social institutions, is a social construct. It is not physically real in the sense that Denali in Alaska, the pyramids in Egypt, and the musician Enya are real, existing independent of whether or not someone believes they are real. Religion is, like government, laws, and families, something that exists only because humans agree to believe and behave as though it exists. How such social constructs come into existence and are maintained is detailed in Berger and Luckmann's book.

In other work, Berger extended his ideas on religion.[32] He argued that religion was a social construct and was also not necessary for society, an idea that contrasted with some social theories from the 1930s, namely structural functionalism as detailed by Talcott Parsons.[33] Based on this perspective, Berger argued that religion would greatly diminish. In making that argument, he offered a specific mechanism that would lead to secularization: religious pluralism.

For Berger, religion was maintained because people are socialized into a comprehensive worldview, which he called a "sacred canopy," envisioning it like a tent being held up by poles. That sacred canopy provided people with an understanding of the world that was filtered through the lens of their religion. For instance, a Mormon would understand that humanity exists as a trial of their worthiness and devotion to their

Heavenly Father. In order to prove their worthiness, Mormons believe they must not only take advantage of the sacrifice of Jesus, who paid for their sins, but must also undergo a number of religious rituals, including baptism and confirmation, receiving the priesthood if male, marrying in a Mormon temple, and participating in additional rituals that take place in Mormon temples. They must also follow the behavioral dictates of the religion. Only if all of those requirements are met do Mormons believe they can pass the test that is mortality and earn exaltation, which involves them eventually becoming gods and goddesses. That is a highly condensed version of their sacred canopy.[34]

The poles that hold up the sacred canopy, according to Berger, are called a "plausibility structure." A plausibility structure is what makes belief in that sacred canopy seem reasonable. Per Berger, the plausibility structure is made up of all the aspects of daily life—and the multitude of social relations and interactions—that reinforce the veracity of the sacred canopy. Returning to our example of Mormons, elements of a plausibility structure would include: family members and friends who are also faithful members of the religion and regularly reinforce their belief in and reliance upon the sacred canopy, the leaders of the religion, the books and other materials that educate and provide information about the sacred canopy, serving a mission, and the regular activities that Mormons engage in—like daily prayers and scripture study, attending religious services, summer programs, family home evenings, participating in various rituals, evangelizing or sharing their beliefs with others, and interpreting events and phenomena in such a way that they reinforce the sacred canopy of Mormonism.[35]

Berger argued that the mechanism of secularization was the dissolution of the plausibility structure through religious pluralism. Religious pluralism, to be more explicit, is many different religions existing in the same geographical space. If the plausibility structure is what makes it possible to maintain a sacred canopy, then the destruction of the plausibility structure will result in the collapse of the sacred canopy. What might begin to pull down the tent poles that make up the plausibility structure that holds up someone's sacred canopy? For Berger, the mechanism was coming into contact with, and gaining an appreciation for, people who adhere to a different religion.

At a fundamental level, Berger's argument makes sense. A young Amish individual who has a large family, works on their family farm, has all Amish friends, and interacts almost exclusively with other Amish people—thus occupying a comprehensive Amish sacred canopy—is only rarely going to experience threats to their plausibility structure. In their daily life, their plausibility structure is regularly reinforced, leading to the maintenance of their sacred canopy, that is, their religious world. Contrast this young Amish person with someone who grew up and lives in New York City where there are not only millions of people, but there are also many different sacred canopies. Unless this New Yorker grows up in an Orthodox Jewish enclave, they are highly likely to be exposed to Muslim, Jewish, Catholic, Hindu, Buddhist, and various versions of Protestant sacred canopies just by attending public school. For our hypothetical New Yorker, Berger would argue that the exposure to all of these sacred canopies, thrust into the same geographical location, undermines their plausibility structure.

It's very challenging to maintain an exclusive religious worldview, believing that you live within the one true sacred canopy and everyone else is wrong, when you live in a metropolitan environment with close friends who have different sacred canopies.[36] For Berger, then, religious pluralism was the fundamental mechanism of secularization—it undermined plausibility structures, causing sacred canopies to collapse.

Interestingly, for a time, some scholars thought Berger was wrong. The primary problem with religious pluralism as a mechanism for secularization is that humans prefer homogenous social networks. Most of us like to surround ourselves with people who are just like us.[37] As a result, it is possible for someone to live in a metropolitan city like New York but only build close relationships with other Muslims (or Catholics or Pentecostals). Such an individual could be surrounded by religious pluralism at the meso level but, in their personal life, never experience any meaningful threats to their plausibility structure because it is constantly being reinforced by their intimate social network. The implication is that societal-level religious pluralism need not trickle down to individual level religious pluralism, which means Berger's proposed mechanism functions only at the micro level—with individuals, not at a societal level. Higher levels of pluralism at the macro level may or may not result in secularization, but higher levels of pluralism at the micro level are highly likely to result in secularization. Leading to the following proposition:

- *Definition*: Religious pluralism refers to the amount of diversity in religiosity in a given population.
- *Proposition*: The greater the religious pluralism of an individual's social network and contacts, the greater the likelihood that this individual will secularize.

For a brief period in the 1990s and early 2000s, some scholars suggested that religious pluralism might have the opposite effect of what Berger proposed—increasing religiosity as a result of religious organizations (i.e., denominations and congregations) competing for adherents.[38] That research was wrong.[39] Recent findings using methods that are able to overcome some of the methodological limitations to capturing religious pluralism show that higher levels of religious pluralism do seem to trickle down to individuals, reducing their religiosity.[40] Likewise, there is compelling research suggesting that the more nodes in someone's social network that are nonreligious, the greater the odds that the individual will be nonreligious.[41] Despite his later reversal on the question of secularization,[42] current research suggests that Peter Berger's earlier ideas on secularization have some merit and religious pluralism may be a mechanism of secularization. Thinking about it in the context of the broader theory, pluralism results from differentiation in a society, which then leads to secularization, as illustrated in Figure 1.2 below.

Existential Security

Another suggestion as to a mechanism for secularization was offered by Pippa Norris and Ronald Inglehart in their 2004 book, *Sacred and Secular*, which was later further developed by Inglehart in his 2021 book, *Religion's Sudden Decline*.[43] They argued that the key element of modernization that is responsible for secularization is what they called "existential security." They defined existential security as "the feeling that survival is secure enough that it can be taken for granted."[44] Drawing upon World Values Survey data, Norris and Inglehart then illustrated that the countries with the most robust social safety nets—universal health care, public education, social welfare, etc.—were also the countries that had experienced the most secularization.

Norris and Inglehart's approach was particularly compelling because of one specific finding—the US was an outlier when it came to secularization despite being a highly developed, modern country, and they argued that existential security helped explain why the US was an outlier. Unlike other highly developed countries, the US did not have the same degree of social welfare. Yes, there were elements of a social safety net, like Social Security and Medicare, but the US did not offer (and still does not offer) universal healthcare, paid parental leave, and robust unemployment benefits, among other differences. As a result, when illustrating the relationship between societal development and secularization, Norris and Inglehart were able to explain why the US was an outlier— the lack of existential security that existed in the US.

Like religious pluralism, it appears as though existential security may contribute to secularization. This leads to the following proposition:

- *Definition*: Existential security is the feeling that survival is secure enough that it can be taken for granted.
- *Proposition*: Societies with higher levels of existential security will be more likely to secularize.

However, the underlying social process that leads to existential security is not differentiation but rather rationalization, as illustrated in Figure 1.2 below.

Religious Transmission

Recent scholarship proposes another mechanism through which secularization may take place—socialization and parent/child relationships.[45] There is a large body of research examining the transmission of religion from parents to children.[46] Religious socialization is the primary means of spreading religion. Given the challenges involved in convincing others to adopt a sacred canopy with its concomitant beliefs, values, and behaviors, it makes sense that it is far more effective to simply raise children within a sacred canopy rather than try to convince adults to adopt a sacred canopy.

However, since at least the 1960s,[47] a shift in parenting has taken place in many societies. Jörg Stolz and colleagues have shown that many parents now grant their children more autonomy than parents did 40-plus years ago.[48] These children have a greater say in whether they want to participate in religion. When given such autonomy, a sizable percentage of children opt for lower levels of religious participation or none at all. Some religious sociologists frame this as a "failure" of religious transmission, belying their personal values.[49] We prefer to focus, instead, on the modern sensibilities and values that are reflected in granting children autonomy, which derive from general processes of rationalization in society. Parents who grant their children autonomy when it comes to decisions about religion reflect these modern values.

The result of this autonomy is a clear pattern in secularization in many countries—successive generations are less religious than previous generations.[50] This proposed mechanism of secularization, then, is the autonomy granted to children that shapes the transmission of religion (or lack thereof) from parents to children. This leads to the following proposition:

- *Proposition*: Children who are granted higher levels of autonomy regarding their religiosity will generally be less religious than are their parents.

Figure 1.2 illustrates these mechanisms inside the broader theoretical framework of secularization, showing that pluralism derives from differentiation while existential security and autonomy for children derive from rationalization.[51] All three of these ideas can serve as specific mechanisms that can lead to secularization.

A Comprehensive Theory of Secularization

What we have laid out above is a general theory of secularization with some specific mechanisms. Other scholars, notably Steve Bruce,[52] have provided book-length treatments of the theory. Our model differs from his in some ways, but our model and his understanding of secularization

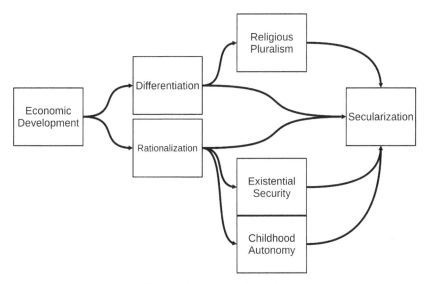

Figure 1.2: The Processes and Mechanisms of Secularization.

theory are largely in agreement about the broader underlying forces that lead to secularization.

We turn now to criticisms of secularization theory.

Challenges to Secularization Theory

Religious Economies and Supply-Side Arguments

The major competitor to secularization theory in the US emerged in the 1980s[53] but really gained steam in the early 1990s.[54] It was an amalgamation of arguments that some labeled "the religious economies model," though it is also often referred to as "the supply-side argument."[55] There are two general ideas that underlie this argument. First, advocates for this idea argue that the demand for religion is constant. Second, they also frame religion as a pseudo-economic marketplace, the key idea being that religions compete for adherents. The theory places the onus for religiosity on the religions since the demand for religion is constant. Thus, the factor that matters when considering changes in religiosity in society is not demand but supply, making this a supply-side economic argument.

How does supply matter? According to this theory, religiosity goes through cycles based on religious competition. Over time, some religions will outcompete others in the religious marketplace, gaining most of the population as adherents. However, once religions become dominant in the marketplace, they become lazy and stop trying to compete (i.e., they are like economic monopolies; with limited competition, they have no incentive to innovate). The lack of innovation opens the door for smaller religions that are willing to innovate. These smaller religions will eventually begin gaining market share—assuming the economy is not regulated by the government through legal measures that prevent smaller religions from competing (more on this below). Since the smaller religions have an incentive to grow, they will outcompete the bigger, lazy monopolies and eventually take over. Of course, once the new religions become dominant, they will start the cycle over again. The implication is that religions and religiosity will cycle over time, with some religions dominating for a time only to be replaced by others. And when there is meaningful competition in the market, that will drive up religious engagement as people are invigorated by religions that are innovating.

Where the supply of religion is regulated, such as the state-church monopolies of Europe, low levels of religious participation is then, according to the religious economies argument, not a result of secularization or a limited demand for religion, but rather caused by restrictions to the supply. Once state churches are disestablished and multiple religious firms are able to compete in a free market, the religious economies model proposes that religiosity will increase.[56] However, this has not happened, as we will demonstrate in subsequent chapters. Rather, religious deregulation tends to be accompanied by continued secularization, and societies with the highest levels of government regulation of religion remain the most religious.

As we have an entire chapter dedicated to the question of whether demand for religion is constant (spoiler alert: it's not), we will not focus on that devastating flaw in the religious economies model here. Instead, we will briefly examine the idea of religions competing in a marketplace. Other scholars have argued that there are religious marketplaces in societies where there is religious freedom and religious pluralism is allowed.[57] It is certainly the case in such marketplaces that religions compete for adherents. Thus, the idea of a religious marketplace in and of itself is not problematic. However, the idea that people are more or less religiously engaged based just on the supply of religion is highly unlikely and not in line with empirical reality.

At the heart of this claim about religiosity increasing and decreasing in cycles of supply and competition in the marketplace is a criticism leveled at secularization theory that is a logical fallacy. Advocates of the religious economies model claimed that there never was a golden age of religiosity in which orthodoxy and orthopraxy were widespread.[58] They argued, instead, that during the medieval period in Europe, for instance, few people attended religious services and the widespread intermingling of folk beliefs with Catholicism suggested people were not very ortho-dox in their beliefs.[59] In making this argument, Stark and friends set up a straw man that they were easily able to defeat. The idea behind this straw man, and why Stark and friends considered it so damaging to secularization theory, is that, if there was not a period in the past when religiosity was pervasive, there could not have been a decline in religi-osity. This was coupled with the idea that formal religiosity (really the planting of churches) actually increased in the US over the eighteenth and nineteenth centuries.[60] In other words, if, during the Middle Ages in Europe, people were not particularly religious, to claim that people had become less religious didn't make sense, undermining seculariza-tion theory.

However, the claim about low levels of religiosity was rooted in an idea that Stark attributed to secularization theory but was never actually part of the theory: that people in the past were all orthodox in their be-liefs and that orthopraxy was widespread. This argument is a straw man and has been refuted most compellingly by Steve Bruce.[61]

What, then, does secularization argue about past eras and religios-ity? Note that the definition of secularization at the beginning of this chapter included a shift away from religion but also from supernatural beliefs and values. Secularization does not focus exclusively on shifts away from official Christian conceptions of religion. The theory is much broader than that. The argument is that, as societies modernize, they will move away from beliefs, values, and behaviors rooted in the super-natural *and* religions. In the Middle Ages, many people may not have held particularly orthodox views, but they did hold many supernatural views rooted in folk beliefs. A couple of quick examples can illustrate this. Why would there have been witch hunts both in Europe and the US if people didn't believe in witches?[62] Why would very Catholic Venice have a clock in Piazza San Marco that includes the positions of the zodiac if people didn't believe in astrology and horoscopes?[63] The argument of secularization theory is not that at some point in the past all people were theologians who carefully followed all the behavioral dictates of their religion, comported themselves perfectly in accordance with modern church-attending norms, and disavowed all folk beliefs. No, the argument of secularization theory is that people held beliefs and values and engaged in behaviors rooted in the supernatural—like believing in witches and horoscopes—in past eras and that modernization undermines those beliefs, just like it undermines traditional religiosity.

The religious economies model gained a lot of attention among sociologists of religion in the US for about fifteen to twenty years. Outside the US (mostly in Europe), scholars thought that the religious economies model was misguided and continued exploring secularization. Given the rapid secularization that has taken place around the world (including the US), the fallacious claims made by advocates of the religious economies model have been thoroughly refuted.

Change Not Decline

A second prominent line of attack against secularization theory is the argument that religion, religious authority, and religiosity are not declining but that they are *changing*. Or put another way: by focusing on traditional, organized religion, scholars are missing the bulk of how people do religion in other ways. This argument has taken multiple forms. An early version of this argument was proposed by Thomas Luckmann in his book *The Invisible Religion*.[64] For Luckmann, organized religions were likely to see declines, but individuals would take elements of religion, privatize them, and create their own "invisible religions" (i.e., since they are private, that makes them "invisible"). Thus, while organized religion may see declines, religiosity in general—that is, the ways in which people manifest their religiosity—was unlikely to decline because it would become private.

In a similar vein, Grace Davie proposed that while involvement with organized religion in the UK was declining, this did not mean that people were less religious.[65] Many of the people who were no longer regularly attending religious services or considered themselves members of various congregations were "believing without belonging." Her basic idea was that shifts in UK culture and society have led to a diminution of identification with organized religion and lower levels of practical involvement, but that British individuals are still likely to hold many traditionally religious ideas, like believing in Jesus or God, or even valuing the teachings of the Bible. Additionally, Davie argued that many of the supposedly nonreligious in society were still supportive of religion because they valued that other people continued to both be religious and maintain religions, which she called "vicarious religion." Through the idea of vicarious religion, Davie argued that the nonreligious continued to value religion, supporting the idea that religiosity had changed but not declined. Subsequent work raised a number of challenges to Davie's arguments, particularly that people still claimed to be Christian and/ or hold Christian values because that was part of what it means to be a good member of society, even if, when asked, they admit to not actually believing in Jesus.[66]

Other scholars have made similar arguments under the framework of "lived religion."[67] Lived religion suggests that people take the elements of religions that work for them and customize them, making them their own "religion." For instance, an individual raised Catholic who may not have the time to regularly attend mass because of the need to work long hours might have their own personal shrine in their home where they burn incense and say regular prayers for their family members. Such an individual has created their own version of Catholicism. That version is their "lived religion." Like Luckmann and Davie, scholars who argue for studying lived religion suggest that, if we only examine metrics tied to organized or traditional religion, we miss much of what is happening when it comes to how people actually do or live their religion.

A similar argument focuses on spirituality instead of lived religion.[68] The general argument is similar to those above—people are less and less interested in organized religion and are turning, instead, to spirituality. Since spirituality is notoriously difficult define in a clear and straightforward way,[69] it's rather challenging to refute the idea that people are spiritual if, by spiritual, one could mean virtually anything.

This leads to our response to this line of criticism. We don't disagree with the general argument that people "do religion" in many and varied ways. Of course that is true, as many of these authors have illustrated with their rich ethnographic research, interviews, and thick description. Certainly, people privatize religion, people customize religion, and many people identify as spiritual, even if they use that word in a completely secular fashion, as has been shown with elite scientists, for instance.[70]

However, we disagree that these arguments undermine or challenge secularization for five reasons. First, as noted, secularization takes place at three levels—macro, meso, and micro—and secularization is best conceptualized as declining religious authority at all of these levels. When people "do religion" outside of the framework of organized religion, that is a manifestation of secularization. Religious authority is not dictating how they are doing religion; individuals are dictating how they are doing religion. This is a decline in the authority of religion. Thus, invisible religion, private religion, spirituality outside of religion, spirituality but not religion, and lived religion are all manifestations of secularization, not arguments against it.[71]

Second, some of these authors have argued for very, very broad definitions of religion. McGuire, for instance, gives the example of people gardening as a form of doing religion.[72] If everything people do can be or is religion, then religion is everything. And if religion is everything, *ipso facto*, religion is also nothing, as the word ceases to meaningfully demarcate something in the world that is different from something else.[73] By this line of reasoning, it would be possible to argue that the most strident atheist who actively works toward the destruction of organized religion, does not identify as religious or spiritual, and either rejects all notions of the supernatural or suspends belief toward them, is religious because they find the game Animal Crossing meditative and relaxing. Such a definition of religion does "violence to language," to quote Durkheim.[74] Let us be very clear here: Religion cannot encompass all things. Such an understanding of religion is meaningless.

Third, while we find value in this kind of thick description of how people do religion, it is also important to continue to use traditional and consistent measures of religiosity over time. Without consistent measures of religiosity, it's impossible to illustrate change. A simple example will help. Advocates of the "change not decline" argument might suggest that measuring how often people attend religious services in Iceland fails to capture widespread belief in elves and the various actions people take to protect elves or to illustrate that they believe in elves.[75] Of course that is true. But that does not make measures of religious service attendance worthless or meaningless. Traditional measures of religious service attendance provide scholars with an indication of how often (or, more accurately in the case of Iceland, how seldom) people attend organized religious services and how that has changed over time. If we stop using such measures, there would be no way to illustrate that people's behaviors have changed, increased, or declined.

Fourth, the "change not decline" argument has not, to date, been formulated as a theory. There is nothing theoretical about the claim that people customize religion to suit themselves and this is how they "do religion." That is an empirical observation. But it is not a theory about religious change or about the relationship between modernization and religion or about rationalization, differentiation, or any other social processes. It's literally just describing what people are doing. Descriptive research is perfectly fine. It is widespread in the natural sciences as people describe the behaviors of aardvarks or atoms or asteroids and should be more widespread in the social sciences. But lived religion, invisible religion, believing without belonging, and spirituality are not theories about religion but rather are descriptions of what people believe and do. To be considered theories, these ideas would have to explain the phenomena that they describe, and such explanation is lacking in this body of scholarship today.

Fifth and finally, the "change not decline" argument is a beautiful illustration of the "moving the goalposts" fallacy. It would be apt to describe this as the "change not decline hydra." Whenever a scholar asserts that secularization is happening, the "change not decline" crowd point to a new specific example of someone doing something lived religion/invisible religion/spiritual-esque and assert that religiosity has just changed, not declined. When scholars like David Voas,[76] Steve Bruce,[77] or us[78] muster evidence to challenge these claims, another head of the hydra pops up making the same claim over again but perhaps with a different example. It appears as though the "change not decline" advocates continue moving the goalposts indefinitely when new evidence of religious decline is presented.

What we recommend as a result of this fifth point is that the lived religion and spirituality advocates either simply admit that there is "change *and* decline" or that they meet the following six criteria in order to assert that their specific example of lived religion or spirituality undermines the evidence that scholars have delivered on secularization. First, they must demonstrate that whatever it is that they are observing can be considered religion or religious by well-accepted definitions. In other words, it must have some supernatural component to it and be communal. Gardening alone is out. Building a shrine to a saint in a corner of your house where you and your family burn incense for divine intervention would count. It's notable that the communal element here is a high bar. Most would agree that when one person claims that they are Jesus, people either dismiss them or worry about their mental health, but when many people believe that someone is Jesus, this results in a religion. Isolated, individual behaviors, even with supernatural elements, are *not* religion or lived religion. At best, they can be called spiritual practices. Additionally, if people are moving away from religion toward spirituality, that is still secularization as it is a manifestation of declining religious authority.

Second, those claiming "change not decline" must establish that the function of these lived religion/spiritual activities is largely the same as the functions of traditional religion. Is an athlete crossing himself in order to garner God's favor the same as an athlete not shaving his beard for luck? If one is motivated by religion and the other is individualistic and superstitious, can we call the second "lived religion"? If it is done alone, no. And if this is done without some appeal to something supernatural, it wouldn't even count as spirituality. In order for religion to not be declining but changing, what is replacing religion must be functionally the same.

Third, those claiming "change not decline" must demonstrate that these lived religion/spiritual practices are as meaningful to those engaged in them as were traditionally religious practices. What is the lived religion or spiritual equivalent of Catholic flagellation or being nailed to a cross, as is done in the Philippines to celebrate Good Friday? How committed to these lived religion/spiritual practices are people? Is their dedication equivalent to that of individuals who are traditionally religious? If not, this would at best be "change *and* decline."

Fourth, advocates of the "change not decline argument" must demonstrate that these lived religion/spirituality practices carry the same authoritative weight as did traditional, organized religion in decades past. If the spiritual practice is collective daily meditation, the practitioners should feel as though they have sinned or otherwise harmed themselves or those with whom they meditate if they miss a session when something important comes up at work.

Fifth, advocates of the "change not decline" argument must demonstrate that these lived religion/spiritual practices consume just as much physical or cognitive time as did traditionally religious practices. If an individual replaces active participation in the LDS Church, which can consume anywhere from two to 20 hours per week, with yoga classes, in order for there to only be change and not decline, that individual would have to likewise engage in the equivalent amount of yoga. If there is any decline in the time engaged in lived religion or spirituality compared to traditional religion, that is decline, not simply change.

Sixth and finally, with the mountains of evidence that has accumulated in favor of secularization both from other scholars and what we include in the following chapters, the burden of proof has arguably shifted to the advocates of the "change not decline" argument. Those claiming that there is only change and not decline need to demonstrate that secularization is not occurring. They would need to provide considerable and substantive evidence that the individuals, groups, and societies that they study have *not* secularized. Interestingly, the "change not decline" advocates are much less likely to question meso and macro secularization than micro secularization, and typically only with qualitative data.

Should a scholar be able to muster evidence that meets all six of the criteria that we have detailed above, we will grant that what is occurring is "change and not decline." Until then, there are reasons to be skeptical of the "change not decline" claim.

Conclusion

The goal of this chapter was to provide a clear and succinct summary of what secularization theory is, noting some of the important recent contributions, and addressing some of the major criticisms of the theory. In conclusion, we want to address a few additional questions that come up regularly about secularization: Is it possible for secularization theory to be wrong? Can secularization be reversed? Is secularization inevitable? Aren't macro theories passé?

Can Secularization Theory Be Wrong?

From the discussion above, it may seem to readers that we are all in when it comes to secularization theory and that, given how secularization theory is formulated, it's possible to interpret any scenario as being supportive of secularization theory. We certainly don't want to run afoul of supporting a theory that is true by definition (i.e., a tautology), meaning it isn't really a theory. In order for secularization to truly warrant being called a theory it has to be falsifiable. There has to be a way to illustrate that the theory is wrong. This is true for evolution. If, for instance, we were to find fossils of fully formed *homo sapiens* in rock strata that were dated to, say, 70 million years ago and those humans were fossilized on a saddle on the back of a *Tyrannosaurus rex*, that would raise some serious concerns about evolution. What might raise some serious concerns about secularization theory?

If we could find a society that was: a) highly differentiated such that religion has been separated from all major aspects of that society (government, education, law, healthcare, welfare, etc.) and b) highly rationalized, with a clear understanding of technology, science, and modern, egalitarian values; and c) the vast majority of the people were devoutly religious, granting religion influence and authority over many of their actions, allowing religion privilege to influence society at the macro and meso level, then such a society would cause problems for secularization theory. The two core underlying aspects of modernization that lead to secularization—differentiation and rationalization— would be in place, but the outcome would not be what is expected. If such a society were to exist, that would be a clear exception to the theory and would lead us to reconsider whether secularization is a compelling theory.

We are unaware of such a society.

Can Secularization Be Reversed?

The short answer is yes. However, other scholars have suggested that secularization cannot be reversed.[79] We agree that it is unlikely that it will be reversed, but, as detailed above, secularization as a process is contingent upon modernization and the subsequent processes of differentiation and rationalization. It does not challenge the imagination to envision scenarios in which those processes are reversed. Here are two possible scenarios.

Imagine a populist government takes over a country that is quite modernized and, up until the election of that government, is highly differentiated and very rationalized with a sizable percentage of the population having secularized. The new populist government, as part of its platform and to reinforce its authority, begins de-differentiating the government, putting religious clergy into positions of power and recognizing religious authority in various aspects of the society.[80] This is not that far-fetched, as governments of this sort have taken over in Hungary, Turkey, Poland, the Philippines, and Russia (among others) in the early twenty-first century and have attempted to institute religiously conservative policies (as we will examine in later chapters). They have not gone as far as just suggested, putting religious clergy in charge of, say, education, healthcare, and the law. But these governments have pushed a conservative religious agenda, restricting the rights of LGBTQ+ individuals, women, and the media, and generally curtailing democracy and equality. Should such a situation occur in which a government undoes differentiation, it is possible that secularization could reverse itself.[81]

Likewise, should a rationalized society experience de-rationalization, it is possible that secularization could be reversed. That scenario seems both less likely and more catastrophic. To de-rationalize in light of the technology and scientific advances we have would probably have to involve some sort of apocalyptic scenario: a meteor strike that wipes out much of humanity, a viral outbreak leading to a zombie apocalypse, a mega volcano that kills much of humanity, etc.[82] If the end result of such an apocalypse was the collapse of the power grid, the shuttering of the internet, a loss of much of the technology and scientific understanding we have, and a turn to might-makes-right ethics as people struggle for survival, it is absolutely possible for secularization to be reversed. Alternatively, if a government were to be elected (or otherwise assume power) and remove the social safety net that provides existential security, it is also possible that we could see a reversal of secularization.

The above scenarios are not common or particularly likely, but possible. Without such dramatic reversals of differentiation and rationalization, we do not think it is likely that secularization will be reversed.

Is Secularization Inevitable?

There are two elements to this question. First, will all countries eventually go through a secular transition?[83] And, second, will religion and supernatural beliefs, values, and behaviors decline?

The answer to the first question is: it depends. If all countries eventually modernize, then yes. If they do not, then no. Certainly there are many countries that are holding out against differentiating, maintaining close ties between religion and the government, and prohibiting secularization through punitive laws that restrict freedom of religion. As long as such governments continue, those countries are unlikely to experience open and widespread secularization (see our penultimate chapter on exceptions to secularization).

As for the second question . . . It would be rather stupid of us to suggest that religion and supernatural belief will completely disappear. Scholars who have made such claims in the past are now heavily criticized, particularly if they suggested a time frame for religion to disappear. Our position on this is more nuanced. We believe that religiosity and supernatural beliefs, values, and behaviors will continue to decline in light of widespread differentiation and rationalization. The discussion of religious transmission above provides pretty compelling justification for that prognostication. In almost every country where secularization is occurring, young people are less religious than are their parents and are substantially less religious than are their grandparents. Barring a massive reversal of either differentiation or rationalization in those countries, there is no reason to think that those young people will reverse course and suddenly become more religious or credulous. Thus, we believe that secularization is going to continue for the foreseeable future.

Even so, we can also envision scenarios in which a smaller percentage of populations in highly modernized countries remain somewhat religious. We are reticent to give specifics on what that might look like, but, following Guyau,[84] we can see the beginnings of one trend brought about by secularization. It seems to us as though exclusive religions that used to consider all other religions to be the competition and the enemy are changing their position. They appear to be realizing that they all have a common enemy—secularization. As a result, formerly exclusive religions are now teaming up with other religions on initiatives like efforts to push "freedom of religion," by which they mean they do not want governments to restrict their abilities to discriminate against minorities or regulate their behaviors or actions.[85] That religions are forming a coalition to oppose secularism and secularization is telling. It suggests that religions are suffering from secularization and are willing to change to fight their common enemy.

Aren't Macro Theories Passé?

Finally, it sure seems as though macro theories are passé these days, and we can understand why when we consider, say, structural functionalism. Such theories are often too big and unwieldy, with far too many exceptions or problems. We actually consider secularization theory to be a mid-range theory. It is not a theory about all of society but rather about one aspect of society—religion.

The major criticism here is that secularization does not play out the same way in every country, leading some people to suggest that a broad, overarching theory is simply not very useful in understanding what happens inside countries. Such criticisms are fine, but they do not undermine secularization theory. If the specific details for how a country secularizes varies such that secularization looks a little different in Argentina, Austria, and Angola, that does not undermine the overarching theory. To the contrary, we see that as an opportunity for scholars to dig deeply into the specifics of how secularization develops in individual countries. Just as there are many ways that democracy develops, there are many ways that secularization plays out in countries. Sometimes secularization is delayed, or a catastrophic event might lead to a brief, short-lived reversal, or there may be specific phenomena that facilitate or retard secularization in specific countries. There may be cultural nuances in countries such that people are less likely to adhere to "religion" in the westernized sense but retain elements of supernatural belief, like praying to ancestors (e.g., China) or participating in manifestly religious rituals that are part of local and national identity (e.g., Japan). All of those nuances are important. But none of those nuances undermine secularization as the broad, overarching process. The nuances offer scholars opportunities to illustrate how secularization occurs in varied cultures, contexts, and situations.

2

The Evidence, Part I

A Global Overview

In 1697, in the Scottish city of Edinburgh, a young college student named Thomas Aikenhead discussed religion with some of his friends. He told them that he thought that the Bible was a bunch of fables, that theology was a rhapsody of nonsense, that Jesus was probably just a skilled magician, and that he simply didn't believe in the religion of Christianity.

For giving voice to such sentiments, Aikenhead was arrested, charged with blasphemy, and publicly hanged.[1]

The idea that someone would be executed—let alone arrested—for expressing skepticism toward religion in Scotland today is unimaginable. Christianity has shrunken so severely in relevance and religious authority has become so diluted in Scottish life,[2] that nonreligious people hardly merit a yawn, and those expressing anti-religious sentiments barely raise an eyebrow.

If anything, it is the devoutly religious people in Scotland today who are the outcasts, the nonconformists, and the social deviants. Of course, secular individuals have not completely turned the tables on the religious—religious zealots aren't arrested, tortured, or hanged. However, they are increasingly not fully welcomed, either. For example, when a Bible-toting evangelist took up a megaphone in the central square of the Scottish town of St. Andrews, on September 20, 2015, and began fervently preaching, a 14-year-old named Daniel Boyle decided to silence him by playing bagpipes right next to him, drowning out his pious pontifications. The young teenager was heartily cheered on by the other people in the crowded square, with many applauding his novel approach to countering the evangelist—who soon gave up and left the square.[3]

Daniel Boyle, this bagpiping Scottish teenager who drove out a Christian preacher, represents just how much has changed over the last three centuries in Scotland: from a land almost completely dominated by

Christianity, to today, where only 32 percent of Scottish people identify with the Church of Scotland (down from 42 percent in 2001),[4] and a Bible-thumper in the central square of St. Andrews is a pariah.

The secularization of Scotland is acute.[5] For example, since the 1980s, over 400 churches have folded,[6] with the number of Scottish people who regularly attend church plummeting by half, and of the Scottish people who still regularly attend church, nearly half of them are over age 65.[7] The Church of Scotland has been shedding adherents at an almost unbeliev-able rate: between 1966 and 2015, membership fell from over 1.2 million down to just over 350,000.[8] To put these numbers in even starker terms: the Scottish church currently loses about 320 members a week,[9] which is close to 5 percent of its membership per year. This loss is also reflected in the number of wedding ceremonies that the Church performs, with more Scots now marrying in Humanist ceremonies than in weddings officiated by the Church of Scotland.[10] Simultaneously, the number of Scots who identify as non-religious has increased dramatically: nearly 73 percent of Scottish people now say they have no religion, up from 56 percent in 2011,[11] which means that—for the first time in the nation's history—the overwhelming majority of Scottish people identify as secular.[12]

As for Jesus—he is far less of a significant person to the average Scot than the likes of singers Beyoncé or Adele, or soccer players Matt Phil-lips or Kylian Mbappé, or national/political heroes like Nelson Mandela or Malala Yousafzai. Even God, that central pillar of religion, has faded significantly from Scottish life. God is rarely at the forefront of Scottish people's minds as they make personal decisions, go about their daily work, interact with family and friends, travel, cook, shop online, stare at TikTok or Instagram, swipe on Tinder or Grindr, hike, bike, ride their motorcycles, order pints, vape, binge watch TV shows, diet, download, or seek to find meaning in this or that aspect of being. In fact, for mil-lions of Scots, God isn't even at the *back* of their minds: a 2018 study[13] found that 57 percent of Scottish people lack any belief in God, and of those in Scotland today who do still believe in God, only 18 percent hold that belief with real certainty.

If Scots aren't that religious anymore, perhaps they are spiritual? Is it the case that many people who eschew organized Christianity seek out other alternative spiritual fulfillment in new-age beliefs or Eastern religious practices?

No.

As Scottish professor and distinguished sociologist of religion Steve Bruce has demonstrated, only about 16 percent of Scots currently describe themselves as "spiritual," and the percentage of those who are actually committed to alternative spiritual activities or Eastern traditions, or who regularly participate in new-age spiritual groups, hovers at around 5 percent.[14]

Religion is clearly dying in Scotland, and spiritual practices are not taking its place. We've begun this chapter highlighting Scotland because the secularization that has occurred over the course of the last century there is deep, dramatic, and historically unprecedented. But what is perhaps more important to note is that Scotland's secularization is not some isolated, rare sociohistorical anomaly. As the remainder of this chapter will demonstrate, the significance of Scotland's secularization is that it has taken place amidst a larger and more widespread global process. Indeed, secularization is taking place throughout the modern world.

International Data

Using cross-national survey data, this chapter will illustrate the spread of secularization internationally. We use data from the World Values Survey (WVS) (1981–2020) and the European Values Study (EVS) (1981–2020)[15] to present both current levels and changes in the three Bs of religiosity: belief, behavior, and belonging, in over 100 countries over the past four decades. These surveys have been selected because they consist of representative samples of the adult population in each country; having been described as "the largest non-commercial, cross-national, time series investigation of human beliefs and values ever executed,"[16] the WVS is particularly useful for investigating global trends. Although we recognize that there is an overrepresentation of European countries in our sample, data are available and presented from a wide range of nations around the world well beyond Europe.

Below, we explore patterns in these measures globally by presenting current levels and changes over time in the three Bs. Religious *belief* is measured with a survey question on belief in God; *behavior* is measured with a question on attendance at religious services; and *belonging*

encompasses individuals' self-identification with a religious organization. While such measures and questions are admittedly broad, and certainly do not accurately reflect various ambiguities and nuances within
countries, they are useful in providing a clear and accessible overview
of the global situation. We offer more nuance and specificity in more
detailed analyses of specifically featured secularizing countries—
presenting a broader range of additional measures of belief, behavior,
and belonging—in chapter 3.

Behavior

Sociologically speaking, individuals adopt their religious identity
through the process of socialization, whereby they learn the beliefs, values, norms, expectations, and activities associated with this identity.[17]
Although family is the primary mechanism through which religion is
passed on to future generations,[18] religious institutions are necessary for
reinforcing and sustaining religious ideologies and beliefs.[19] If people
do not attend religious services, religious beliefs and belonging subsequently dissipate and fade over time and across generations. Thus, of
the three Bs, a decline in *religious behavior* is often the first indication of
secularization. When enough people stop *doing* religion, religion strug-
gles to retain its authority, dominance, and even relevance in society.[20]

To examine religious behavior, we use a very common measure: frequency of religious attendance. Similar to other scholars,[21] we focus on
regular attendees—those who attend religious services at least monthly.
Figure 2.1 shows monthly attendance at religious services for the most
recent year that each country participated in the survey. Less than half
of the population attend monthly in 63 percent of the countries. In other
words, church attendance is not the contemporary norm in a majority of
the countries represented in the survey data.

With few exceptions, the lowest levels of religious service attendance
can be seen in Europe, and in particular in western and northern Europe. However, eastern and southern Europe—regions that are typically
viewed as more religious than their northern and western European
counterparts[22]—show clear signs of weakening religious behavior; less
than a quarter of the population attends church monthly in Estonia, the
Czech Republic, Albania, Latvia, Hungary, Bulgaria, Belarus, Serbia,

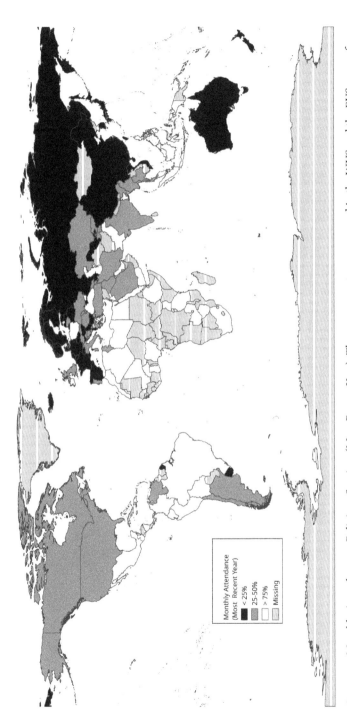

Figure 2.1: Monthly Attendance at Religious Services (Most Recent Year). The most recent year surveyed in the WVS and the EVS ranges from 1996 to 2020, with a mean of 2015.3; a median of 2015.3; a standard deviation of 5.28 years. Data from the European Values Study and the World Values Survey.

Spain, and Slovenia. Outside Europe, countries in which less than a quarter attend at least monthly include Uzbekistan, Japan, Azerbaijan, Hong Kong, New Zealand, Russia, Vietnam, Australia, Uruguay, Taiwan, South Korea, China, and Macau.[23]

In a minority of countries, primarily located in Africa, Southeast Asia, and Central America, more than half of the respondents attend at least monthly. In Europe, the only populations to fall into this category are those of Cyprus, Ireland, Poland, and Malta. Thus, low levels of religious participation are clearly not exclusively a western European—or even a European—phenomenon.

While we can see that levels of regular participation are low, the important question is: what is the trend over time? Are people attending religious services less frequently now than they did in the past? We examine this issue by exploring changes in church attendance between the first year a country participated in one of the surveys and the most recent year that same country participated. Although the EVS and the WVS began collecting data in some countries in 1981, in the larger sample of all countries, the mean and median number of years between first and most recent participation in the surveys were 22.2 and 22 years, respectively. In the context of measuring secularization, which can be a very slow process, this time span is relatively short. Even so, substantial changes are observed in many contexts. We also take a somewhat conservative approach here when considering change, in that any country with a difference in monthly attendance between time one and two that is smaller than plus or minus 2.5 percentage points we classified as having experienced "no change."

Figure 2.2 displays changes in monthly attendance over time. More than half of the surveyed countries—52 percent—have seen religious attendance diminish. In Europe, the trend of decline is particularly strong. Some specific examples help illustrate the large declines. In 1981, 54 percent of Spaniards attended religious services at least monthly; in 2017, that had fallen by more than half, to 23 percent. In the Netherlands, monthly attendance decreased from 40 to 16 percent between 1981 and 2017. The apparent lack of a decline in religious attendance in some of the most secularized countries—Finland, Estonia, and Iceland—is explained by a "floor effect": These countries secularized early and attendance already appears to have stabilized at a very low level.[24] In the case

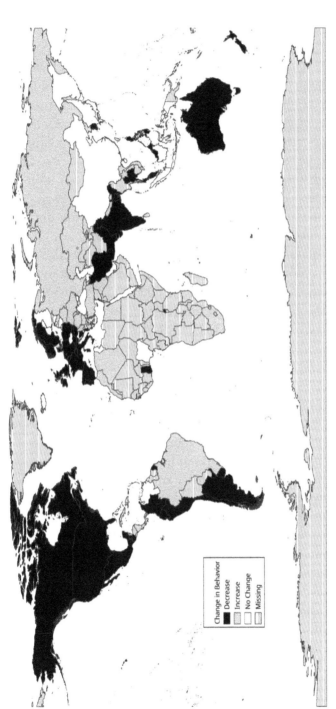

Figure 2.2: Changes in Monthly Attendance at Religious Services. Mean number of years between first and most recent measure: 22.2; Median: 22 years; Standard Deviation: 9.8 years. Data from the European Values Study and the World Values Survey.

of Finland, for example, only 13.1 percent of the population attended church monthly in 1990; that dropped to 11.2 percent in 2017. Similarly, in Iceland, 10.6 percent attended church monthly in 1984, which declined to 8.5 percent in 2017. It's possible that attendance in these countries will continue to decline slowly in the future, but it may also be the case that a small percentage of people will continue to find some value in religion into the foreseeable future, suggesting attendance may not drop to zero anytime soon.

The trend of declining attendance is also seen in Malta, Poland, and Ireland, which were three of the four European countries noted above that have more than 50 percent monthly attendance, and are arguably the least secularized countries in Europe on this particular measure. In Malta, monthly attendance declined from 94 to 82 percent between 1983 and 2008. In Ireland in 1981, 88 percent attended at least monthly, but Irish religious attendance fell by 34 percentage points by 2008, to just 54 percent of the population attending religious services at least monthly. Poland has seen a similar decline in religious service attendance, dropping from 84 to 65 percent between 1990 and 2017. The trends in Ireland and Poland are particularly important as they make it clear that there is a considerable weakening of the influence and authority that the Catholic Church has in these societies, as will be discussed in a later chapter in greater detail. Declining religious behavior in these countries also illustrates that, even in the most religious European countries, people are increasingly less likely to spend their time attending religious services.

While religious service attendance among Europeans has seen pretty steep declines in the past couple of decades, we see similar changes in countries around the world, particularly in countries located in Asia, Oceania, and North and South America, where the decline has also been rapid and substantial. For example, South Korean monthly attendance declined from 45 to 23 percent between 1982 and 2018. Chilean attendance declined from 46 to 32 percent between 1990 and 2018. In Mexico, monthly attendance decreased from 81 percent in 1981 to 61 percent in 2018. Argentina also experienced a decrease from 56 to 36 percent between 1984 and 2017. Although Africa remains the most religious continent in the world, there are modest signs of changes there, too.[25] There are now established secularist/nonbeliever organizations in countries such as Ghana and Kenya.[26] WVS data from the African continent are sparse, and while some northern African countries have increased their religious service attendance,[27] Ghana and Rwanda show small declines in monthly attendance.

Our data also indicate that the United States is not an outlier, as some critics of secularization theory have suggested.[28] In 1981, 60 percent of Americans attended religious services monthly. In 2017, that had fallen to just 39 percent, a number we also know to be inflated by social desirability biases in the US.[29] The decline in religious attendance in the US has been confirmed with other sources, such as the ISSP[30] and reports from the Pew Research Center.[31] David Voas and Mark Chaves used data from the General Social Survey to show a decline in American religious attendance resulting from cohort replacement where each generation in the US is generally less religiously engaged than their parents.[32]

Among the countries that have seen *increases* in church attendance, many, including Armenia, Belarus, Georgia, Latvia, Moldova, Russia, Ukraine, Kazakhstan, and Kyrgyzstan, are countries that were republics of the former Soviet Union. An increase in such countries can be explained by the fact that the previous lower levels of religion were not a result of modernization of free societies, but of religion being artificially and forcefully suppressed in this region by an undemocratic, anti-religious regime.[33] Additionally, the growth in religiosity in these countries appears to be a reflection of nationalism[34] and, to some degree, fascist tendencies that tend to draw upon the supernatural, the misogynistic, the traditional, and the religious for justification of their brutal and anti-modern policies. We discuss in much greater detail the perceived uptick in religiosity in former Soviet countries in chapter 6.

Belonging

In most countries around the world, a majority of people identify with a religion. Figure 2.3 shows religious affiliation for the most recent year available for each country. In only a minority of nations—China, Estonia, the Czech Republic, Vietnam, Hong Kong, Macau, Japan, South Korea, the Netherlands, Great Britain, Uruguay, France, Hungary, and Australia—does less than half of the population identify with a religion. Many modern and modernizing countries also fall into the second category: countries with between half and three quarters of their populations

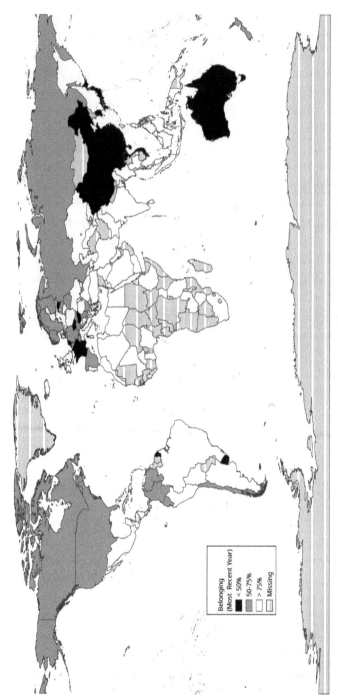

Figure 2.3: Belonging to a Religion (Most Recent Year). The most recent year surveyed ranges from 1996 to 2020, with a mean of 2015.2, a median of 2018, and a standard deviation of 5.4 years. Data from the European Values Study and the World Values Survey.

belonging to a religion. In the least developed countries, religious identification is often closer to 100 percent.

What do these results tell us about secularization, secularity, and religious identities? We know from previous research that nominal affiliation to a religion carries a wide range of meanings in diverse contexts.[35] Although religious belonging may typically signify a person's commitment to the supernatural beliefs, values, and doctrines of a particular religion, in other contexts, religious organizations perform what many people may consider to be predominantly secular functions. That is, identifying with a given religion can sometimes be a national, political, or ethnic identity marker without concomitant religious beliefs or behaviors. In the Nordic countries, for example, *cultural religion* prevails, where the national churches carry a cultural and historic heritage even though its members do not necessarily believe in God or ever attend religious services.[36] This would explain why religious belonging remains unusually high in Finland (73 percent), Denmark (82 percent), and Iceland (82 percent)—countries that are, on measures of belief and attendance, among the most secularized in the world. However, in all of these countries, there has been an undeniable drop in religious affiliation (see Figure 2.4) following the disestablishment of state churches and an increase in religious diversity. As will be demonstrated in a later chapter, the decline of religiosity in these countries after disestablishment and the introduction of less regulated markets illustrates that Rodney Stark's theoretical arguments detailed in the religious economies model[37] were erroneous.

While most of the world remains religiously identified, such religious identification has experienced a steep decline in diverse global contexts. As illustrated in Figure 2.4, in terms of religious affiliation, the world is not as religious as it has ever been, and, while a vast majority of European countries have seen sharp declines on this measure, decline is not limited to this region, for the decline of religious identification in the Americas is also clear. In North America, Mexico saw a decrease of nine percentage points between 1981 and 2018. The highly modernized and wealthy countries of Canada (1982–2006) and the United States (1982–2017) experienced declines of 22 and 37 percentage points respectively, and a modest decline can also be seen in Guatemala.

In South America, all surveyed countries, with the exception of Peru, show evidence of diminishing religious affiliation. This includes

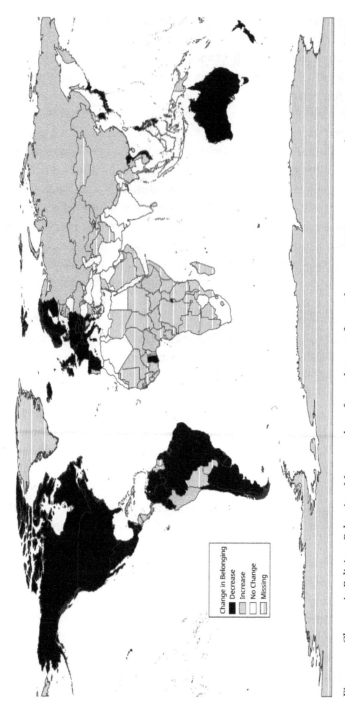

Figure 2.4: Changes in Religious Belonging. Mean number of years between first and most recent measure: 22.4; median: 22.5 years; standard deviation: 9.3 years. Data from the European Values Study and the World Values Survey.

Change in Belonging
■ Decrease
▨ Increase
□ No Change
▥ Missing

Colombia, Ecuador, Venezuela, Chile, Brazil, Argentina, and Uruguay. In many of these countries, the decline is substantial. Colombia, Venezuela, Ecuador, Chile, and Uruguay have all seen a decline of at least 10 percentage points between the earliest and the most recent surveys. Among African countries, Ghana and Rwanda have noted lower levels over time, just as we saw on religious service attendance. In Asia and Oceania, we see decreasing levels of religious belonging in highly modern contexts such as in Australia, Japan, New Zealand, and South Korea. We also note a decline in Vietnam and the Philippines. Once again, where religious belonging is increasing, it is almost exclusively in countries where religion has historically been highly suppressed by authoritarian regimes, such as in the former Soviet Union and in China.

Belief

Of the three Bs, religious beliefs remain the highest across the world. As seen in Figure 2.5, more than 75 percent of the population believe in God in all surveyed countries in North and South America, Africa, the Middle East, and in most countries in eastern Europe. In Sweden, Norway, the Netherlands, the Czech Republic, Great Britain, Estonia, China, Macau, Vietnam, Thailand, and South Korea, less than half of the population believes in God. However, sizeable secular populations exist in a range of modern and modernizing countries: Between a quarter and half of the population are nonbelievers in Denmark, Hong Kong, France, Japan, New Zealand, Finland, Australia, Germany, Slovenia, Iceland, Belgium, Andorra, Switzerland, Spain, Luxembourg, Hungary, Slovakia, and Austria.[38]

Does the high level of belief in God mean that secularization is not occurring? Are the critics of secularization correct that the world is more religious than it has ever been? Our answer to these questions is an unequivocal no. Figure 2.6 on changes in belief in God shows that out of 81 countries, 34 experienced a decline (of at least 2.5 percentage points) in belief in God between the earliest and the most recent measure, and simultaneously, belief in God did not increase in any country in the West or in South America, except for in Argentina. In fact, almost all countries in western Europe saw a decline in belief in God—a

Figure 2.5: Belief in God (Most Recent Year). The most recent year surveyed ranges from 1996 to 2020, with a mean of 2015.4, a median of 2018, and a standard deviation of 5.6 years. Data from the European Values Study and the World Values Survey.

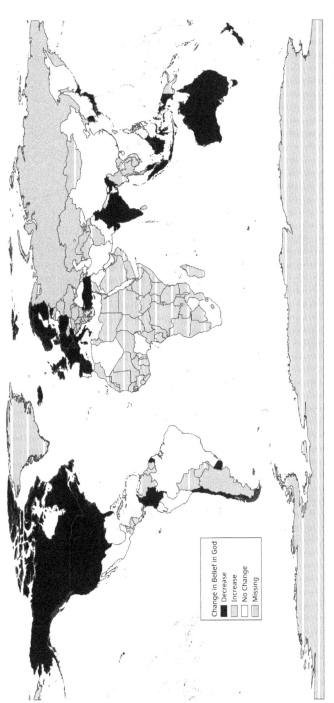

Figure 2.6: Changes in Belief in God. Mean number of years between first and most recent measure: 22.9; median: 22.5 years; standard deviation: 9.2 years. Data from the European Values Study and the World Values Survey.

secularizing phenomenon that many scholars in the field of sociology of religion consistently maintained wasn't occurring.[39]

Having demonstrated that Europe has indeed seen a decline in belief in God, is this decline limited to western Europe—the region of the world that critics of secularization have often claimed to be the only one that is experiencing a decline?[40] Again: No. The wide variety of countries that have seen declines in belief in God is striking: Sweden, South Korea, the Netherlands, Estonia, Norway, Great Britain, Denmark, Hong Kong, France, Japan, New Zealand, Finland, Australia, Germany, Iceland, Belgium, Switzerland, Spain, Luxembourg, Austria, the United States, India, Uruguay, Singapore, Italy, Chile, Canada, Ireland, Northern Ireland, Poland, Malaysia, Turkey, Colombia, and Indonesia all witnessed declines of at least 2.5 percentage points. Countries with a decrease of more than 20 percentage points include the Netherlands, Norway, Australia, Belgium, Sweden, Great Britain, Spain, New Zealand, the United States, Iceland, and South Korea. In some of these countries, the drop was astonishing. For example, between 1982 and 2018, belief in God in Great Britain declined by 34 percentage points, from 82 to 48 percent. Sweden saw a decline from 60 percent in 1982 to 36 percent in 2017. And in Belgium, 87 percent believed in God in 1981, which subsequently declined to 61 percent in 2009. Clearly, even though levels of belief in God are high in most of the world, secularization has occurred in the realm of belief, and is *not* limited to religious practices and identification.

Secularization and Modernization

In chapter 1, we laid out the key premises of secularization theory, explaining that what drives religious decline is modernization, including industrialization, economic development, and the subsequent differentiation of religion and rationalization of society. So far in this chapter, we have demonstrated that religiosity is diminishing in a wide range of countries around the world. In this section, we provide a brief overview of the link between this decline on the one hand and development (urbanization, employment, and income) and government regulation of religion (as a measure of religious differentiation) on the other. Here, we use data from the most recent year that a country participated in the EVS or the WVS since 2010. In addition to variables on religion and employ-ment from these surveys, we also draw on statistics from the World Bank for data on urban population (percent of total population) and GDP per capita (in constant 2010 US dollars), and the Cross-National Socioeconomic and Religion data from the Association of Religion Data Archives[41] for a measure on government regulation of religion (GRI).[42]

Countries were organized into groups based on their scores on gov-ernment regulation of religion and development (a composite measure of a country's urban population, GDP per capita, and full-time employ-ment). Cluster analysis[43] was performed to create four clusters of countries, generally characterized by a combination of high–high, high–low, low–high, and low–low scores on development and on regulation of religion at the macro level.

As seen in Table 2.1, when these four groups were compared on mea-sures of religiosity, we find that the most modernized group—made up of the countries with high scores on development and low scores on regulation of religion, which includes most countries in the West—is substantially and significantly less religious than the other three groups. Generally, the most religious group of countries is also the least mod-ernized, with low levels of development and high levels of regulation, which includes countries such as Bangladesh, Yemen, and Rwanda. The countries in this group have a mean monthly attendance level of 49.5 percent, compared to just 18.6 percent for the most modernized. The same figures are 95.5 and 57.8 percent for belonging and 96.8 and 60.4 percent for belief in God.

TABLE 2.1: Religiosity across Four Clusters of Countries (Percent)

	Low Development, High Regulation	Low Development, Low Regulation	High Development, High Regulation	High Development, Low Regulation
Monthly Attendance	49.5	52.2	40.3	18.6
Belonging	95.5	86.9	81.7	57.8
Belief in God	96.8	92.3	86.9	60.4
	e.g., Bangladesh, Yemen, Rwanda	e.g., Ghana, Albania, Guatemala	e.g., Kuwait, Qatar, Belarus	e.g., Japan, Sweden, Australia, Uruguay
N	20	31	10	26

Although countries with low development and high regulation are the most religious overall (scoring the highest on two of the three dimensions), the group of countries with low development and low regulation, such as Ghana, Guatemala, and Albania, overall show slightly higher attendance levels, but with somewhat lower levels of belonging and belief. The group of countries with high development and high government regulation of religion, such as Qatar and Kuwait, also remain highly religious—even if less so than the two groups with low levels of development. In other words, it is only in countries that have freedom of religion (i.e., differentiation) *and* high levels of development (i.e., rationalization) where we see more substantial secularization take place. As argued in chapter 1, countries with high development but with a high degree of religious regulation by the government cannot be expected to secularize because they have lower levels of differentiation of religion.

The above analysis illustrates the connection between economic development, religious differentiation, and secularization. It is difficult to argue, based on the data presented here, that there is not a relationship between modernization and religious decline, given the much lower levels of religious belief, behavior, and belonging in countries that are more developed and where religion is not regulated by the state. As this relatively simple but compelling analysis illustrates, when people live in modernized societies and have the freedom to choose not to be religious, secularization is more likely, supporting the propositions from chapter 1.

Conclusion

This chapter has provided an overview of religious changes, globally. The data are clear and the implications obvious: past critics of secularization were simply mistaken. Is Europe an exception to a world that is more religious than ever? Do people continue to believe, even if they aren't going to religious services nearly as much as they did in the past? And does religiosity increase in nations with former state churches? Nope, nyet, and nej. The data make the answer plain: The modern world is NOT more religious than it has ever been. On the contrary, most modern or modernizing countries have seen a steep decline in three key dimensions of religiosity: belief, behavior, and belonging—exactly as secularization theory predicts.

Along with the highly modern and modernizing nations in Asia and Oceania, the Americas in particular have also seen noteworthy decreases in all three dimensions of religiosity. This also includes the United States, which has previously been touted as a major exception to the secularization thesis.[44] As is explored further in the next chapter, the United States is not an exception.

Additionally, the hypothesis that religious vitality will increase when European state churches are disestablished—that is, cut off from government support and regulation—has now been falsified. Virtually all European countries have seen substantial declines in the three Bs over the past few decades, with or without the deregulation of state churches. Secularization is also not limited to attendance and belonging, as some critics of secularization have argued; belief in God is declining throughout most of the West.

To be precise, countries such as Great Britain, Canada, Ireland, Northern Ireland, Belgium, Uruguay, Switzerland, Sweden, the United States, the Netherlands, Spain, Denmark, Colombia, Austria, Germany, Chile, Poland, Norway, South Korea, Australia, Italy, France, and New Zealand, have something interesting in common: These nations are all religiously differentiated and economically developed or developing and have all experienced a decline, of at least 2.5 percentage points, in religious belief, behavior, and belonging between the first and the most recent years that they participated in these surveys. For most of these countries, the decline is substantial. Spain provides a compelling illustration. In 1981, 92 percent of Spaniards believed in God; in 2017 that number had declined to 68 percent. There was a similar decline in belonging, from 91 to 63 percent, and in behavior, from 54 to 23 percent of Spaniards attending religious services at least monthly. In the Netherlands the percentage of the population that believed in God in 1981 was 72 percent; this fell to 44 percent in 2017. At the same time, belonging decreased from 64 to 38 percent and monthly attendance from 40 to 16 percent. Beyond Europe, Chile serves as an example of a more recently secularizing country that has seen noteworthy declines: Belief has decreased from 95 to 86 percent between 1990 and 2018, belonging from 83 to 73 percent, and monthly attendance from 46 to 31 percent. In 1982, 60 percent of South Koreans believed in God, a figure that declined to just 41 percent in 2018. At the same time, belonging decreased from 53 to 36 percent, while attendance saw a drop from 45 to 23 percent. Secularization is not a European phenomenon; it is a global phenomenon.

It is certainly reasonable to argue about the nuances of secularization theory. How it manifests, what drives it, and when it occurs are all issues that warrant ongoing investigation. But denying secularization in light of the evidence is a denial of reality at this point. Modernization causes problems for religion, even if the nature of those problems is subtle. In the next chapter, we examine additional measures of religiosity that provide nuance and finer detail to the global picture presented in this chapter.

3

The Evidence, Part II

A Closer Look

Located on four different continents, Norway, Chile, South Korea, and the United States are highly distinct sociocultural contexts. From the long history of a Protestant state church in the modern welfare state of Norway, to South Korea with its religious diversity traditionally rooted in indigenous Shamanism (*Sindo*), Buddhism, and Confucianism, to the United States—once held up as a notable exception to Western religious decline—and to the Catholic colonial history of Chile, each country represents a unique religious and cultural landscape. However, despite their differences, we can observe two important similarities across the four countries: they all allow freedom of and from religion and all are modernizing countries with high or increasing levels of economic and human development. As a result, they are all secularizing on all three dimensions of religion.

While the previous chapter provided a global overview of countries that have secularized on religious belief, behavior, and belonging, this chapter takes a deeper dive into religion in Norway, Chile, South Korea, and the United States, specifically. We chose these four countries precisely because they are so different culturally but still demonstrate notable trends of religious decline. We summarize a wide range of evidence to show not only how these countries have secularized on religious identification, belief in God, and attendance at religious services—as we saw in the previous chapter—but also on measures such as belief in life after death, heaven, hell, miracles, spirituality, and more. In addition to the data from the World Values Survey and the European Values Study explored in the previous chapter, we also use additional data from the International Social Survey Program's (ISSP) religion modules (1991, 1998, 2008, and 2018).

Norway

"This change is something that we have wanted for a long time," proclaimed the Church of Norway's communications director, in 2012, in response to the Norwegian Parliament's decision to put an end to the tax-subsidized Church of Norway's 500-year-long history as a state church.[1] This decision came after a century of steady religious decline, as demonstrated by the diminishing authority of the national church alongside decreasing levels of religious beliefs and practices of Norwegians.[2] Nonetheless, rather than deeming the break with the state as a lethal blow to this once powerful social institution, the Church argued that its newfound independence would afford them the opportunity to reemerge with their own ideas, values, and practices that would in turn strengthen the Church and its mission.

A decade has passed, and we can evaluate whether the Church of Norway has succeeded. Rodney Stark argued that because church monopolies are sluggish and inefficient, all that is needed for a weakened national church to become a flourishing organization is a formal separation of its ties to the state.[3] Perhaps contradictorily or perhaps just to give themselves some leeway on this assertion, Stark and his fellow critics of secularization theory also suggested that a separation of church and state may, at least initially, result in some decline in individual religiosity,[4] perhaps as some nominal members leave when membership becomes a matter of active choice (and a "flourishing free market" is not yet established). As is often the case with claims made by these critics, no timeline for this is specified. Thus, it's not clear if former state churches should expect one or one hundred years of membership decline before their newfound independence supercharges the clergy and leadership and they become highly competitive in the religious marketplace, resulting in rapid growth. While it's possible that Stark and colleagues will be vindicated at some time in the future, given what has happened since the Church of Norway became independent, we think that is highly unlikely.

As seen in Table 3.1, between 2008 and 2018, the percentage of Norwegians that belonged to the national church declined from 77.9 to 62.2 percent. If advocates of the religious economies model were correct, this drop off of 15.7 percentage points could be temporary and should be

TABLE 3.1: Religious Belonging in Norway in Percent (1991–2018). Data from the International Social Survey Program

	1991	1998	2008	2018
Church of Norway	87.6	83.3	77.9	62.2
Other Religion	6.3	6.4	5.9	11.6
Humanist or Other Worldview	–	2.7	4.8	4.1
No Religion	6.1	7.3	11.2	22.2

TABLE 3.2: Beliefs among Church of Norway Affiliates (Percent)

	1991	1998	2008	2018
God	41.6	42.7	40.6	34.1
Life after Death	49.2	43.1	42.0	35.2
Heaven	37.1	33.2	33.6	26.8
Hell	16.7	13.3	12.4	10.9
Religious Miracles	32.6	30.2	33.6	25.9

Data from the International Social Survey Program. Total sample includes "don't know/can't choose." For Life after Death, Heaven, Hell, and Religious Miracles: Yes = Yes, definitely, and Yes, probably.

primarily made up of adherents who were not fully committed to the church or its creed, leaving just the most dedicated adherents. However, evidence since the separation of the Church of Norway from the government tells a fascinating story. Contrary to Stark's predictions, there has been no revitalization of religious supply resulting in a resurgence of religiosity in Norway. Additionally, the remaining members—those who ought to be the most pious—have in fact become *less* religious.

This is demonstrated in Table 3.2, which shows the percentage of Church of Norway affiliates who believe in God, life after death, heaven, hell, and religious miracles; among all national church adherents, only a minority hold any one of these beliefs, with the highest percentage being the 49.2 percent who believed in life after death in 1991. For each measure of belief, there is a substantial decline, *in particular* between 2008 and 2018—the very decade during which the state church was disestablished. In 2018, around a third of the adherents believed in God or life after death, with about a quarter believing in heaven and religious miracles, and only 1 in 10 believing in hell. It is now quite clear that the separation of church and state did *not* reinvigorate the church. If

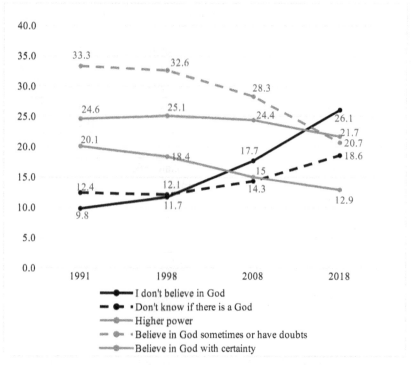

Figure 3.1: Beliefs about God in Norway (1991–2018). Data from the International Social Survey Program.

anything, the Church of Norway appears to be struggling, more than it ever has, to retain followers. It is also struggling to transmit basic Christian beliefs to those who remain adherents. In short, while nominal affiliation remains relatively high,[5] it is merely a remnant of the cultural heritage of the Church of Norway's position as the *folkekirke* and does not, in and of itself, change the picture of Norway as one of the most secular countries in the world.

But what about "other" religious and/or spiritual beliefs? Perhaps Norwegians no longer subscribe to conventional Christianity, but believe in a higher power? Indeed, this is an argument that is frequently made by critics of secularization theory.[6] The trends displayed in Figure 3.1 provide a response to the claim that individualized understandings of the supernatural are a sustainable replacement to traditional religious beliefs. Similar to the patterns presented above, the data show that atheistic and agnostic dispositions[7] increased sharply between 1991 and 2018. In 1991, 9.8 percent did not believe in God and 12.4 percent did not know if there is a God. By 2018, these figures had increased to 26.1 and 18.6 percent, respectively. In the same time period, belief in God with certainty declined from 20.1 to 12.9 percent, and belief in God with doubts declined from 30.3 to 20.7 percent. Furthermore, as displayed in Figure 3.2, among Church of Norway adherents, a higher percentage of individuals hold no belief in God (13.4 percent) than believe in God with certainty (10.4 percent). We thus see robust evidence for secularization in terms of belief in God.

What happened to alternative religious beliefs? Have they replaced the fading beliefs in God? The answer is a clear no. In fact, belief in a higher power remained relatively stable between 1991 and 2008 (24.6 to 24.4 percent) then declined marginally (to 21.7 percent) between 2008 and 2018. In other words, traditional religious beliefs have *not*

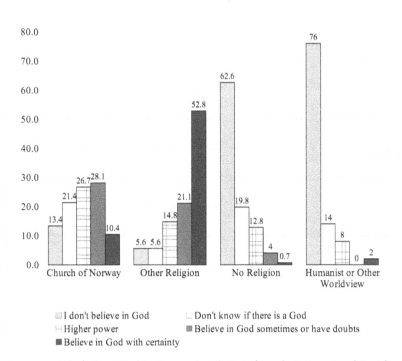

Figure 3.2: Beliefs about God in Norway (2018). Data from the International Social Survey Program.

been replaced by alternative forms of supernatural beliefs, but rather with nonbelief. Notably, atheism was the smallest category in 1991 and, almost three decades later, it was the largest. As demonstrated in Figure 3.2, among the unaffiliated, which is the fastest growing group in Norway—only 12.8 percent stated that they believed in a higher power, and those who believed in a higher power made up a relatively small group across all categories of religious belonging.

Although more people have adopted atheist or agnostic perspectives, it does not necessarily mean that they *identify* as atheists or agnostics. In fact, and as discussed in detail in chapter 5, in the most secular societies, most nonreligious individuals tend to be indifferent about their lack of religious beliefs and eschew taking on specific atheist or agnostic labels or identities.[8] Yet, as we can see in Table 3.1, we do have a comparatively large body of secular humanists in Norway. In fact, *Human-Etisk Forbund*, the Norwegian Humanist Association, is the largest humanist association in the world, with over 100,000 members.[9] However, the share of humanists and individuals who identify with other secular worldview organizations is not growing nearly as fast as "non-organized" secularity—in line with the argument that secularity, in the most secular countries, is characterized by indifference. When religion increasingly becomes a nonissue in society and in social interactions, the need to explicitly express or identify with an irreligious identity fades.

Finally, on the matter of *spirituality*, we can see in Figure 3.3 that this type of identification has *not* increased as a result of the decline of conventional religion and the disestablishment of the state church. In fact, in the typology of religiosity and spirituality that includes "spiritual and religious," "spiritual but not religious," "religious but not spiritual" and "neither religious nor spiritual," the two categories of spirituality ("religious and spiritual" and "spiritual but not religious") are the two smallest (13.5 and 17.9 percent respectively). Between 2008 and 2018, the *only* category to increase was the "neither religious nor spiritual," which is also the largest category in both 2008 and 2018 (38.2 and 45.6 percent).

This overview of recent trends of secularization in Norway makes it easy to reject the propositions a) that the disestablishment of a state church reinvigorates religiosity, b) that secularization ought to be associated with substantial increases in explicit irreligion, and c) that alternative forms of belief replace conventional religion in secularizing

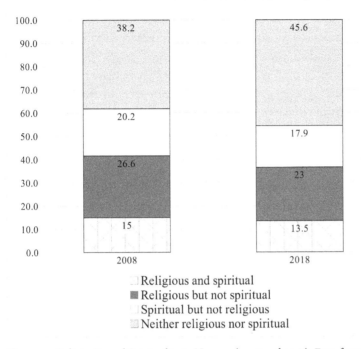

Figure 3.3: Religiosity and Spirituality in Norway (2008 and 2018). Data from the International Social Survey Program.

societies. The data presented here show that the group of individuals who identify with the Church of Norway has become less pious after the disestablishment of the state church, and belief in a higher power and spirituality have not replaced the decline in traditional religious beliefs. As a world-leading country in terms of economic and human development,[10] Norway is an important case study illustrating the trajectory of secularization following religious disestablishment.

Chile

The growing disenchantment with the Catholic Church was evident in the lukewarm response that Pope Francis received from the Chilean people on his visit to the country in 2018.[11] On his arrival in Santiago, he was greeted by "small crowds of well-wishers" alongside protesters.[12] The protests targeted the Church's inadequate and highly criticized reaction to the clergy sex abuse scandal. This incident has contributed to the decreasing interest in the Pope and the Catholic Church in Chile[13] and to a record-low 36 percent of the population that report trusting in the Church—the lowest level in Latin America.[14] A similar trajectory is observed in the ISSP data, where the percentage of Chileans who have complete or a great deal of confidence in churches or religious organizations declined from 52.2 percent in 1998 to a surprisingly low 13.3 percent in 2018. Similarly, in 1998, only 10 percent stated that they believed the church had too much power—a figure that increased to 30.3 percent in 2018.

It would, however, be wrong to assume that Chileans were enthusiastic about the Church before these scandals were at the center of public scrutiny.[15] Chile has been secularizing rapidly in recent decades, and the once ubiquitous Catholic Church is facing significant difficulties in retaining followers. According to a report from the Pew Research Center,[16] in 1910, 96 percent of Chileans were Catholic. In 2014, this had declined to 64 percent. While many Chileans have left the Catholic Church for other religious traditions—such as Pentecostalism—many have simply become less religious or nonreligious altogether. For example, only eight percent of Catholics in Chile say that religion is very important in their lives, that they pray daily, and that they attend religious services weekly—another figure that is among the lowest in Latin America. The continuous decline is also confirmed with data from the ISSP. As seen in Table 3.3, in 1998, 74.3 percent of the respondents identified as Catholic. Twenty years later, only 56.7 percent did so. In the same time period, the religiously unaffiliated increased from 5.2 to 21.6 percent. The trend of disaffiliation seen in this data looks similar to what we saw in the data from the World Values Survey in the previous chapter, where religious belonging decreased from 82.7 percent in 1990 to 73.0 percent in 2018.

TABLE 3.3: Religious Belonging in Chile in Percent (1998-2018). Data from the International Social Survey Program

	1998	2008	2018
Catholic	74.3	69.8	56.7
Protestant	19.4	16.9	16.4
Other Religion	1.1	3.3	5.3
No Religion	5.2	10.0	21.6

The secularization of Chile follows global trends of religious decline with increasing levels of development. Chilean society has transformed rapidly in the past few decades as a democratic society. Compared to the high levels of poverty during the military regime of the seventies and eighties, Chile is now seeing increasing economic development with diminishing poverty[17] and has, in fact, become one of the most economically developed nations in Latin America.[18] In terms of its GDP per capita, Chile is not far behind some European countries with moderate economic development, such as Greece, Latvia, and Croatia.[19]

A majority of Chileans do still believe in God, life after death, heaven, hell, and religious miracles (Table 3.4). At 57 percent, belief in hell is the lowest of these measures. Except for belief in hell, all of these indicators declined between 1998 and 2018. Belief in God declined from 91.3 to 86.9 percent, belief in life after death from 75.0 to 68.2, belief in heaven from 81.0 to 69.0, and belief in religious miracles from 79.0 to 69.8. When compared to the equivalent measures for Norway (Table 3.2), it is clear that Norway is further secularized than Chile, but both countries are experiencing a similar secularizing trend. Considering that Norway is also further down the path of modernization, these differences are not surprising—in fact, they are exactly in line with the premises of secularization theory.

When examining beliefs about God further (Table 3.5), we can see that, in 2018, 69.5 percent believed in God without any doubts, declining from 80.1 percent just 10 years prior. The approximately 10 percentage point decrease in belief in God with certainty seems to be replaced by modest increases in nonbelief, uncertainty, and alternative beliefs, as all other categories but belief without doubts are seeing small growth. For

TABLE 3.4: Beliefs in Chile (Percent). Data from the International Social Survey Program. Total sample includes "don't know/can't choose." For Life after Death, Heaven, Hell, and Religious Miracles: Yes = Yes, definitely, and Yes, probably

	1998	2008	2018
God	91.3	93.3	86.9
Life after Death	75.0	75.8	68.2
Heaven	81.0	78.3	69.0
Hell	57.0	58.8	57.0
Religious Miracles	79.0	79.7	69.8

TABLE 3.5: Beliefs about God in Chile (Percent). Data from the International Social Survey Program

	1998	2008	2018
I don't believe in God	2.1	2.0	4.3
Don't know if there is a god	0.7	1.3	2.5
Believe in higher power	2.9	4.6	8.0
Believe in God sometimes or have doubts	14.2	11.9	15.7
Know God really exists and have no doubts about it	80.4	80.1	69.5

TABLE 3.6: Religiosity in Chile (Percent). Data from the World Values Survey

	1990	1996	2000	2006	2012	2018
A religious person	76.8	74.5	70.8	64.7	52.2	49.9
Not a religious person	20.0	24.3	27.8	32.0	43.4	41.8
An atheist	3.1	1.2	1.4	3.3	4.4	8.2

example, belief in a higher power increased from 2.9 percent in 1998 to 8.0 percent in 2018, following the argument that earlier stages of secularization see a move away from institutionalized religion to privatized religious beliefs. However, as demonstrated in the data on Norway (Figure 3.1), a country that is further secularized will begin to see more substantial increases in nonbelief and a move away from both conventional and alternative religious beliefs. In other words, if Chile continues its current trend of modernization, we will likely see Chileans secularize even further, with increases in doubt and declining confidence in the existence of a higher power.

Table 3.6 demonstrates that the percentage of Chileans who identify as "a religious person" has declined from 76.8 percent in 1990, to just 49.9 percent in 2018. This decrease corresponds with growth primarily in the "not a religious person" category (from 20.0 to 41.8 percent), coupled with a modest increase (from 3.1 to 8.2 percent) in the "self-defined atheist" category. As previously noted, advanced stages of secularization do not result in widespread atheism and/or irreligion but rather indifference, though countries often experience an increase in atheism in the earlier stages of secularization,[20] just as we see in Chile in the first two decades of the 2000s.

If we look deeper at the percentage of Chileans who described themselves as a "religious person" (Figure 3.4), we see clear changes both over time and across generations. Older birth cohorts are more likely to be religious than are younger cohorts, in line with the theory that secularization is often a result of the unsuccessful transmission of religiosity across generations.[21] We can see that for each of the three time points included here (1990, 2006, and 2018), the oldest birth cohort is the most religious. However, it is also important to note that we do not just observe lower levels of religiosity between birth cohorts; religiosity is not static within birth cohorts. In fact, if we compare the same birth cohorts at the three different time points, we see that almost all of them are less religious in 2018 than in 2006 and 1999. This observation also refutes Stark and Finke's argument that people tend to *become* more religious as they get older, when the possibility of being rewarded in an afterlife starts to outweigh the costs of religious commitment.[22] Contrary to this assumption, older birth cohorts in Chile have become *less* religious as they have aged.

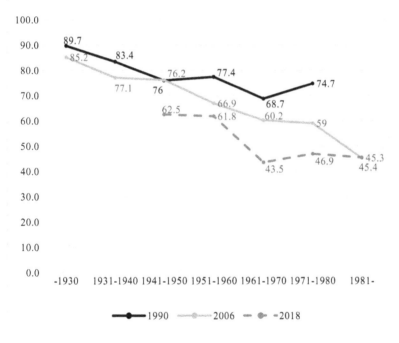

Figure 3.4: Percentage of Chileans Identifying as a "Religious Person" by Birth Cohort (1990, 2006, and 2018). Data from the World Values Survey.

As a case study of the secularization process, Chile illustrates that religious decline is not limited to the highly developed West. Although it is not as secular as Norway, it is also not as modernized. Assuming that Chile continues to follow the same trend of development that it has over the past few decades, we have no reason to assume that the religious decline in this country will subside. Given the growing number of Chileans who are skeptical of the Catholic Church and its power, it is likely that differentiation between religion and other institutions in Chile will continue. In sum, Chile is where secularization theory predicts it would be in relation to its level of modernization.

South Korea

In the city center of Seoul, the capital of South Korea, Yoido Full Gospel Church operates the largest megachurch in the world.[23] This Pentecostal church opened in 1958 and has since grown to 800,000 members. Close to 200,000 of them attend Sunday worship each week, with services taking place throughout the day—from early morning until dinner time.[24] Although Yoido Full Gospel Church is the largest, it is not unique in being a Christian megachurch in Seoul. The capital is home to 17 additional megachurches,[25] which is perhaps not what one would expect to see in an Asian society that is not historically Christian.

At first glance, South Korea could appear as a counterexample to secularization theory. In fact, Rodney Stark and others have argued that increasing industrialization, urbanization, and rationalization have not reduced religiosity there.[26] These claims initially seemed accurate given that South Korea is a prosperous and modern society, with the world's eleventh largest economy,[27] but it also saw some growth in Christianity during its period of rapid economic development. Data from the World Values Survey, presented in Table 3.7, show that in 1982, 46.7 percent of South Koreans were religiously unaffiliated, and 8.7 and 15.3 percent identified respectively as Catholic and Protestant. Just over two decades later, in 2005, the unaffiliated had declined to 29.2 percent and the share of Catholics and Protestants had increased to 21.2 and 22.1 percent respectively. During this time period (1982–2005), South Korea would appear to be a distinctive case of an Asian country that experienced a substantial rise in Western religiosity.

However, not all scholars interpret this uptick in religiosity in Korea as a flaw in secularization theory or a triumph for the religious economies model. Christianity is closely intertwined with capitalism, neoliberalism, and the Americanization and modernization of South Korea.[28] As described by Hyaeweol Choi:

> At a time when Korea was struggling to cope with imminent threats from imperial forces and find ways to build a modern nation-state, Protestant Christianity offered an alternative belief system and worldview . . . Koreans viewed this new religion as the embodiment of an advanced civilization . . . and even the proper foundation of modern development.[29]

Modeling themselves and their country on the United States, the country that was intimately involved in the war that divided the peninsula, South Koreans came to believe that the key to Western prosperity could be found in the adoption of Christian beliefs and practices. As a result, Protestant congregations in South Korea, including Yoido Full Gospel Church, preached prosperity theology and the notion that economic success and wealth would come to the faithful, similar to what had supposedly been seen in the West—and in particular in the United States. This message "appealed to the South's desire to modernise and differentiate itself from the North"[30] and Christianity became a tool with which South Koreans could "westernize" and create a "modern identity" distinct from their neighbors. As a result, religion came to function as a defense of South Korean culture during a time of conflict, threat, and change. As detailed in chapter 6, when religion is used for purposes other than what it has traditionally accomplished, the result can be higher levels of religiosity.

Even so, the surge in Christianity did not last. As seen in Table 3.7, since 2005, Christianity has seen a sharp decline in South Korea. In 2018, the shares of Catholics and Protestants were, at 6.8 and 14.9 percent, the lowest they had been since before 1982. At the same time, the unaffiliated made up a record-high 64 percent of the population, which is a growth of 34.8 percentage points since 2005, just 13 years earlier, and 17.3 percentage points since 1982, which was the previously highest level.[31] Buddhism has also seen a recent decline in South Korea. In 1982, 28.2 percent identified as Buddhist. At the time, this was the most

TABLE 3.7: Religious Belonging in South Korea (Percent). Data from the World Values Survey

	1982	1990	1996	2001	2005	2010	2018
Catholic	8.7	16.3	12.8	13.9	21.2	15.8	6.8
Protestant	15.3	21.6	17.6	23.7	22.1	21.2	14.9
Buddhist	28.8	25.4	26.8	20.9	24.9	20.7	14.0
Other Religion	0.5	7.5	3.8	4.8	2.7	0.8	0.2
No Religion	46.7	29.2	39.1	36.8	29.2	41.6	64.0

common category after "no religion." In 2005, this figure was at 24.9 percent and in 2018 at 14.0 percent. At 14 percent, Buddhists are only marginally smaller than Protestants, who are the largest of the "religious" groups at 14.9 percent of the population. In addition to the trends in religious affiliation, data from the World Values Survey show that religious service attendance is also in decline in South Korea. In 1982, 26.8 percent "never or practically never" attended. Although this went down in the early 2000s, by 2018, this had grown to 52.2 percent.[32]

In relation to the recent challenges that Christian congregations have encountered in growing their membership in South Korea, Jemima Baar argues that economic security and general stability may have "reduced the psychological and practical needs for religion."[33] Very recent data on changes in religiosity during the COVID-19 pandemic show that the religiosity of South Koreans has, as a result of the pandemic, largely remained unaffected.[34] Offering an alternative explanation, Steven Borowiec maintains that the religious decline is particularly sharp among younger Koreans and that religious organizations, with old-fashioned structures and leadership styles, fail to appeal to a generation that largely does not find religion helpful in addressing contemporary issues, supporting our argument in chapter 1 that one of the mechanisms of secularization is the inability to transmit religiosity across generations.[35] Similarly, the popularity of the Pentecostal megachurches has also stagnated, with decreasing levels of trust in these religious organizations following a number of public scandals, including the embezzlement of $12 million by a pastor at Yoido Full Gospel Church.[36] These negative sentiments are also growing alongside a rise in skepticism surrounding neoliberalism, imperialism, and the Americanization of South Korea.[37]

TABLE 3.8: Religiosity in South Korea (Percent). Data from the World Values Survey

	2001	2005	2010	2018
A religious person	31.0	30.0	32.5	16.1
Not a religious person	41.1	37.5	37.6	29.0
An atheist	31.3	28.6	29.9	54.9

TABLE 3.9: Percentage of South Koreans Identifying as a "Religious Person" by Religious Denomination (2001–2018). Data from the World Values Survey. Other religions are excluded due to a very small sample size (N = 4 in 2018)

	2001	2005	2010	2018
Catholic	45.2	34.4	54.3	47.1
Protestant	64.4	58.9	71.4	63.2
Buddhist	36.0	36.6	40.7	16.7
No religion	0.7	0.3	0.0	1.5

Moving beyond religious affiliation to other measures of religiosity, we can see just how weak religion has become in South Korea. In terms of self-described religiosity (shown in Table 3.8), only 16.1 percent of Koreans would consider themselves a religious person, with 29.0 percent identifying as "not a religious person" and 54.9 percent as convinced atheists. South Korea now has the distinction of being the country with the highest percentage of convinced atheists per World Values Survey data. The percentage of self-defined atheists is similar to the percentage of individuals who state that they do not believe in God (59.4 percent in 2018). The high proportion of atheists also suggests that South Korea is seeing rapid religious decline, even though religion still has a strong presence in the country. Additionally, this suggests that secularization in South Korea is not yet characterized by religious indifference that can be seen in countries like Norway that modernized and secularized earlier.

Intriguingly, even among those who report a religious affiliation, a large proportion do not consider themselves religious. As shown in Table 3.9, in 2018, just 47.1 percent of Catholics, 63.2 percent of Protestants, and 16.7 percent of Buddhists stated that they were "a religious person." Around half of all Catholics and 4 in 10 Protestants consider themselves either "not a religious person" or "an atheist," suggesting that, for many South Koreans, their religious affiliation is not a highly salient aspect of their identity.

Importantly, South Korea differs from the other case studies in this chapter in that the adoption of Christianity has been quite recent. This raises the question of whether South Koreans think about and practice religion differently from people in countries with a longer history of Christianity, where it is assumed that religious practice is "rather rigid."[38] In other words, do South Koreans include or combine elements of Eastern spirituality into their westernized religious beliefs or behaviors? Although he provided no data on such practices nor cited any studies to support his claim, Rodney Stark argued about South Koreans that "most people claim to have no religion, although most of these Koreans probably take part in Buddhist activities, including worship in temples, and the statistics make no mention of folk practices such as ancestor worship, although they are quite common."[39] In order to be as comprehensive as possible in addressing such unfounded claims, we also examine non-Western measures of religiosity/spirituality.

As seen in figures 3.5 and 3.6, even when a wider range of measures of beliefs and practices are examined, these are not widespread among South Koreans. Specifically, for each birth cohort, less than half of Koreans believe in life after death, religious miracles, or supernatural powers of deceased ancestors (Figure 3.5). The measures fluctuate across birth cohorts, and although individuals born in the seventies and eighties appear more religious than those born in the sixties, in particular on the measure of life after death, we see lower levels among the youngest birth cohort (those born after 1990). Data from the World Values Survey show that in 1982, 52.2 percent of Koreans believed in life after death, a percentage that had declined to 33.7 in 2018. The overall trend across cohorts is a decline.

We see a similar pattern regarding Eastern religious practices (Figure 3.6). None of the measures attract a majority of Koreans of any birth cohort. The most popular activity appears to be the Western measure of religious service attendance that varies fairly substantially between cohorts. Among those born in 1940 or earlier, 42.6 percent attend at least monthly, whereas just 17.6 percent among those born in 1991 or later attend at least monthly. Very few Koreans, of any birth cohort, frequently visit a holy place outside of regular religious services, and between one in five and one in three Koreans read or listen to religious scripture

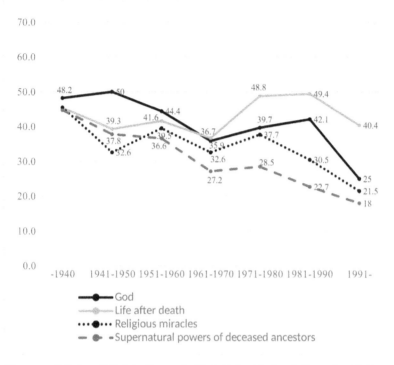

Figure 3.5: Religious Beliefs in Percent by Birth Cohort in South Korea (2018). Data from the International Social Survey Program. Total sample includes "don't know/can't choose." For Life after death, Supernatural powers of deceased ancestors, and Religious miracles: Yes = Yes, definitely, and Yes, probably.

outside of worship or have a shrine, altar, or religious object on display in their home. Examining actual data suggests that the story that Stark is telling cannot be supported.

This brief overview of religion in South Korea shows a unique pattern of religious change that involves both a rise and a fall of Christianity during a period of economic development, in line with prior research suggesting that economic development can increase religiosity initially before more advanced development undermines religiosity.[40] The temporary rise, in particular of Protestantism, was related to modernization processes in South Korea that were linked with a desire to create a prosperous, westernized cultural identity different from its neighbors rather than a pursuit of religious beliefs and practices in their own right.

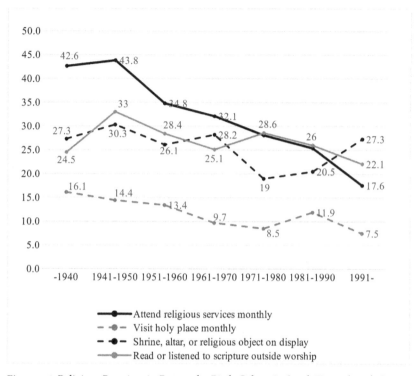

Figure 3.6: Religious Practices in Percent by Birth Cohort in South Korea (2018). Data from the International Social Survey Program.

This interpretation seems most closely to align with the data given that a large portion of Christians in South Korea do not consider their religion as salient to their identities. Additionally, now that modernization is widespread in South Korea, Christianity is experiencing a significant decline. The decline of Christianity is taking place alongside a growing criticism of the Americanization of South Korea. The youngest cohort of South Koreans is largely detached from both organized religion and alternative beliefs and practices. With the highest percentage of atheists in the world, widespread secularization in South Korea is beyond doubt.

The United States

As mentioned earlier, the United States has regularly been held up as the greatest exception to—and thus refutation of—secularization theory.

For decades, the US has been a modern, wealthy, industrialized nation but was still religious. Peter Berger and colleagues wrote in 2008 that the continued religiosity of the United States represented "a big nail in the coffin" of secularization theory.[41] That same year, Philip Gorski and Ates Altinordu agreed, insisting that the United States constituted "a fatal anomaly" for secularization theory because it was indisputably modern—urbanized, democratic, and rationalized—but showed no signs of secularizing.[42] The timing of those claims is somewhat surprising as survey data released around that time[43] made it clear that these scholars were wrong. Granted, Peter Berger was never much of an empiricist, but the trends in the US were coming into focus even in the late 1990s and were hard to deny by the end of the first decade of the twenty-first century.[44]

Anyway . . . That was then. This is now.[45] What all the best data show as of 2021 is that not only has religion been declining in the United States—even as Berger and Gorski were publishing their erroneous assertions—but it has been declining more markedly than ever in recent years.[46] According to the empirically robust analysis of Ronald Inglehart, since 2007, the United States "has been secularizing at a more rapid rate than any other country for which data is available."[47]

While much has been written about secularization in the United States, and while we already presented data illustrating the decline of religiosity in chapter 2, in this section we draw from a plethora of different studies, in addition to data from the ISSP and the WVS, to highlight the most obvious and explicit ways in which this nation, too, is secularizing.

Church membership in the US is at an all-time low. In 1940, 73 percent of Americans said that they were a member of a church, mosque, or synagogue. In 2020 that was down to 47 percent.[48] In 1986, just 10 percent of young adult Americans (those between the ages of 18 and 29) were unaffiliated with a religion, but by 2020, that was up to 36 percent.[49] According to the CIRP "Freshman Survey," which gathers information on incoming college students, in 1986 only 10 percent of first year college students said they had no religion. In 2016, 31 percent were religiously unaffiliated.[50]

When Americans are asked *if* they belong to a religious denomination (rather than *which* religion), religiosity is even lower. As seen in Figure 3.7, in 2017, only 43.4 percent of Americans born in 1981 or later

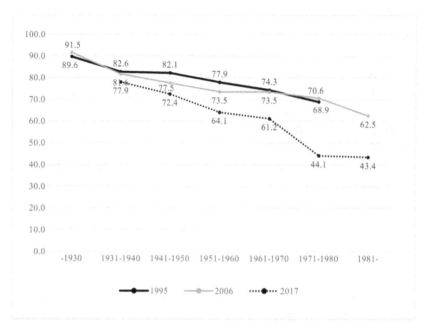

Figure 3.7: Religious Belonging in Percent by Birth Cohort in the United States. Data from the World Values Survey.

stated that they belonged to a religion. This figure had been 62.5 percent in 2006, showing a steep decline in religious belonging among the youngest respondents. Similar declines are observed for the cohort born between 1971 and 1980. In 1995 and 2006, around 7 out of 10 of the members of this cohort indicated that they belonged to a religion. In 2017, this had fallen to below half, just 44.1 percent. Similar to what we observed with Chile, religion appears to be declining both within and across generations in the US, with a particularly sharp downturn between 2006 and 2017. Importantly, even though each cohort is less religious than the one before it, during the decade from 2006 to 2017, religious belonging declined for all generations. The generational declines in religious belonging also reflect the fact that fewer Americans are being raised with religion: According to the American Perspectives Survey, only three percent of US adults over the age of 65 were raised without religion and remained non-religious as adults. However, 19 percent of Americans between the ages of 18 and 29 were raised as children without religion and remain nonreligious today.[51]

On the *behavior* front, the drop in religious weddings is a good indicator of the decline of religious hegemony in people's lives. According to the American Perspectives Survey, while 27 percent of married Americans over the age of 65 had a secular wedding that was not held in a religious venue nor officiated by a religious person, 48 percent of married Americans between the ages of 18–35 had secular weddings.[52] Similarly, according to national data provided by Facts and Trends, religious congregations hosted 41 percent of all weddings in 2009, but that was down to 22 percent in 2017.[53] As for rituals around death, while 50 percent of Americans felt that having a religious component in the funeral of a loved one was very important in 2012, that had fallen to 35 percent in 2019.[54]

When examining changes in other religious behaviors in ISSP data, we observe an increase in the group of people who never attend religious services, who never attend church activities, and who never pray. For example, in 1991, 13.5 percent of Americans never attended religious services. In 2018, this figure was 29.3 percent. In 1991, 7.9 percent never prayed and in 2018, this had gone up to 14.5 percent. Similar data from the WVS (Table 3.10) show that in 1995, 41.8 percent of the respondents stated that they attended religious services at least weekly, with 17.5 percent never attending. In 2017, 29.3 percent claimed to attend weekly, with 33.4 percent never attending.

The increase in the category of Americans who reject religious practices altogether has been steady, and previous research has indicated that survey questions on religious service attendance tend to overestimate the frequency of attendance in the United States.[55] In fact, when comparing attendance levels from surveys to findings from time use studies—when individuals use a diary to write down their day-to-day activities—actual

TABLE **3.10**: Religious Service Attendance in the United States (Percent). Data from the World Values Survey

	1995	1999	2006	2011	2017
Weekly	41.8	45.2	36.1	33.8	29.3
Monthly	13.3	15.0	12.9	9.8	9.7
Less often	27.4	25.0	25.5	25.9	27.6
Never	17.5	14.9	25.5	30.6	33.4

attendance is consistently 10–18 percentage points lower, with "real" levels of US church attendance that are similar to European countries like Italy.[56] While the share of people who claim to regularly engage in religious practices is higher than the percentage in very secular countries like Norway, what the data make clear is that it is a minority of Americans who are in services on a weekly basis. Claiming that Americans are highly religious when at least 70 percent (and perhaps as much as 85 percent to 90 percent) are not at religious services every week is rather absurd. Yet, many scholars continue to make such claims.[57]

Given the decline in church membership as well as church attendance, religious weddings, and religious funerals, it is not surprising that many churches are closing in the US. One of the authors (Ryan) attends religious services several times a year to observe what is happening in congregations. In a recent church visit in fall 2021, he attended a Baptist church that had been in existence since 1950 and was a cornerstone of the neighborhood. In attendance that day were eight women, ranging from mid-sixties to late eighties. Two entered the sanctuary with the aid of walkers. There was also one male attendee in his fifties, a nurse assistant at a local hospital who was also the secretary of the congregation. The pastor, a middle-aged male, explained in a brief interview before the service that it was not a matter of *if* the congregation was going to close but *when*. And the when was not a distant consideration. The very day Ryan attended the service the pastor was meeting with those in attendance to determine whether they would close after their Christmas service or hang on until Easter. Those were the two options. Declining religiosity in the US is observable in the closing and shuttering of religious buildings.

As mentioned in chapter 2, between 6,000 and 10,000 US churches are closing every year.[58] Admittedly, some congregations open every year, but related research suggests that many more congregations close than open every year.[59] Such decline is historically unprecedented. If the US was as religious as many scholars seem to suggest, thousands of congregations would not be closing their doors every year.

In terms of *belief*, Table 3.11 shows that there is a modest but noticeable trend toward a decline in conventional religious beliefs. In 1991, 62.8 percent of Americans believed in God without doubts. In 2018, this was 54.6 percent. The percentage of nonbelievers and agnostics also

TABLE 3.11: Beliefs about God in the United States (Percent). Data from the International Social Survey Program

	1991	1998	2008	2018
I don't believe in God	2.3	3.2	3.1	4.6
Don't know if there is a god	4.5	4.9	5.0	6.0
Believe in higher power	6.9	9.8	10.5	12.5
Believe in God sometimes or have doubts	5.2	4.7	3.1	3.4
Know God really exists and have no doubts about it	62.8	62.8	61.1	54.6

increased marginally in the same time frame, and the share of believers in a higher power rose from 6.9 to 12.5 percent. There was a clear decline in religious beliefs among young Americans during this time. In 1988, among Americans between the ages of 18 and 34, 58 percent claimed to know, with surety, that God existed. That dropped to 39 percent in 2018.[60]

Other studies, data, and measures echo the trends presented here. While 50 percent of older Americans (those born between 1927–1945) believed that the "universal purpose for all people is to know, love, and serve God with all heart, mind, strength and soul," only 19 percent of millennials (born between 1984–2002) believed that; while 67 percent of older Americans believed that the "universe was designed and created, and is sustained by God," only 30 percent of millennials believed that; while 27 percent of older Americans said that they "Don't know, care, or believe that God exists," 43 percent of millennials hold this agnostic, ap-atheistic, or atheistic position.[61] According to the American Perspectives Survey, 65 percent of older Americans said they believe in God without ever having doubts, but only 30 percent of young adults aged 18 to 29 reported they believed in God without ever questioning their belief.[62]

Not surprisingly, the declines in religious belief, behavior, and be-longing have also led to a shift in how Americans describe themselves in relation to religion (Table 3.12). In 1995, 81.1 percent of Americans iden-tified as "a religious person." This percentage declined to 58.5 in 2017. "Not a religious person" increased from 18.0 percent to 33.6 percent in that same time period. Interestingly, identifying explicitly as an atheist has increased to 8.0 percent in 2017 when, in 1995, it was close to zero (0.9 percent).

TABLE 3.12: Religiosity in the United States (Percent). Data from the World Values Survey

	1995	1999	2006	2011	2017
A religious person	81.1	82.5	72.1	67.9	58.5
Not a religious person	18.0	16.0	24.4	27.6	33.6
An atheist	0.9	1.4	3.5	4.5	8.0

The increase in self-identified atheism and in secular identities more broadly shows that it has become more socially acceptable to admit to being nonreligious in the US. For much of the 20th century, the US was engaged in a cultural war with the USSR. Of course, the Cold War was tied to nuclear weapons and economic systems—capitalism versus communism. But overlaid on these issues was also religion versus irreligion. As will be discussed in detail in chapter 6, the USSR and the Marxist-Leninist leadership were strongly opposed to religion. To counter that narrative, the US government embraced religion, making religiosity normative in the US. When the Cold War ended, it became possible in the US to identify as nonreligious or even atheist without your loyalty to the country being called into question.[63] Not surprisingly, then, the seismic declines in religiosity have largely occurred since the end of the Cold War in 1989 and 1990 when it became more socially acceptable to admit one's secularity.

Is religion important to Americans? Yes, but decreasingly so. In 1952, a Gallup survey asked Americans (over the age of 18) how important religion was in their lives; 75 percent said "very," but that dropped to 48 percent in 2021, the lowest percentage on record.[64] In 1957, a Gallup poll found that 82 percent of American adults felt that religion could answer today's problems; that fell to 46 percent in 2018—the lowest level on record. Conversely, only 7 percent of American adults said that religion was "old-fashioned and out of date" in 1957. That rose to 39 percent in 2018—also a record high.[65] Although the United States may not be as secularized as other highly developed countries and declines in religious beliefs may be relatively modest at this point, all measures appear to point in the same direction—toward decline.

Conclusion

This chapter focused on Norway, Chile, South Korea, and the United States to examine the nuances of religious decline in varied cultures. What we learn from the findings from these countries is that secularization is not simply a European phenomenon, as was strongly argued by Peter Berger, Grace Davie, and Effie Fokas.[66] The case study on Norway illustrated how mistaken Rodney Stark and colleagues were in their prediction that religious deregulation would increase religious vitality.[67] We also demonstrated that alternative religious beliefs may increase modestly at earlier stages of secularization, but that in countries like Norway, these measures do not replace a decline in conventional religiosity. This chapter also presented examples of clear trends of religious decline both within and across generations, suggesting that people are unlikely to become more religious as they age. All of the arguments that we reject here have previously received broad support in the sociology of religion, even though the evidence and the data available tell a very different story.

As mentioned at the start of this chapter, we chose to focus on these countries to show that secularization is happening in modernizing societies around the world regardless of cultural, historic, and geographic differences. It is important to note that we did not cherry-pick the best or easiest examples for this chapter; we did not purposefully select the "most linear" illustrations of secularization. In Scandinavia, Sweden and Denmark are, on most measures, more secular than Norway. In North America, Canada is more secular than the United States. Uruguay is regularly referred to as Latin America's most prominent example of religious decline, and in Asia, there are countries, such as Japan, that are highly secularized and that, unlike South Korea, do not have a previous uptick in religiosity that warrants explanation. Thus, while we selected four different countries from four different continents to focus on in this chapter, we could have easily focused on many more, all of which would have revealed similar—or even more robust—patterns of secularization.

There is no doubt that the paths and experiences of secularization are highly dependent on historic backgrounds and unique social and political forces at play in each country. We are not claiming that religious decline is a uniform process the world over. But what we have shown in this chapter is that despite numerous differences—and even with the complex and context-dependent patterns of religious change—religion is nonetheless clearly trending down as a result of modernization in these four countries.

4

Is Being Secular Unnatural?

One of the strangest assertions to emerge within the debate over secularization, is the claim that religion is an innate, natural, and therefore, universally unalterable aspect of the human condition. This position essentially argues that—to quote the unambiguous words of psychology professor Justin L. Barrett—humans are literally "born believers."[1] As such, secularization ought never get very far, since people who are nonreligious are, at root, living unnaturally. To be secular, according to this perspective, is to live in conflict with—or in violation of—an innate predisposition that is a fixed part of our humanity.

The assertion that religion is an innate, natural, and unalterable phenomenon is strange because, generally speaking, most social scientists—or, at least most sociologists and anthropologists—are rather reluctant to characterize the specific beliefs that humans hold, the various cultural behaviors that they engage in, and the socially significant identities that they ascribe to as being the result of some inborn, static biological component of the species homo sapiens. Rather, as social scientists, we are much more likely to emphasize and focus on the degree to which such things are largely the result of arbitrary historical developments, idiosyncratic cultural patterns, and various social forces, and not inherent, instinctive mechanisms.[2]

It is not that we outright deny the existence of universal human traits or shared, natural proclivities common to all people that result from our collective evolutionary development as a primate species.[3] Rather, we recognize that actually determining what they are is a matter of much fraught debate. Furthermore, we believe that the specific content of human beliefs, the varied forms of human behaviors, and distinctive associational bonds that humans construct are very much shaped, determined, suppressed, and/or enhanced, by when we happen to live, where we happen to live, and who we happen to live among.

Hence, it is peculiar that some contemporary social scientists make the claim that religion is a common, unvarying aspect of the human condition. But it is actually much more than peculiar; it is empirically unsupportable. As this chapter will reveal, 1) there have always been nonreligious people throughout recorded history, 2) a large number of people today are not religious, 3) a growing number of societies are increasingly secular (as also shown in the previous chapters), and 4) when children are raised without religion, they tend to stay secular as adults. These facts counter the contention that secularity is some abnormal or unnatural aberration and render problematic the strange thesis that religion is a universally unalterable, innate, natural phenomenon.

Religion as Natural, Innate, and Universal

When someone describes religion as "natural," it can mean many things. Let's start here with the most basic interpretation of this phrase. It can simply mean that the underlying biological origins and foundational roots of what would eventually become our religious beliefs, practices, and concomitant identities grow out of the natural human condition: the kinds of brains we have and the ways in which we have evolved as social animals. In this sense, religion has to be natural because it derives from "human nature." How could it be otherwise? This is effectively a tautology: religion is part of human nature because religion is part of human nature. Anything and everything that humans do and believe is—at base—the result of our neurology, sociality, and evolutionary development. Thus, when writer Nicholas Wade publishes a book called *The Faith Instinct*,[4] in which he claims that religion is "natural to humanity"[5] and an "ingrained part of human nature,"[6] all that he is really arguing is that "the mind's receptivity to religion has been shaped by evolution . . . [and that] . . . religious behavior evolved because it conferred essential benefits on ancient societies and their successors."[7] Since any and every observable aspect of humanity has only natural sources—undoubtedly resting on bio-evolutionary foundations—this is an innocuous, uncontroversial position, and one widely shared by most scholars.[8] Indeed, given the obvious lack of empirically sound evidence for any supernatural forces at play, *all* human activities, beliefs, and identities throughout history—and in the contemporary world—develop out of, draw upon, and reflect our species' naturally evolved origins, capabilities, and proclivities.

However, there is another, more loaded and more problematic meaning that comes with employing the term "natural" to describe or understand religion. It is one that implicitly argues that religiosity is somehow more normal, more healthy, more properly human—and inevitably more in line and more in accordance with our essential human nature—than secularity is. When the term "natural" is employed thus, secularity is constructed as unnatural and something counter to normal, healthy, and proper human living; religion is characterized as appropriate and immutable, while secularity is viewed as being inevitably limited in scope and inherently "artificial."[9] We can call this the "religion as correctly natural and secularity as problematically unnatural" thesis.

For an example of this curious perspective, consider the work of sociologist of religion Christian Smith, who describes religion as being "irrepressibly natural to being human."[10] According to Smith, humans are so primordially and innately religious, that secular humanism cuts against the very "grain" of "nature's reality structure."[11] In fact, religion is such a genuine, natural human tendency that, according to Smith, to live secularly is analogous to "crab-walk[ing] backwards."[12] Sure, it can be done—but it is clearly awkward and unfeasible, if not downright futile. Smith goes even further and compares people living secularly to individuals who might choose to "repeatedly hit themselves in the head with sharp objects."[13] Again, people can do so if they really want to—but it is obviously inimical to natural human well-being. For Smith, when it is "understood rightly" that humans are "naturally"[14] religious, "we should not expect human societies to become thoroughly secular on any long-term basis. Secularization as a process will likely be limited, contingent, and susceptible to long-term reversals."[15]

Smith is far from alone in this viewpoint. In the latter half of the twentieth century, formidable sociologist and Catholic priest Andrew Greeley wrote extensively on the supposedly manifest, eternal unsecular-ness of humanity, arguing that religious needs are "inherent in the human condition."[16] "Man," by his very nature, "needs faith" and "religious leadership" to facilitate an interpretation of the meaning of life.[17] Thus, according to Greeley, given that such religious needs are so unshakably innate, "there is no evidence to show that the need is any less now than it was in the past."[18] In other words, anything so natural does not diminish or decay: hence religion's inevitable persistence. Peter Berger, another giant of the sociological study of religion, came to the same conclusion later in his career, arguing that the "religious impulse" is such a "perennial feature of humanity" that a lack of religiosity would entail a "mutation of the species."[19] A secular state of human life, according to Berger, would be "an impoverished and finally untenable condition."[20] According to Robert McCauley, "religious expression in beliefs and practices is nearly inevitable in most people."[21] Justin Barrett characterizes a lack of supernatural, religious faith—specifically in God—as constituting not merely a state of "unnaturalness,"[22] but as a true "oddity";[23] a secular, naturalistic worldview is, according to Barrett, so abnormal that it is "only" found among the "privileged" and the "elite."[24] Laurence Iannaccone goes even further, insisting that without a bedrock, core religious faith undergirding all our morality, customs, and institutions, people would "cease being recognizably human."[25]

In sum, according to the "religion as correctly natural and secularity as problematically unnatural" thesis, religiosity is framed as properly normal, inevitable, irrepressible, perennial, unshakable, and innate, while secularity is characterized as artificial, untenable, impoverished, unnatural, odd, a mutation—almost *unhuman*.

Fortunately, a growing group of evolutionary psychologists and cognitive scientists are debunking this argument, illustrating that secularity is just as normal, natural, and innate to humanity as is religiosity. They show that while religious needs are truly deep and widespread, they are no more inborn than their absence, that religious faith is no more rooted in our nature than skepticism and rationalism, and that a supernatural worldview is no more inherently human than a naturalistic worldview.[26] As Armin Geertz and Guðmundur Ingi Markússon have argued, "[A]theism . . . draws on the same natural cognitive capacities that theism draws on" and both "religiosity and atheism represent entrenched cognitive–cultural habits where the conclusions drawn from sensory input and the output of cognitive systems bifurcate in supernatural and naturalistic directions."[27] As Ara Norenzayan and Will Gervais argue, "religious belief and disbelief share the same underlying pathways and can be explained within a single evolutionary framework that is grounded in both genetic and cultural evolution."[28] Or in the strong words of historian Tim Whitmarsh:

> The notion that a human is an essential religious being . . . is no more cogent than the notion that apples are essentially red. When most of us think of an apple we imagine a rosy glow, because that is the stereotype that we have grown up with . . . and indeed it is true enough that many apples are tinctured with red. But it would be ludicrous to see a Golden Delicious as any less "appley" just because it is pure green. Yet this is in effect what we do to atheists . . . we treat them as human beings who are not somehow complete in their humanity, even though they are genetically indistinct from their peers.[29]

Sociological evidence additionally debunks the "religion as correctly natural and secularity as problematically unnatural" thesis, as the remainder of this chapter will lay out.

Secularity in the Past

To begin with, it is crucial to recognize that—*yes*—there have always been secular people—at least as long as there has been religion. We have plenty of evidence of secularity going back as far as we have written records of human civilization. This is important to stress, because it counters the myth that being secular is some new, artificial, modern "mutation."

The earliest documentation of ancient secularity is probably found among the Indian writings that contend with a group of skeptics known as the Carvaka—also referred to as the Lokayata—who lived in India during the seventh century BCE. The Carvaka expressed a decidedly naturalistic worldview, rejecting the supernaturalism of primordial Hindu religion. They refused to engage in religious rituals and mocked religious authorities. As materialists and atheists, they saw no evidence for the existence of gods or karma or an afterlife. "Only the perceived exists," they argued, and "there is no world other than this."[30]

Additional evidence of secularity in the ancient world can be found within the teachings of Xunzi, who lived in China in the third century

BCE, and who argued that there is no heaven other than this natural world and that morality is a social construct, with no divine component. Also, in ancient China, some 2,000 years ago, was the secular, naturalistic skepticism of Wang Ch'ung and Hsun Tzu, who both argued that there is nothing supernatural or spiritual behind the wonders of the world, that chance alone determines fortune and misfortune, and that immortality is not possible.

Early forms of atheism, agnosticism, anti-religiosity, and an all-around naturalistic orientation are extremely abundant among many of the sages of ancient Greece and Rome; individuals such as Protagoras, Xenophanes, Carneades, Lucretius, Epicurus, Democritus, Anaxagoras, Prodicus, Critias, Anaximander, Hippo of Samos, Clitomachus, Celsus—and so many others[31]—insisted that the gods did not exist, or that it was impossible to know if they did or did not exist, or that there was no life after death, or that morality was a purely human matter, or that everything that we experience and that exists is essentially natural, without any divine intervention at play.[32]

From ancient Israel, Psalms 14, written sometime around the third or second century BCE, explicitly attests to the existence of atheists. The ancient Jewish philosopher known as Kohelet, from the third century BCE, voiced a serene existentialism and skeptical doubt, arguing that all life is ultimately meaningless and that there is no life after death. In Central Asia, in the ninth century, Jewish philosopher Hiwi al-Balkhi was a skeptic who openly questioned the divinity of the Torah, and whose secular wisdom caused many other people to lose their faith.[33]

Among the most prominent thinkers of early Islamic civilization, there were some notable secular voices. Muhammad Al-Warraq, of the ninth century, doubted the existence of Allah and was skeptical of religious prophets; Muhammad al-Razi, of the tenth century, was a freethinking, anti-religious man who criticized religion and sought to advance the sciences of physics, chemistry, and medicine; Omar Khayyam, of the eleventh century, expressed a decidedly naturalistic worldview.[34] "Men talk of heaven," he observed, yet "there is no heaven but here."[35] Averroes, of the twelfth century, was also known for his secular skepticism.

In short, evidence of what we today would refer to as agnosticism, skepticism, atheism, naturalism, secularism, humanism, and irreligion—throughout history, going back even thousands of years—is quite plentiful and rich.[36] By providing the above examples, we are not making the claim that historical illustrations of nonbelievers demonstrate *definitively* that secularity is just as natural as is religiosity. Such historical evidence simply bolsters our position that secularity has always been around, and as such, is just as much a normal, natural part of the human condition as religiosity.

But weren't these secular individuals from the past quite rare? Weren't they excruciatingly few and far between? Perhaps. It is hard to know for sure just how widespread secularity was in ancient times—especially since most people did not read or write, and thus we have no record of what they thought or believed. Additionally, dominant religions—throughout the millennia—have almost always been tied to political power and oppressive authority, making any public expression of secularity often taboo, if not dangerous or downright deadly.

However, even if a lack of religious belief, a disinterest in religious behaviors, or a reluctance to identify with a religious tradition were rare in centuries past—for whatever reasons—they are certainly rare no longer. A massive proportion of humanity is now openly secular and societies where secularity is widespread have not collapsed into chaos, further undermining the "religion as correctly natural and secularity as problematically unnatural" thesis. As detailed in chapter 2, a quick perusal of secularity around the world in the early twenty-first century illustrates how absurd it is to argue that religion is uniquely innate or inevitable and that secularity is somehow artificial and thus unsustainable.

So Many Secular People

As of this writing, there are hundreds of millions of people in the world today, maybe even over a billion, who are not religious, to varying degrees. The existence of so many secular people in the world renders unsustainable any suggestion that secularity is unnatural or strictly limited to some fringe population. It surprises us that those who insist religiosity is natural ignore this evidence. Whatever the reason, we find it necessary to counter such a perspective by laying out the numbers, as we did in chapter 2.

If we totaled up the unaffiliated, non-practicing, and non-believing populations of most of the countries in the world, the number of secular humans—according to Pew international data—would skyrocket up to somewhere over one billion.[37] Not all are self-identified atheists or agnostics, not all desist from each and every form of religious observance, but they do not identify with any religion—even when presented with numerous options—and a significant proportion of them do not engage in regular religious worship or maintain faith in anything supernatural.[38]

To further make the point, here are some snapshots from countries that we have not explored in depth in previous chapters: In China, over 500 million people lack a belief in God.[39] About 3.5 million Taiwanese individuals[40] and at least 60 million people in Japan are secular.[41] In the Czech Republic, there are six million people alive today who are secular.[42] In the Netherlands, there are at least 10 million secular people.[43] In France, at least 30 million people are nonreligious today.[44] In Australia, 58,000 identify specifically as atheist or agnostic.[45] In Argentina, around 1.5 million people are secular.[46] In Tunisia, Libya, and Algeria, many claim to be "not religious."[47] We do not know how many of the residents of these Maghrebi nations are actually atheist or agnostic, but even if it is only a mere 2.5 percent,[48] that amounts to over 1.2 million individuals. In nearby Israel, there are around 1.75 million secular Jews.[49] In Botswana and Mozambique, over two million people do not identify with a religion.[50] In South Africa, another two million people are secular, of varying degrees.[51]

Given the demographic reality, it is irrational to characterize secularity as unnatural, artificial, odd, or unhuman. Yet, as the beginning of this chapter noted, there are a number of studies that appear to ignore all the evidence that counters the "religion as correctly natural and secularity as problematically unnatural" argument. Do the authors truly believe that over one billion people are effectively "crab-walking backwards" or repeatedly hitting themselves in the head with sharp objects because they are not religious? And, if they do, would they also be willing to admit that they have no evidence to support such claims? We can only wonder.

Likewise, we are surprised that scholars have argued that a lack of belief in God is something that one only finds among atypical circles of privileged elites.[52] But when seeing how widespread secularity is in many nations around the world—it is hard to take such an assertion seriously. Do they honestly believe that the over 60 percent of Czechs or the 56 percent of Dutch people who do not believe in God[53] are all part of a privileged elite? Given that some of these scholars are such well-respected, widely-cited, and prolifically-published social scientists, we must take their assertions seriously—even if only to refute them. They are incorrect in their dismissal of secularity as constituting some odd, tiny, marginal, fringe, or elitist element of humanity.

Of course, it remains true that most humans are religious, and only a minority are secular. No question about that. But just because a minority of humans are left-handed, or have perfect-pitch, or are over six feet tall, or are monolingual, or are illiterate, or are homosexual, or are vegetarian, or colorblind, or have 20/20 vision, or are secular, does not make *any* of these traits, characteristics, or orientations unnatural, artificial, or manifestly untenable.

Furthermore, even though most people in the world are religious, there are now a handful of societies in which it is the other way around: secular people constitute the majority and religious people comprise the minority. More specifically, as shown in chapter 2, a number of countries—such as the Czech Republic, the Netherlands, Japan, China, Estonia, Vietnam, Hong Kong, Macau, South Korea, Uruguay, France, Hungary, and Australia—have religiously unaffiliated majorities.

Scotland, with a population of 5.5 million, has already been discussed earlier, in chapter 2. But it bears repeating that somewhere between 58 percent[54] and 72 percent[55] of the population—depending on what surveys you look at—currently has no religion, constituting either a small majority or a whopping majority. Either way, it illustrates the possibility of secularity being a predominant orientation in a given society, and religiosity being atypical.

In Estonia, a Baltic country of 1.3 million, religion has faded into a truly minority phenomenon, where widespread indifference towards religious beliefs and practices reigns.[56] In addition to the low levels of belief in God (46 percent), belonging (19 percent), and monthly attendance (8 percent) presented in chapter 2, other research has found that only 17 percent of Estonians claim that religion is important in their life; nearly 90 percent never talk about religion with their friends or family; nearly 80 percent never think about religion; 75 percent never pray; only 4 percent engage in daily prayer; and only 1.8 percent of schools in Estonia are affiliated with a religion. And while some superstition and supernaturalism clearly exist—over half of Estonians believe in some sort of spirit or force, over half believe in astrology, and around two-thirds believe in the powers of psychics—when it comes to religious beliefs, only 21 percent believe in a personal god, 14 percent believe in heaven, and 12 percent believe in hell.[57]

How this widespread secularity plays out in Estonian culture is succinctly captured by the words of Atko Remmel, who discusses his research among Estonians:

> When my interviewees talk about religion, what is most striking is their grasping for words—they often go silent or mumble while trying to describe feelings, thoughts, or opinions, compensating this with gesticulation. Furthermore . . . many students were even puzzled by the meaning of the word "religion," and their answers reflected their distance from the concept. As a result, they rarely appear to acknowledge religion in their everyday life . . . Lack of contact with religion was one of the central findings during my interviews: many participants claimed to have met religious people only one or two times *in their entire life.*[58]

There are no countries in North America, Africa, or the Middle East that have a majority secular population, and in Latin America, Uruguay is the only country where more than half of the population is religiously unaffiliated. However, one Muslim majority country is of interest: Azerbaijan, a Muslim nation of 10 million in the Caucasus region. Azerbaijan is widely considered "the most secular country in the Muslim world."[59] Granted, the vast majority of Azerbaijanis believe in Allah, and most identify nominally as Muslim—even if this is essentially an ethnic or cultural identity marker.[60] But what stands out is the degree to which religion plays such a muted, marginal role in Azerbaijani society: even among those Azerbaijanis who consider religion to be highly or rather important in their lives, only 1 in 20 attend religious services at least weekly.[61] According to the World Values Survey from 2018, when Azerbaijani parents were provided with a list of qualities that could possibly be important to foster in children at home, 86 percent did not choose religious faith as one of the top five qualities; only 16 percent regard religion as "very important" in their lives; and 40 percent "never or practically never" attend religious services.

IS BEING SECULAR UNNATURAL? | 107

While the countries discussed here comprise only a handful of nations, their existence proves—a word we use carefully but intentionally—that countries can be predominantly secular and still function. This fact further erodes any suggestion that religion is uniquely natural and perennial, while secular life is unnatural and only to be found among small, privileged circles of elites, as Barrett claims.

Some readers might wonder: Haven't these handful of highly secular nations only had a nonreligious majority in recent years? Isn't this a new historical phenomenon? Most likely, yes and yes. But even these facts can be interpreted to indicate that religion is not irrepressibly/universally natural and secularity artificial/unnatural. For if religion can be widely abandoned and secularity widely emergent *in such a short time period*, then this speaks to the former not being so intrinsic to humanity after all, and secularity not being as unnatural or unsustainable as some assert.

Socialization

When it comes to understanding and explaining the long-term, ongoing existence of religion, there are basically two matters to address: genesis/origin and reproduction/maintenance. That is: 1) how religion initially arose, and 2) why religion continues to exist. While these questions may appear related, they are actually quite distinct. For example, how and why the holiday of Halloween originated is very different from how and why people celebrate it today. Centuries from now, people will probably celebrate Halloween quite differently, and for different reasons—or they may not celebrate it at all.

Concerning the genesis, origin, or "start" of religion—this is a matter for anthropologists and historians to debate, and to debate endlessly, because we will never really know for sure; the data are simply unattainable and unverifiable. Religion—supernatural beliefs and concomitant ritualistic behaviors and forms of association—emerged long before reliable, recorded history. Of course, that has not kept countless scholars from speculating.[62] Theories of religion's genesis abound, including such possibilities as: religion began when small bands of hunters and gatherers came together in large seasonal assemblies and experienced a feeling of collective effervescence; religion started when people had dreams of their dead relatives; religion arose as a way to create powerful in-group allegiances while trading and bartering; religion started when people first heard thunder; religion emerged as a way to justify the position of those in power; religion was sparked by humans' experiences of awe in the face of nature's mighty wonders; religion developed out of humans' instinctive impulse to anthropomorphize, attributing human-like qualities, traits, and desires to non-human things; religion was what occurred when humans first tried to explain and control the workings of nature; religion arose out of early humans' unconscious need and wish for a loving and protective father-like, parental figure who can provide comfort and protection throughout life; religion is what humans created in order to handle their fear of death; and so on.

Maybe some of the above speculations are correct, maybe not. We'll never know for sure. But what we can know—and measure and observe—is what keeps religion going. In our view, the most important engine of religion's ongoing maintenance and continued reproduction is socialization, which we touched upon briefly in chapter 1 in considering the transmission of religion from parents to children.[63]

Socialization is the process whereby we learn the norms and values of our culture. It is how we learn—passively, informally, and often unconsciously—how to behave in school or at the dinner table, what it means to be in love or to be a good citizen, how to act when meeting your boyfriend's parents or a police officer, whose job it is to raise kids or skin elk, what sorts of animals are acceptable to eat and what sorts are not, how to dance, how to express anger, what careers are respectable, what it means to be brave, cowardly, attractive, funny, and so forth. In short, socialization is all the ways—both subtle and overt—whereby we learn how to become and function as members of our society.

Our experience of socialization is most profound and powerful when we are young, as we are growing up. And the people who most directly and most potently socialize us are those who raise us, keeping us fed and safe—usually our parents and other immediate family members. But any humans we come into contact with—either in-person or virtually—can socialize us, to varying degrees: neighbors, friends, teachers, coaches, nurses, or those we see in TV shows, in movies, on TikTok, and on Instagram.

Socialization is fundamental to religion's maintenance and reproduction. Babies do not start out religious; they have to be taught religion. The process, in short, goes like this: small children are raised by religious people, who teach them the norms, beliefs, and rituals of their religion. Those children internalize that religious socialization and go on to be religious themselves as they grow up. They accept as true the religious beliefs that have been presented to them as such by their loved ones; they come to practice and value the religious rituals they have been socialized to perform; they come to personally identify with the religious group in which they were raised. And when these kids grow up and have kids of their own, the cycle is repeated (or not, which is what is happening today).

Evidence of Religious Socialization

In the 1980s, a team of social psychologists, Helt, Ikke, and Sandt,[64] undertook an amazing experiment. They gathered 275 infant orphans, all under the age of six months, from eight different countries from different continents, and randomly divided them into two groups. One group of orphan babies was placed on a remote island where they were raised by foster parents who exposed them to no religion at all—no supernatural beliefs, no concomitant rituals, and no religious group identity. The other group of orphan babies were placed on three different islands: one group was raised by foster parents who belonged to a community of devout Mormons, the second group was raised by devout Catholics, and the third group was raised by devout Muslims. These children—the three groups raised by and among religious people from early on—were taught by their parents, extended family members, and larger social circles that the supernatural beliefs of their respective religions were true. These children were also raised with everyone in their immediate family and community performing various rituals, engaging in body-modifications and bodily adornments, and celebrating certain holidays related to their supernatural beliefs. The team of researchers visited all the islands periodically for thirty years—the last time being in 2015. What did they find? Over 95 percent of the children raised completely secular—without any religion—were secular as adults and had little knowledge of or interest in any religion; over 95 percent of the children raised as Mormon, Catholic, or Muslim were believing, practicing, identifying members of those respective religions.

Pretty strong evidence for the powerfully determining effect of socialization on religiosity, no?

As you may have suspected, the study described above never took place. We made it up. It is the kind of "imagined pure experiment" that is both unfeasible and unethical, for numerous obvious reasons. But the underlying premise of the imagined experiment puts into clear focus what we might expect to find if socialization really is the powerful engine that maintains and reproduces religiosity generationally. And while we don't have such "babies raised on different islands" data, we *do* have decades of studies—realistically limited by methodological feasibility and ethical considerations—that provide compelling evidence concerning socialization's key role in maintaining and reproducing religion in various societies over generations.

For example, in 2016, the Pew Research Center[65] found that, within the United States, parents' religiosity is a very strong predictor of people's religiosity. Of Americans who identify as Protestant Christians, 80 percent of them were raised by two Protestant Christian parents; however, if one parent was a Protestant Christian and the other identified with no religion ("none"), then only 56 percent identify as Protestant Christian, with 34 percent being religiously unaffiliated. Among those who were raised by a Protestant parent and a Catholic parent, 38 percent now identify as Protestant, 29 percent as Catholic, and 26 percent as non-religious. We see similar correlations within Catholicism: of people who were raised by two Catholic parents, 62 percent are Catholic today, but of those who had one parent who was Catholic and one parent who was not, only 32 percent are Catholic today. As for people raised by two non-religious parents, 63 percent are non-religious themselves. There are more permutations within this Pew study, but the primary finding is obvious: our parents *strongly* shape our religiosity, or lack thereof.

As Stark and Finke have rightly observed, "children usually adhere to the faith of their parents and relatives . . . [and] most people do remain within the religious organizations in which they were raised."[66] Or as Scott Myers puts it, "parents' religiosity is the primary influence on the religiosity of their adult offspring."[67] Numerous studies—spanning over a century—bear these assertions out: people generally adhere to the religion in which they were raised; such is the unparalleled power of religious socialization.[68]

But what is most relevant for our discussion, is that when children are raised secularly, without religion, they generally don't become religious as adults. As Stephen Merino found in his analysis of various generational cohorts in the USA, "those with religiously unaffiliated parents as children are significantly less likely to express a religious preference as adults."[69] Hart Nelsen found—looking at American families back in the 1980s—that if both parents were secular, then about 85 percent of children raised in such homes grew up to be secular themselves.[70] These findings were confirmed in a British context by Steve Bruce and Tony Glendinning, who also found that children raised without religion rarely grow up to become religious themselves; only about 5 percent of people raised in secular homes by nonreligious parents ended up being religious themselves later in life.[71] A similar figure of 6.6 percent is found in the 2015 data from the Scottish Social Attitudes Survey.[72]

Consider the work of Vern Bengtson, perhaps the leading authority on religious generational transmission within families before his untimely passing. Since 1970, with his Longitudinal Study of Generations, Bengtson and his team followed 3,500 respondents, representing four generations from over 350 different families in the United States. Since 1970, the percentage of people in his sample who no longer identified as religious increased by more than 300 percent (from 11 percent up to 36 percent), and the main force at play is—you guessed it—family socialization. "We find," Bengtson reports, "nearly 6 out 10 unaffiliated young adults come from families where their parents were also unaffiliated, indicating that nonreligion is indeed transmitted from one generation to the next."[73]

Clearly, we have an innate, natural propensity to believe what our parents teach us, to accept the reality presented to us by those who care for us, to internalize the worldview of our immediate culture, and to enjoy, value, and despise what we have been socialized to enjoy, value, and despise. If religion is part of our socialization, we will most likely be religious. If it is not, then we will most likely be secular. And thus, if religiosity can evaporate in just one generation—as a result of secular socialization—it is quite erroneous to speak of it as irrepressibly innate. Barrett is mistaken to characterize humans as "born believers," given the evidence showing that children's religiosity is something that they get socialized into, and when that socialization is secular, children tend to remain secular.

What about the Soviet Union?

In their ongoing insistence that secularity be understood as unnatural— and thus secularization is always doomed to be limited in scope, as the likes of Professors Smith and Stark argue—many scholars cite the Soviet Union as their main evidence.

Although we will delve into the former Soviet Union in greater length in chapter 6, a quick discussion of this argument is warranted. It essentially goes like this: in the former USSR, the government tried to eradicate religion. It did so by various forceful means, such as arresting, torturing, and murdering religious leaders; blowing up religious buildings; teaching and lecturing about the folly of religion and superiority of science; producing various forms of art, media, and propaganda that mocked religion; changing religious holidays into socialistic/nationalistic holidays; making certain religious gatherings and rituals illegal; and so forth. For seventy years, the Soviets tried to wipe out religion. The result? *Failure.* Although some nations that were under Soviet domination are quite secular today—such as the Czech Republic, Estonia, former East Germany, and Hungary[74]—as seen in chapter 2, many former-Soviet nations have seen an uptick, or rather, reassertion, of religious belief, behavior, and belonging since the collapse of the communist regime.[75] This, according to some, proves that religion is so natural, so innate, so irrepressible, so fundamental to humanity, that secularization is clearly an impossibility—as the "Soviet Experiment" shows.

Leading this line of argumentation is sociologist Paul Froese. In his book *The Plot to Kill God*, Froese argues that the Soviet attempt to forcefully secularize its citizens failed not merely because the methods were coercive and inhumane, but because "a religious sentiment is deeply ingrained in human nature"[76] and that "a basic demand for a religious worldview is universal."[77]

But the case of the Soviet Union does not teach us that secularization, in and of itself, is impossible, an argument we return to at length in chapter 6. All it teaches us is that *forced, coercive secularization* doesn't take: you can't eradicate religion by means of state-sanctioned repression; you can't imprison, torture, or murder religion away. And there have been very few social scientists who ever theorized that religion could be stamped out Soviet-style or that secularization could successfully occur under such oppressive conditions.[78]

Rather, long-lasting and likely permanent secularization is most likely to occur in organic ways as a sociocultural process that is aligned with modernization. It usually occurs in relatively free, democratic societies where there are no sanctions or punishments for being religious. It would thus occur largely as a by-product of other social changes—such as increased access to technology, greater existential security, more women in the workforce, etc.—and not because some dictator forcefully imposes atheism on a captive people.

Such secularization occurs when people simply stop being religious of their own volition. And that is exactly the kind of secularization we now see taking place the world over, from Canada and Uruguay to Germany and Japan.

Conclusion

This chapter has refuted the "religion as correctly natural and secularity as problematically unnatural" thesis that views religiosity as a natural, normal, innate, inborn, and essential component of the human condition that is preferrable and superior to secularity, which is viewed as some sort of unnatural, artificial, or odd state of being. Living a secular life is not akin to people repeatedly hitting themselves in the head with sharp objects, as Christian Smith has maintained; most secular populations around the world are not made up of privileged elites, as Justin Barrett has claimed; nor do societies that are largely secular constitute a mutation of our species, as Andrew Greeley has argued.

In the previous pages, we have shown that 1) the historical record offers evidence that there have always been secular people going back thousands of years; 2) there are currently hundreds of millions of secular people in the world today; 3) there are some societies in which the majority of the population is secular; 4) there exists multi-generational evidence showing that religion reproduces itself through socialization, so when children are raised secular, they almost always stay secular as adults—with religiosity evaporating often in a matter of one generation. All four of these facts counter the claim that religion is somehow natural and secularity unnatural. The sooner social scientists understand this, the sooner will our understanding of both religiosity and secularity improve and advance.

5

What Secularity Looks Like

"I just don't really understand religion."

So declared Ju, during a discussion that took place on the third or fourth week of a class that Phil was recently teaching on the sociology of religion.

Ju is twenty. She grew up in Hong Kong, a society of over seven million in which the majority of people are non-religious.[1] Ju's father is a writer and her mother is an engineer. She was majoring in biology but wanted to take a class on religion so she could "better understand Americans." On this particular day, the topic was new religious movements, such as Scientology and OSHO. Some students expressed surprise at the novel beliefs and practices of these religions, while others took the position that there was nothing qualitatively different between these religious groups and more mainstream religions, like Catholicism or Islam. This set off quite a discussion.

But it was Ju who really took the class into uncharted territory. She said that she was having a hard time really comprehending much of what people were saying about faith, spirituality, worship, religious community, heaven, and so on. She explained that she had grown up without any religion whatsoever. Her parents were nonreligious, her aunts and uncles were nonreligious, and so were all of her neighbors, schoolmates, and friends. She had never set foot inside a church or temple, had never prayed, had never been told to worry about heaven or hell. She simply found the entire enterprise of religion distinctly alien. She was having a genuinely hard time understanding how people could be religious.

The other students tried their best to explain religiosity to her, drawing mostly upon their own personal, varied experiences with religion in doing so. But what they eventually came to realize was that here was a living, breathing, well-adjusted, intelligent young woman—a peer—who was a sort of person that none of them had ever witnessed before:

someone who had grown up and been raised completely secular in a secular enclave of an almost completely secular society.

While the main argument of this book is that the core pillars of the secularization thesis are robustly supported by the best available evidence, this chapter's specific goal is to provide a multi-faceted portrait of what secular life actually looks like in highly secularized contexts.

Religious Indifference

What does secularity look like in the *most* secularized societies?

Some readers may picture a society with powerful secularist organizations, outspoken irreligious sentiments in the media and in politics, and a majority of individuals adopting explicitly secular identities, such as atheist, agnostic, antitheist, and/or secular humanist. However, empirical evidence of such societies is actually hard to find, which has ironically been used to illustrate a presumed flaw in secularization theory: that the end result of secularization is supposed to be widespread opposition to religion—or active irreligion—which doesn't seem to occur.[2]

However, what secularization theory *actually* predicts—and what we have shown elsewhere[3]—is that advanced secularity assumes that *both* religion and irreligion are hard to find. Irreligious organizations, religious criticism, and atheist activism are signs of secularization—in particular at the earlier stages. When religion still has some authority in society, there is a need for irreligious or secularist activism. But that is not the endpoint of religious decline.[4] In fact, secularization ultimately leads to religious indifference where religion *and* irreligion become non-issues.[5] After all, it is generally when religion is a strong and pervasive force in society that one finds active and engaged anti-religiosity, but when religion itself is weak and diminished, so too is opposition to it.

Religious indifference, theologically, can be characterized by "apatheism"—a lack of interest in whether there are gods or supernatural entities at all.[6] For many apatheists, the driving motivation is that the question is irrelevant to their lives. Whether Vishnu, Aphrodite, or Yahweh exists or not will not change their morality, their relationships, their job, or their day-to-day decision-making. Religion just does not matter to them in any meaningful way, except perhaps to annoy them when: a) people use religion to justify harming others, b) religious people try to force their morality on others, or c) religious people or organizations receive privileges that are not also extended to nonreligious individuals. Ju, described above, is a perfect illustration of religious indifference and the end stage of secularization: she is not knowledgeable about religion, nor is she actively anti-religious, precisely because religion is irrelevant to her life.

A sheer disinterest in religion is a common sentiment that we have encountered when doing fieldwork in secular Scandinavia.[7] There, we have come across common statements like "I have never talked to my friends or family about religion"; "I have no idea what my friends believe, but you assume that they don't believe"; and "It's just not interesting to talk about." Religion is not a controversial or sensitive topic. It's just that it is "weird" to talk about it because it is "outdated" and "boring." Just like most Scandinavians rarely talk about the existence or nonexistence of the Norse gods, they also don't talk about Jesus either, as they don't find the topic relevant in a modern, secular society. Our impressions from Scandinavia are similar to accounts of religious indifference in Estonia, which is, as mentioned in the previous chapter, another one of the most secular countries in the world. When asking school children how often they speak about religion, Atko Remmel notes that most never do because they are not interested in it and that "some students even expressed astonishment that religion could be a topic of discussion."[8] In that sense, in addition to a lack of interest in religion, indifference is, in a secular society, often manifested as a lack of awareness or knowledge about religion—similar to the experience of Ju who was mentioned at the beginning of this chapter.

In explaining why indifference is a decisive threat to religion or the ultimate sign that religion is on the verge of irrelevance, Johannes Quack and Cora Schuh[9] proclaim that "showing *indifference* towards something challenges its symbolic power." In other words, when people do not care about religion, when they have a lack of awareness of it, when they don't talk about it, when they don't think about it, and when it has no place in their life neither in a positive nor a negative sense, this means that religion has largely become insignificant. The position of indifference is in stark contrast to explicitly anti-religious sentiments that are usually present where religion still carries a high degree of authority. After all, criticizing religion acknowledges its presence and gives it a symbolic space that has largely vanished in places where religious indifference has prevailed.[10]

An analog to religious indifference might be debates over wagons pulled by oxen. We invite readers to think back to the last time you debated whether wagons pulled by oxen were good or bad. If you're like the authors, you've never had this debate. You've never had this debate because wagons pulled by oxen largely do not exist in highly developed countries and have not since the development and spread of internal combustion engines nearly a century ago. The vast majority of people in highly developed countries are completely indifferent to the benefits or detriments of wagons pulled by oxen because such vehicles are not part of our lives. We are aware that they did exist and may still exist in some less developed countries or in some esoteric enclaves (e.g., among the Amish). But to oppose such wagons would require that the wagons be an important part of our society. Since wagons are not, it's hard to

Figure 5.1: Oxen Pulling Wagons in Dröpstad, Hallingeberg, Sweden, around 1920. Isabella's ancestor is holding the reins.

muster up opposition to them. The vast majority of us are indifferent to the question of wagons drawn by oxen. Likewise, when religion has been differentiated from most spheres of society such that people do not need any knowledge of religion to function on a day-to-day basis and rationalization is widespread, the end result is indifference, not opposition to religion.

One of the authors (Isabella) encountered the tension between irreligion and religious indifference when she attended a meeting of an atheist organization in a highly religious town in the United States. At that meeting, she described religiously indifferent Scandinavia, specifically reciting a conversation with a secular humanist in Sweden who encountered benign objections when attempting to distribute humanist pamphlets—not because the people who objected were religious, but because they were so secular that they saw no reason to engage with religion at all. Several participants at the meeting, who were highly antagonistic toward religion, largely disapproved of the religious indifference expressed in her account of Scandinavia and did not seem to understand this position, even after explaining that it took place in a context with a weak social presence of religion.

Discussing these dynamics, David Nash states that "in some respects, both atheism and religion have recognized that one task in their imagined present and future is to entice individuals from the indifferent space, into spending more time embracing and following the religious or the secular narratives on offer."[11] Ultimately, showing indifference toward religion also means rejecting religious counter-identities like atheism, antitheism, and secularism. On this note, it may be the case that, in some respects, the religious and the explicitly irreligious have more in common than either of them have with the indifferent—namely as different opinions and positions within a shared discourse.[12]

Following the reasoning expressed here, self-defined atheism, on the one hand, and nonbelief in God, on the other, are thus two distinct and complex identities with different meanings and dispositions. As we have discussed in depth elsewhere,[13] calling oneself an atheist in a highly secular context can come across as "confrontational" and as an indication that religion still holds a high degree of authority and social significance. Being an atheist but not adopting the label fits the description of Anna, a thirty-one-year-old Scottish woman. While she does not believe in God or a higher power, she doesn't call herself an atheist as she finds it a bit "hardlined." At the same time, she asserts that it doesn't make her "confused about it" or any more religious than someone who does. This is why it is not productive to assume that a society with low levels of self-defined atheists is religious. As stated by Stephen Bullivant,[14] "After all, it would be strange to take one's atheism seriously in a society where no one took theism seriously."

This aspect of secularization theory is important enough to formalize as a proposition:

- *Definition*: Religious indifference is when an individual has no interest in religion.
- *Definition*: Irreligion is opposition to religion.
- *Proposition*: The end stage of secularization is not widespread irreligion but rather widespread religious indifference.

Secular Values

When people live secular lives, and are either anti-religious or indifferent to religion, does this mean that they live empty, nihilistic lives devoid of any values or ethics? Lived experience—and ongoing social science—suggest not.

As noted in chapter 4, Vern Bengtson spent his career studying how religion is passed down from one generation to the next. In the last decade of his life, he became aware of the growing number of nonreligious people in American society and started including secular families in his research. In his last book, *Families and Faith*, published in 2013, he offered the following observation:

A large number of our nonreligious respondents said that their parents (or grandparents) taught them or exemplified the values they chose to emulate . . . it was clear that most of the nonreligious parents in our sample were quite articulate about their nontheistic ethical standards and moral value systems. In fact, many nonreligious parents were more coherent and passionate about their ethical principles than some of the "religious" parents in our study. The vast majority appeared to live goal-filled lives characterized by moral direction.[15]

Numerous studies of secular people deepen and affirm Bengtson's observations.[16] Far from leading nihilistic, meaningless, or immoral lives—as is often the pejorative stereotype[17]—most secular people find meaning, value, and purpose in their family relationships, friendships, community involvement, work, hobbies, nature, artistic endeavors, sports, pets, political interests, films, music, education, and so forth.[18] Furthermore, secular individuals are clearly not prone towards immorality or criminality, as they are markedly under-represented in US prisons,[19] and those democracies with highly secular populations tend to have very low violent crime rates and excellent, humane social welfare systems.[20]

But what are some of the specific and prominent guiding ethical principles, moral precepts, virtues, and values common within secular culture?

Empathy and compassion are key.[21] Whereas many religious people—particularly devout Christians and Muslims—tend to think that morality is sustained through fear of an ever-watching deity who rewards good behavior with a heavenly afterlife and punishes bad behavior with eternity in hell, most secular individuals consider morality a natural matter of empathetic understanding for others' experiences and a compassionate desire to alleviate unnecessary suffering. For example, Laura Saslow found that nonreligious people are more strongly motivated by compassion than strongly religious people,[22] while Jared Piazza found that the more religious people are, the more likely they are to exhibit a morality based on following rules, rather than on how their behavior might or might not affect someone else's state of suffering or well-being.[23] Furthermore, survey results show that when parents are asked what characteristics they desire to see their children exhibit, secular parents are much more likely to choose "being considerate of others" than religious parents.[24]

The secular emphasis on empathy and compassion manifests in clear political and social values. For example, studies[25] have shown that when it comes to things like wanting to help refugees,[26] supporting affordable healthcare,[27] wanting to fight the climate crisis,[28] supporting women's reproductive rights,[29] being sensitive to racism,[30] homophobia,[31] and transphobia,[32] supporting death with dignity,[33] and supporting animal rights[34]—secular people, on average, exhibit relatively high levels of empathy and concern for the suffering of others. Indeed, in their presentation of data from Canada, Joel Thiessen and Sarah Wilkins-Laflamme show that secular people are more likely than the religious to support government aid to the disadvantaged and the right of homosexuals to marry.[35]

In his in-depth analysis of over five hundred secular Americans, Jerome Baggett found that nonreligious people also place a high value on empiricism—basing their beliefs on demonstrable evidence. They also accept an essentially agnostic, humble position ("I don't know") when confronted with existential mysteries.[36] Other researchers have found additional values significant for secular people, including: a predilection for rationality and a desire to live in reality, while avoiding magical thinking and superstition;[37] an emphasis on living in the here and now, rather than pining for an afterlife;[38] a cosmopolitan orientation that focuses on the unity of all humans, resulting in lower levels of tribalism, nationalism, or patriotism.[39]

Finally, it should be noted that during the COVID-19 pandemic, secular people in the United States—especially atheists—were much more likely to get vaccinated than their religious peers, suggesting somewhat distinct value systems between the strongly secular and the strongly devout when it comes to both accepting scientific findings and related public health initiatives aimed at saving lives.[40]

In short, the idea that atheists and other nonreligious, non-believing individuals are valueless, immoral, or amoral is a well-used canard that is possibly designed to frighten religious people so they avoid contact with the nonreligious, reducing the odds that they will leave religion as well. Empirical evidence does not support the idea that nonreligious and non-believing individuals are any less moral or ethical than are the religious.

Organizations and Community

One positive aspect of life that religions have been shown to contribute to is social support through the building of community.[41] While perhaps not true for all incarnations of religion everywhere, for many religions, the idea of community lies at the heart of what they do. Individuals come together to celebrate and share what they have in common, and being part of a group and sharing a culture provide a sense of belonging and identity.[42] As much of the rest of this chapter and this book illustrate, many elements of religion are not necessary for society to function, but it does appear as though a sense of belonging, identity, and community are important elements of social life for humans.[43]

How, then, do nonreligious individuals find a sense of community without religion? The most obvious way is by building intentional communities around the aspect of their identity that they have in common: their nonreligion or nonbelief.[44] In the US, thousands of local atheist, Humanist, and freethought groups (collectively, "secular groups") have been founded to provide community for the nonreligious.[45] Thousands of similar groups exist around the world, from India[46] to Kenya.[47] As García and Blankholm found in their research on secular groups, they are more likely to exist in locations in the US where there are higher numbers of evangelicals, suggesting that a perceived need for such groups is higher where the nonreligious feel threatened. This finding also reveals the primary function of such groups: to provide support to the nonreligious. Galen and Kloet showed that individuals affiliated with secular groups tend to receive the same social health benefits as do individuals associated with religious groups.[48] In short, secular groups can replace the social support provided by religions.

However, secular groups are unlikely to be the option of choice for the vast majority of nonreligious individuals for two reasons. First, most people who leave religions do so not because they engaged in a careful and detailed examination of their religion's beliefs, history, or policies and found them to be out of line with their own values, but because religion just ceased to matter to them.[49] As noted above, most people who leave religion or who were never affiliated with a religion are indifferent to religion, not irreligious or anti-religious. Those who are angry or feel as though they were victimized by religion may join a secular group where they find support as they work through their anger and other issues related to or caused by religion.[50] The one study of which we are aware that was able to estimate the percentage of a population that was affiliated with secular groups was conducted in Switzerland and found that just 0.1 percent of the population was affiliated with a secular group in 2017.[51] We are unaware of any countries or societies where a sizable percentage of the population (e.g., greater than five percent) is affiliated with secular groups.

Second, secular groups are often organized around what the members oppose, not necessarily on what they value. Admittedly, Humanist groups may be organized around shared values, but atheist and freethought groups are organized around their opposition to religion and religious belief and practice. There is, of course, a place for such groups, particularly as watchdogs to police violations of secular law by religions, as do many of the larger secular organizations around the world.[52] But many of the smaller secular organizations primarily function as support groups for individuals who have had traumatic experiences with religion. As people work through their issues, it is not uncommon for them to eventually move on (or "graduate") from these groups and then turn to other organizations for community.

This leads to our last point in this section. In highly secular nations like Norway and Scotland, there are many who utilize the services provided by secular organizations. As noted in chapter 3, in Norway, more than a hundred thousand people are members of *Human-Etisk Forbund* (the Norwegian Humanist Association)[53] and many more take advantage of the ethical training and rituals of the organization. Likewise, in Scotland, as we note below in greater detail, thousands of Scottish people now marry in Humanist rituals rather than in churches. But regular, day-to-day involvement in these secular groups is limited because nonreligious people are able to find communities and social support elsewhere. Returning to Norway, while there are 105,000 members of *Human-Etisk Forbund*, there are over 260,000 members of the Norwegian Trekking Association.[54] The Norwegian Trekking Association organizes group hikes, provides information on trails, routes, and cabins, and helps maintain hiking trails all over Norway. Joining the Norwegian Trekking Association is a quick and reliable way to build a community around a shared interest—hiking.

Building communities outside the confines of religion takes some work, admittedly. Religions have evolved over millennia to be good at this. Belonging to a congregation with a highly engaged pastor or priest who is paid to shepherd their flock by actively working to build a community can be a powerful source of social support. But so, too, can bowling leagues, Dungeons & Dragons gaming groups, tailgater groups at sporting events, book clubs, music fandom, national or ethnic enclaves, and community gardens. People can find and build community around nearly anything. One of the author's (Ryan's) favorite examples of this is a community that has arisen around model horse competitions. Ryan was incredulous when he found out that his staff assistant was part of NAMHSA, the North American Model Horse Shows Association, where people take model horses they have bought to shows and compete to see who has the best model horses. Yet, his staff assistant showed him the blue ribbons she had won for her plastic and ceramic model horses, and he had to concede that this, too, is a real community. She has gained numerous friends through the competitive model horse community. Seriously!

Granted, religious communities have an innate capacity to link generations, providing rituals and culturally significant experiences specifically designed for family life over time; such secular analogs exist, but are much more rare, at least in the West.

Again, religions are very good at building community and providing social support. But with a little creativity—think model horses—communities and support can be built around any shared interest. Secular populations can and do create intentional communities to replace the social support provided by religions with a focus on shared interests that are very wide-ranging. Sometimes those communities are focused on their opposition to religion, but most secular people are not part of secular groups and instead find community in other ways. Secularity still involves community and social support; it is, however, more organic and typically focuses on shared secular interests.

Life-Cycle Rituals

An unfortunate but common misconception of secularization is that without religion, life carries less meaning. This stereotype often encompasses a perception of nonreligious rites of passage as dry and lacking in depth. The assumption that such ceremonies are inferior to religious ones was a sentiment that was expressed by Jacob, a Northern Irish Presbyterian minister. Although he had never attended a secular funeral, he "could imagine it being some sort of sad affair . . . Christian funerals can be happy if that person was willing to join God in Heaven, whereas with the humanist and nonreligious ceremonies, they have nothing to look forward to."

In addition to the fact that secular funerals are fundamentally different in that they do not involve the promise of an afterlife, a source of the perception of secular life-cycle ceremonies as "less than" may be the stereotypical civil marriage ceremony in a registrar's office or a courthouse. Such "ceremonies" are bland, quick, bureaucratic affairs, even taking place in an office cubicle with fluorescent lights. To be fair, such marriage ceremonies remain an option, but reality is far more nuanced than that. When speaking to secular northern Europeans on this matter, a common sentiment was that there is indeed a growing wish for secular life-cycle ceremonies that personalize and solemnize the occasion. After all, secular individuals find the same sense of awe, purpose, and significance in celebrating love, family, and special moments in life as do religious people.

The rising demand for secular life-cycle celebrations is seen in many societies,[55] including in Scotland, where, as noted previously, a growing number of nonreligious Scots turn to Humanist celebrants for weddings, naming ceremonies, and funerals. Although civil ceremonies remain the most common type of marriage ritual in Scotland, Humanist marriage ceremonies are, at 23 percent, more popular than Christian services, which account for 22 percent of all ceremonies.[56] Furthermore, despite the fact that Humanist ceremonies have only been legally recognized in Scotland since 2005, the largest of the Humanist societies, Humanist Society Scotland, marry more Scots than do the two largest Christian churches, the Church of Scotland and the Roman Catholic Church, *combined*.[57] In asking Scottish couples why they chose to be married by a Humanist celebrant, the common response was that they were looking for a secular option that would provide them the opportunity to choose the location, the content, the poems, and the songs—to create a unique ceremony with the same sense of occasion that you would expect in a religious service. In fact, some Scots described the Humanist weddings and funerals that they had attended as *more* personal than a religious service, because they were truly about the people who were recognized in the ceremonies and "not about God or Jesus." Such a view was described by Carrie who had attended a Humanist funeral in Scotland:

Humanist funerals are more centered on the life of the person. And it's really nice to hear the full story of someone . . . At my great aunt's funeral

I learned a lot about her that I hadn't known. Which was really nice . . .
The last church funeral that I went to was really a lot about God and not
about the person.

This contrast in terms of the qualitative elements of religious and
secular funerals was emphasized by Audrey, a funeral director in Los
Angeles,[58] who finds that "the nonreligious funeral ceremonies tend to
be much more personalized and that a lot more thought has gone into it
being specifically about that person."

The preferences surrounding choice and individuality in secular life-
cycle ceremonies described here are largely in line with Agata Rejowska's
findings from Poland,[59] a society that is often viewed as religiously homogeneous, but that is also experiencing secularization (as we discuss
in greater detail in chapter 6).[60] Drawing on a Durkheimian perspective, Rejowska notes that one of the key motivations of couples to have
a Humanist ceremony was this ability to personalize the ceremony and
that "what is marked as 'sacred' is their relationship, and what is marked
as 'profane' is the interference of the external institutions that represent
irrelevant and rejected values."[61]

In some contexts, civil ceremonies can be personalized the same way
that Humanist rites of passage are. For instance, Maja and Henrik live
in a house on the Baltic Sea in Sweden. They are both nonbelievers and
have both left the Church of Sweden. They still value family, traditions,
and celebrating key moments in life, which is why they called the town
hall to inquire about a personalized civil marriage ceremony that they
wanted to be held on a cliff by the water at their home. The appointed
celebrant from the town hall was happy to conduct such a ceremony,
which in addition to the official language that formalizes the marriage,
also included elements that are common in many religious ceremonies
as well, such as songs and poems sung and read by friends and family.
Maja was pregnant at the time of their wedding, and when their first
child was born, they decided to ask the civil celebrant, who they thought
had done a wonderful job at their wedding, to come back to their home
for a naming ceremony. They explained that it wasn't a given that they
would have such a ceremony but that they "wanted to do something"
since "it's tradition to publicly give your child a name and that's usually done with a baptism," but that since they were not religious, they

"still wanted to recognize the occasion with family." They went on to say that the older generation who attended the naming ceremony just saw it as a typical baptism and that they were "not sure they noticed the difference . . . It was not in a church . . . there was no water on the baby's head, but otherwise it was a baptism."

What these accounts tell us is that although individualization is at the core of secular life-cycle rituals, it does not mean that such rituals reject all elements of tradition and community. In fact, recognizing traditional but secular elements of life-cycle rituals creates a solemn character to a ceremony that the many attendees can "identify with," thus generating a sense of meaning and occasion. Like those who are religious, secular individuals also find value in acknowledging secular or secularized seasonal rituals: Midsummer, Yule, Burns Day, Halloween, Thanksgiving, and New Years Eve. All of these holidays serve as meaningful moments of celebrating one's family, culture, and social groups. As noted earlier[62] "sacred, but not necessarily religious, rituals that mark special occasions in life remain a cornerstone of social life even where religion has lost much of its social significance." Ultimately, acknowledging a social past is a fundamental component of socialization and collective belonging,[63] regardless of whether that community is religious or not.

Raising Children

In some parts of the world, long gone are the days when religion was thought to be a fundamental, necessary aspect of rearing and socializing children to become moral, upstanding citizens with honorable character. Table 5.1 shows the percentage of adults in Chile, South Korea, Norway, and the United States who select a specific quality as one of the top five most important for a child to be encouraged to learn at home. The list of qualities to choose from included: 1) good manners; 2) independence; 3) hard work; 4) feeling of responsibility; 5) imagination; 6) tolerance and respect for other people; 7) thrift, saving money and things; 8) determination, perseverance; 9) religious faith; 10) unselfishness; and 11) obedience.

In Norway, the most secular of the four countries, only 6.4 percent of the survey participants selected religious faith among the top five most important qualities. In Chile, South Korea, and the United States,

TABLE 5.1: Most Important Child Qualities (Percent). Data from the World Values Survey and the European Values Study (2017–2020)

	Chile	South Korea	Norway	United States
Religious faith	10.3	10.0	6.4	32.2
Good manners	77.2	74.2	76.5	51.7
Independence	29.5	60.4	85.6	55.5
Hard work	28.2	60.9	19.0	67.8
Responsibility	57.2	87.6	82.9	59.3
Imagination	22.6	52.4	43.0	29.8
Tolerance and respect	54.8	50.8	90.1	70.8
Thrift	22.0	45.0	11.5	27.2
Determination	35.1	49.6	26.9	38.6
Unselfishness	33.6	4.0	21.1	28.3
Obedience	36.8	5.1	16.6	20.5

the same figures are 10.3, 10.0, and 32.2 percent respectively. It is clear that the United States stands out compared to the other three countries on the importance that its citizens place on religion in child rearing. Nonetheless, alongside other measures of religious decline, as shown in chapter 3, this measure also indicates that secularization is occurring in the United States. In 1999, 52.2 percent selected religious faith as an important child quality, in 2006 it was 50.6 percent, in 2011 it was 43.1 percent, and in 2017 it was down to 32.2 percent. The countries where fewer than 10 percent of the respondents selected religious faith as a top-five important quality include China, Belarus, Denmark, Estonia, Finland, France, Germany, Hong Kong, Iceland, Japan, Macau, the Netherlands, Norway, Vietnam, Slovenia, Sweden, and Switzerland. The countries where more than 70 percent selected religious faith are Bangladesh, Indonesia, Jordan, Nigeria, Tunisia, and Egypt—countries that rank low on measures of modernization, just as secularization theory would predict.

When examining the qualities that appear to be the most highly valued in children, in Norway, we see tolerance, independence, and responsibility at the top of the list. Here, 85.6 percent of the respondents selected independence. The same statistic is 14.4 percent in Egypt and 13.8 percent in Iraq. Figures from Sweden and Tunisia provide an interesting contrast on the importance of obedience. In Sweden, only 7.4 percent of the respondents believe that obedience is one of the top five qualities that children should learn in the home. In Tunisia, a highly religious country with relatively low levels of modernization, 76.5 percent say so.

Autonomy, independence, and worldview choice are primary features of secular child rearing. In her study of nonreligious families, Christel Manning found that secular parents were critical of religious indoctrination and let their children develop their own viewpoints, opinions, and beliefs.[64] The propensity for independence of thought among secular individuals is illustrated by studies showing that when parents in the United States are asked what traits they most seek to foster in their kids, secular parents are much more likely to choose "thinking for oneself," in contrast to religious parents, who are much more likely to choose "obedience to authority."[65] This mindset was expressed by Tonya, a secular mother in the US South, who stated, "I want my children to make their own decisions. That's been my focus. What I want for my kids is to let them be their own voice."[66]

This particular outlook was also one that characterized Eilidh's childhood. Eilidh, who lives in the central belt of Scotland, was born in 1976. She grew up with two parents who were active in the Church of Scotland, but who raised their daughter in a secularized society where instilling a sense of autonomy and independence is a primary feature of raising youth. Eilidh noted, "We were never made to go [to church] . . . I probably didn't go very often, so when Sunday school finished when I was like 10 or 11, then I could just come along if I wanted to . . . I suppose I thought it was quite boring. I just thought there were better things to do." Religion never stuck with Eilidh, who ended up a nonbeliever. Her parents, on the other hand, continue to attend church at the local parish. Eilidh's story exemplifies the link between higher levels of childhood autonomy and secularization that was proposed in chapter 1. In societies where autonomy and independence are valued, children will be less likely to develop a salient religious identity. What this effectively means is that most children who are left to "decide for themselves" will not choose religion.

In the most secular societies, raising your child without religion is the default position. As mentioned above, such societies are typically characterized by widespread indifference on matters of religion. This generally means that parents are *passively secular* and that they do not contemplate religious socialization one way or another. They do not raise their child to be religiously active, but at the same time, they usually do not foster *affirmative secularity* either—i.e., where religion is replaced with an explicitly nonreligious alternative like secular humanism. Parents *can* send their children to a nonreligious confirmation in Scandinavia, but the uptake is quite low.[67] Indeed, in our extensive fieldwork in Denmark, Sweden, and Scotland, we have very rarely come across a person who was raised to be affirmatively secular or who would raise their own children as such.

In more religious societies and cultures, it may be common for nonreligious parents to intentionally raise children to adopt atheist, freethought, or secular humanist identities.[68] Yet, even active members of secularist groups are not always raised in affirmatively secular households or even in more passively secular families. Frank Pasquale[69] found that participants in American secularist groups were typically what Bengtson and colleagues[70] called "religious rebels" who were actually raised by religious parents in a normatively religious context where being nonreligious is stigmatized and alienating.[71]

An alternative strategy to child rearing in secular families that is fairly common in some contexts is to encourage an appreciation for *cultural religion* (a phenomenon that was discussed briefly in chapter 2)—a "secular spin" on conventional religion where the family celebrates religious holidays (in a nonreligious fashion) and encourages the reproduction of a cultural or ethnic connection to a religious heritage. This is a common approach among American Jews and in Scandinavia, where the national churches still have a strong (but shrinking) cultural presence.[72] Consider for instance the culturally ubiquitous Swedish tradition of celebrating Saint Lucia Day on December 13 each year. One girl dresses up as Lucia, with a wreath of candles in her hair, wearing a white dress with a red sash. The other girls wear a similar white dress and hold a candle in their hand. Among boys it is common to dress up as a gingerbread person or in a red outfit with a Santa hat. The celebration typically takes place in a church and includes the children singing Christmas carols, which begin and end with the traditional "Lucia song." A smaller group of children recite poems with a Christmas theme. After the procession, saffron buns, gingerbread, and coffee are served to those in attendance. Despite the popularity of the tradition and the clear religious symbolism in the sainthood of Lucia, few Swedes would associate this event with religion. In reality, it is a cultural celebration of Christmas and the winter solstice that is a blend of religious, pagan, and secular folk traditions.[73] Secular parents gladly encourage and look forward to their children taking part in this event as a seasonal rite that transmits a shared sense of cultural belonging.[74] This is similar to the meaning-making and the sense of occasion that was noted in the section on life-cycle rituals earlier in this chapter.

Ultimately, nonreligious parents tend to raise nonreligious children,[75] whether passively or "by choice." As discussed in chapter 1, religious decline is particularly substantial across generations, and religious transmission becomes less and less successful with each generation, particularly in societal contexts where secularity is increasing.[76] After all, as we noted earlier, successful transmission of religion to a new generation requires explicit and sustained effort by parents and other agents of socialization. Raising a child outside of a faith tradition does not.

Aging

Retired couple Britta and Torvald served tea and homemade cookies as one of the authors (Isabella) sat down with them in their apartment in a city in southern Sweden to talk about their secular life and their relationship to religion throughout the life course. Britta and Torvald, both in their mid-seventies, embody the secular older couple in a highly secularized society. They were not brought up with religious practices or beliefs, and even their grandparents, born in the 1800s, were mostly nonreligious. Although Britta and Torvald only had positive things to say about the Church, neither of them had ever had any interest in being involved. Britta mentioned that the last time she went to a religious service (other than to attend life-cycle celebrations) was more than fifty years ago. That was, nevertheless, more recent than Torvald, who had in fact *never* attended a Sunday service. When Isabella asked them if they had friends or family who were religious, they said that they did not, but after a short pause, they remembered the neighbor downstairs who is a practicing Christian. Britta went on to tell the story of a Christmas Eve, a few years earlier, when the neighbor, who was getting ready to head out to midnight mass, stopped by with some birthday cake to celebrate the occasion and Britta wondered, momentarily, whose birthday it could be.

Britta and Torvald had both been married previously. Britta was only nineteen when she married her first husband, and a church ceremony was simply "what you did." But when Britta and Torvald married each other, only years prior to Isabella's meeting with them, they opted for a civil ceremony at the local town hall. They had already been living together for many years, and Britta explained that it doesn't really feel all that different being married or not married when you make a commitment to someone—except that deep down, there is that feeling of security in case the worst were to happen. In fact, after Torvald had a health scare, they decided to marry to avoid the bureaucratic challenges of not being legally linked to each other.

Britta and Torvald had the same committed relationship and life together before they married. Although they married in a civil ceremony for legal and practical reasons, their ceremony was, to them, just as meaningful as anyone else's. They explained that they had come to realize that people place more value on little things and each other (rather than big fancy celebrations) as you age.

> We invited a few of our close friends to the town hall on a Monday. Candles were lit. It was beautiful. After the ceremony, we all went on a cruise to Finland together and ate good food and had a wonderful time . . .

Neither Britta nor Torvald believe in God, although they expressed that this is not something that they ever really talk about, and it is not something that they discuss with their friends or other family either. "I don't believe there is a life after this one," said Britta. Torvald noted that it might be something that "you perhaps want to believe." Nevertheless, it was clear from the conversation with the two of them that they were of the opinion that life is what you make of it here and now.

Britta and Torvald are not unique in being an older couple who are living a profoundly secular life in Sweden. Data from the ISSP show that, in Sweden, eight out of ten individuals aged 70 and older "agree" or "strongly agree" that life is only meaningful if you provide meaning yourself, 9.6 percent believe in God without any doubts, 23.2 percent believe in life after death, 24.4 percent believe in heaven, and 7.2 percent believe in hell. Only 4.1 percent of those who are 70 and older describe themselves as "extremely" or "very religious," compared to the 23.9 percent who are "extremely" or "very nonreligious." It is also evident that the older generation acknowledges the diminishing influence of religion in contemporary society. Around one in five Swedes of this age say that religion is as relevant now as in the past, and only 6.2 percent attend church at least monthly. The historically early secularization of Sweden is also illustrated by the fact that for respondents aged seventy or older, only 16.8 percent said that they attended church at least monthly when they were children.

The figures presented here show a very weak uptake of religious beliefs and practices among older Swedes. In fact, on most of these measures, there is very little difference between this group and those who are younger than seventy, which demonstrates the weak or missing effects of aging on religiosity in a secular society. Given that 9 out of 10 Swedes of this age also state that they are either "very" or "fairly" happy, the data do not suggest that their lives are deficient as a result of their secularity.

The evidence discussed here, as well as the examples in chapter 3 of declining religious commitment with age in several contexts, refute the claim made by advocates of rational choice theory that people become more religious as they age. This claim is based on the idea that, as people age and their life approaches its end, they will be more likely to "make investments" in religious beliefs and practices to increase the likelihood that they will reap rewards in an afterlife. On this point, Rodney Stark and Roger Finke[77] argued that:

> Just as people often delay their investments in a retirement plan, they often delay bringing their afterlife arrangements up to date. We might refer to this as the *principle of religious procrastination*. Evidence of it shows up in the tendency for people to raise their levels of religious commitment as they age.

According to their argument, higher levels of physical and mental health are also a reality for elderly individuals who choose to "invest" in their afterlife.[78] Yet, in the case of Sweden, those aged seventy or older who do attend church monthly or believe in the afterlife are *not* significantly more happy or healthy compared to those who do not. The effect of religion on a person's well-being as they age is clearly context-dependent, just as we show below in terms of how people deal with crises. What we demonstrate here is that in a highly secularized society, people of all ages can live a perfectly happy and fulfilling life without religion—to the point that they do not consider "investing in religion" as they approach its end.

Dealing with Crises

Another aspect of the human experience where religion is often thought to be particularly beneficial is as a coping mechanism when tragedy strikes. When it comes to dealing with cancer, chronic illness, addiction, or the death of a loved one, previous research has indeed shown that for people who are religious, their faith can be a great source of comfort, both in terms of the psychological aspects of coping as well as the practical and emotional support that a religious community can offer.[79]

Given that religious people tend to turn to their faith in times of pain and sorrow, Rodney Stark and William Sims Bainbridge have argued that religion serves as a *compensator* in such moments of struggle,[80] when the real *reward*—i.e., what the person is ultimately hoping for (such as health, longevity, or immortality)—is not readily attainable.[81] On this matter, they state that:

> All societies utilize compensators. Perhaps the most universal is some form of triumph over death. If means were provided to evade death here and now, that would be a reward. But at present immortality is to be achieved somewhere (somewhen?) else, and the validity of the promise cannot be determined.[82]

This argument could explain why, when faced with serious illness, even religious people turn to effective, secular, rationalized treatment options over religious compensators as they seek better health or a longer life when it is clear that such treatments work.[83] The major flaw in this claim is that it assumes that religion is always the natural or universal default option no matter how secular a population appears, because in moments of true despair, when treatments fail, religion will serve as the compensator that secularity cannot provide. This claim about religious compensators is then used to assert that secularity is inherently fragile since, in the event of a tragedy, people will revert to religion to help them cope with their mortality or other life challenges.

There is a growing body of research showing that secular people do not turn to religion in times of crises. Karen Hwang examined research on atheists with disabilities[84] and conducted interviews with atheists who had spinal cord injuries[85] to determine how they coped with these challenges. What she found was that many of the atheists with spinal cord injuries found comfort and support in their atheism and secular beliefs and values following their trauma. They did not turn to religion to compensate for their life-altering injuries. Religious people can draw upon their religion to help with crises, though religion can also be detrimental for religious people in such moments as well by adding a layer of guilt or leading religious people to distrust[86] or be angry at God[87] over what happened.

Building on the idea that people turn to religion during difficult times, Grace Davie maintained that, even in more secularized countries, people turn to religious organizations for public grief. She noted that, in Sweden, following the sinking of the cruise ship MS Estonia in the Baltic Sea in 1994 (that killed 852 people of whom 501 were Swedes) and the tsunami in Southeast Asia in 2004 (where Sweden, with 543 casualties, was the most severely affected country outside of the disaster region[88]), many citizens filed into the churches to mourn and light candles.[89] She argued that these events illustrated that Scandinavians are *vicariously religious*, where religion is normally "performed by an active minority but on behalf of a much larger number who (implicitly at least) not only understand but appear to approve."[90] The religiously active minority make it possible for everyone else to still utilize the churches for certain, more irregular, purposes such as public remembrances. Professor Davie's claim emphasizes a lasting attachment to religion, even in secularizing contexts.

There are some problems with Davie's assertion. While there was a small uptick in the attendance at "other" religious services (i.e., not the regular Sunday service) in the Church of Sweden in 1994, the year of the MS Estonia accident, the total number of church visits that year was still lower than two years prior. There was also no similar increase in the year following the tsunami disaster, given that, in 2005, religious service attendance declined by 2.3 percent compared to the year before, and in the same year, more than 68 thousand members intentionally left the church, ten times the number who joined.[91] Admittedly, these ceremonies of remembrance did involve churches, but churches can and often do serve secular functions.[92] There are very few buildings that have the capacity and capability to quickly allow for large groups of people to come together at no cost to collectively celebrate or mourn, regardless of the religiosity or secularity of the individuals involved. Having served such functions in the past, religious buildings continue to function well in this regard. That does not mean that they will continue to serve in such a capacity indefinitely into the future, only that they are a convenient place for people to gather on certain occasions.

Davie agreed that vicarious religion does not serve as a refutation of secularization theory, but as a way to conceptualize what a changing religious landscape looks like.[93] Nevertheless, as seen in chapter 3, measures of vicarious religion, such as the popularity of national churches in the otherwise secular Scandinavia, are also in decline.

Moreover, even if some people who normally do not go to churches for services were drawn to churches to acknowledge public grief, this does not necessarily mean that such an event is religious in substance.[94] On this matter, Pascal Siegers states that such practices stem from a "habitual association of the specific functions with the churches more than from explicit support for religious practices or teachings . . . individuals rely on churches for specific occasions because they were socialised into this tradition."[95] It is more accurate to assert that secular Swedes pay their respects in churches because "that's what you do" and not because they are deciding to pray to a higher power in those moments or otherwise experience a swelling of religiosity. In fact, findings from a study in Sweden showed that parents of children with a life-threatening heart condition were no more or less likely to pray or hold religious beliefs than a control group who were not facing this hardship.[96]

There is also empirical evidence that nonreligious people in secular societies are no more likely to struggle with mental illness than are religious individuals. Secular people facing challenges in their lives draw on many of the same coping mechanisms that religious people use, such as family, friends, and professional guidance.[97] For those who are religious and live in a society where religion is pervasive and normative, religion is more likely to be a positive tool when managing crises. Without a desire to utilize a religious community, secular coping is typically more individualized and rationalized. In highly religious societies, such an approach could be isolating.[98] If that is the case in more secular societies, this could be a downside of secularity. Secular people may find value in some of the secular elements of religious coping strategies, such as a stronger emphasis on community and support networks. Of note, however, are some studies that show that religion is not always as helpful in processing grief and tragedies as it is portrayed; some people struggle when their prayers do not seem to be answered and feel despair when God does not intervene in a tragic event.[99]

Overall, there is little evidence that secularization reverses when individuals and societies face punctuated crises or natural disasters, aside from perhaps a very short-lived blip in attendance at religious services. Data on religiosity in relation to the COVID-19 pandemic show that, in the United States, although Christians were more likely to say that their faith had strengthened as a result of the pandemic, there was not a religious revival among atheists and agnostics.[100] More secular societies have not seen meaningful change in religiosity following this public health crisis. Like what was observed in the United States, people who already found religion to be important were the ones whose faith was strengthened; the nonreligious did not turn to religion in massive numbers to cope with the COVID-19 pandemic.[101] The fact that fewer and fewer people turn to faith to cope with tragedy shouldn't necessarily be seen as a negative by-product of secularization. Similar to what we saw regarding happiness among older adults in secular societies, the effects of religion are context-specific, and while it is clearly helpful to some people in some societies, secular people are also able to cope with crises, as best they can.

Conclusion

Individuals in countries around the world are shedding their religiosity at historically unprecedented rates. Secularization has advanced so far in certain parts of the world that there are now many countries in which secular people are the majority, and many more countries in which secular people, though not in the majority, still comprise a large percentage of the population. There are now hundreds of millions of people living their lives without religious identification, involvement, or faith. This reality alone—as argued in chapter 4—renders fallacious the argument that widespread secularity is somehow unnatural or untenable. Claims that social life would be unsustainable, calamitous, immoral, or otherwise debauched without religion are no longer legitimate. Secular people live their lives in pursuit of love, joy, friendship, family, and compassion. Many are actively involved in social causes surrounding human rights, poverty, the relief of suffering, and global warming. They also enjoy and find meaning in rituals, traditions, and a sense of community. Secular life is not just possible—for hundreds of millions of people, secularity is preferred, positive, and pleasurable.

6

Exceptions?

Some scholars have suggested that there are exceptions to secularization.[1] Typically, what is meant by an "exception" to secularization is a society that should be experiencing secularization given its level of modernization, but is not; or a society that has seen an increase in religiosity. Theories can, of course, include caveats for when they do not work or when they are not relevant. In this chapter, we explore three scenarios that may impede secularization: cultural defense, government restrictions (or artificial religiosity), and forced secularization (or artificial secularization). Below, we explain what these presumed exceptions entail and then consider each in light of the theory of secularization that we delineated in chapter 1, as well as the data we have presented throughout this volume.

We are reluctant to consider these true exceptions since, when properly understood, secularization theory is actually capable of explaining each of these scenarios. Even so, it is important to examine these phenomena, as it helps to clarify the theory of secularization.

Cultural Defense

The first exception that has been proposed is that secularization may be unlikely to occur in modern societies where religion finds "something else to do" other than serve its traditional roles and/or functions.[2] Traditionally, religion has helped people communicate with and supplicate the supernatural and has provided a sense of understanding of the natural world, like believing earthquakes are caused by angry gods.[3] By finding "something else to do," religion is being used beyond these traditional functions to, for instance, provide a sense of common identity for a group of people. This has been referred to as the "cultural defense" exception and the most common examples *were* Ireland and Poland.[4] The cultural defense exception is typically understood to mean that if the beliefs, values, and behaviors of a given society are under attack or are being threatened—usually by a political or military force external to that society—religion provides one of the key means to organize those under threat and provide a unified sense of identity. As a result of religion's expanded role in these countries, despite experiencing modernization and rationalization, secularization is less likely to occur.

With Ireland and Poland, external forces threatened both societies. Ireland was conquered by England in the twelfth century and made a kingdom in the sixteenth century by Henry VIII, the King of England. It was later merged with Great Britain in 1801 to form the United Kingdom of Great Britain and Ireland. However, Irish agitation for independence—which was violently repressed—eventually resulted in the Anglo-Irish Treaty of 1921. Under that treaty, Ireland was separated into Northern Ireland and what would become the Republic of Ireland. Conflict over Northern Ireland, which remained part of the United Kingdom, continued until the 1990s. The conflict within Northern Ireland was heavily tied to religion; militant Republicans from the Catholic minority were fighting militant Unionists from the Protestant majority.

Following World War II, the Soviet Union was able to orchestrate the implementation of a communist government in Poland, resulting in the country being swallowed into the Eastern Bloc. During the period of forced communist rule, there was regular agitation against the state by workers, the intelligentsia, households, and the Catholic Church, much of which was rooted in economic and political problems resulting from the centrally planned economy.[5] The rise of the Solidarity movement, starting in the 1980s, led to an election in 1989 in which the Solidarity Party was able to participate as a viable alternative to the Communist Party. The victory of the Solidarity Party was one of the first manifestations of the collapse of the Soviet Union.[6]

In Ireland and Poland, external forces, the UK and the Soviet Union, respectively, threatened the autonomy and culture of the citizens. Religion—in both cases, Catholicism—became a culturally defensive tool that the citizens of these countries used to aid in their fight against the external forces that threatened them. In Ireland, Catholics made up the majority of the citizens of the Republic of Ireland but a minority in Northern Ireland, which had experienced substantial immigration from England and was majority Protestant—a mixture of Presbyterian

Church, Church of Ireland, Methodist Church, and other Christian de-nominations.[7] Support for a unified Ireland, as opposed to a divided Ireland with Northern Ireland aligned with the UK, was tied to religion: Catholics tended to want a unified Ireland, while Protestants wanted Northern Ireland to remain part of the UK. In the Republic of Ireland, then, religion "found something else to do" by strengthening the na-tional, political, and cultural identities of both Catholics and Protestants during the Troubles.

In Poland, the Catholic Church initially helped the communist Polish Workers Party gain power by reinforcing Polish/Catholic ethnonational-ism in the wake of changed borders and intentional efforts on the part of the Soviet Union to turn Poland into a homogeneous society.[8] However, once communism was firmly entrenched in Poland, the communist gov-ernment turned on the Catholic Church, which, until then, had retained substantial influence over the Polish people. The communist govern-ment began imprisoning priests and confiscating Church lands.[9] The Polish communist government even tried to suggest that the then Pope, Pius XII, held greater sympathies for displaced Germans who had been forced out of the realigned borders of Poland than he did for the Polish people, attempting to drive a wedge between the Catholic Church in Po-land and the Papacy. Eventually, the communist government came to an agreement with the Catholic Church that would ensure that the Church functioned as an arm of the government, legitimating communism in Poland despite the leadership of the Catholic Church in Rome openly opposing communism.[10]

While there were many forces involved in weakening the grip of communism and the Soviet Union in Poland—particularly workers' unions, an underground economy, and intellectuals—the Catholic Church provided substantial support for the movement by allowing dissenters to utilize their presses, providing dissenters safe havens, and creating venues wherein dissent could be expressed openly.[11] The election of Cardinal Karol Wojtyła, who was the archbishop of Kraków when elected to the Papacy as John Paul II, helped solidify both the alignment of Catholicism with Polish identity and the support of the Catholic Church in the Polish people's fight against communism.[12] Thus, religion found "something else to do" in Poland as well.

By defending the cultures of Ireland and Poland, religion moved beyond its limited role of helping to supplicate the supernatural and became an integral part of nationalist identities in both countries. During these periods, being Catholic was synonymous with being Irish and Polish. When religion is used to defend a society's culture, some scholars have argued that secularization may be less likely to occur.[13]

Our perspective is that, while religion certainly can and does bolster cultural identity and/or ethnic movements in the face of external threats as in the cases of both Poland and Ireland, we aren't actually seeing an "exception" to secularization, but rather, an illustration of a key aspect of secularization theory: differentiation. When religion is used as part of an ethno-nationalist agenda to strengthen centripetal identity,[14] there are lower levels of differentiation between religion and other aspects of society. The 1937 Constitution of Ireland privileged the Catholic Church while allowing the existence of other religions. In Ireland, the Catholic Church ran many of the schools, orphanages, hospitals, and provided numerous social services that, in countries with higher levels of differentiation, would be provided by a secular government. Likewise, in Poland the Catholic Church ran numerous hospitals and a university, and was required to legitimize the communist government. In both Poland and Ireland, there was minimal differentiation between religion and other aspects of social life. When national identity and religious identity are closely intertwined, it is difficult to be, for instance, a good Irish citizen and not be Catholic.[15] As noted in chapter 1, lower levels of differentiation in a society will result in lower levels of secularization. Thus, rather than exceptions to secularization, Poland and Ireland are, in fact, illustrations of the general theory of secularization: religion was instrumental in their defenses of their cultures against external threats, limiting religious differentiation, which otherwise delayed secularization.

Of course, Ireland and Poland are no longer held up as exceptions to secularization, for both have now started to secularize, as shown in Figures 6.1 and 6.2. While the end of the Troubles in the 1990s in Ireland reduced the importance of cultural defense, this also coincided with a period of rapid modernization. The Celtic Tiger refers to the economy of the Republic of Ireland from the mid-1990s into the early 2000s when it experienced substantial growth.

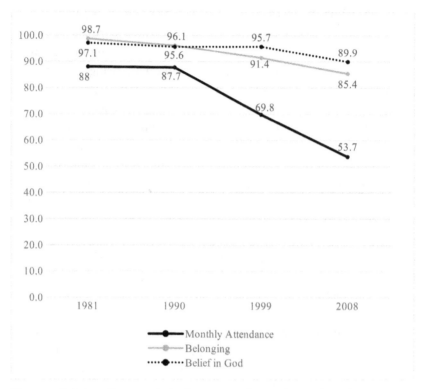

Figure 6.1: Religious Change in Ireland, 1981–2008 (Percent). Data from the European Values Study.

Additionally, a number of revelations concerning abuse at the hands of the Catholic Church and Catholic clergy came to light during this period. Collectively, all of these developments resulted in a period of rapid secularization with concomitant reductions in belief, behavior, and belonging.[16] Similarly, with the end of communism in Poland there has been a decline in religiosity, particularly in religious service attendance, and growing opposition to Catholic dominance in the country; the Catholic Church has once again aligned itself with the government in an attempt to implement Catholic values as part of an authoritarian, populist agenda.[17]

Arguably, a similar style of cultural defense was at play in the United States during the Cold War, delaying the rapid secularization that has occurred since the 1990s while "God-fearing Americans" fought the "godless communists." Even as several court cases removed religious in-struction from schools, the American government minted God on the currency and added it to the Pledge of Allegiance.[18] Yet, just as occurred in Ireland and Poland, once religion was no longer required to defend American culture and values, secularization has advanced. All three of these cases support our earlier proposition: *The greater the differentia-tion at the societal, institutional, or individual levels, the more likely secu-larization is to occur.* When religion is used to defend a culture from external threats, differentiation in that society will be lower, reducing the odds of secularization. Rather than exceptions, the delayed onset of secularization in each of these countries is fully explainable by the theory of secularization.

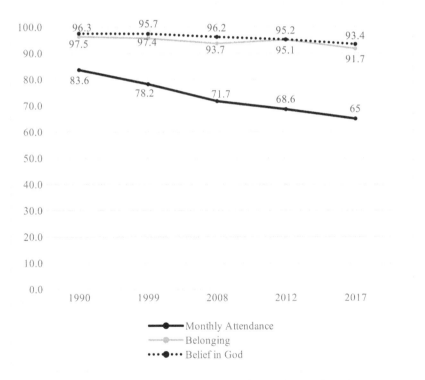

Figure 6.2: Religious Change in Poland, 1990–2017 (Percent). Data from the European Values Study and the World Values Survey.

Government Restrictions/Artificial Religiosity

Another exception to secularization that some scholars have suggested is when governments prohibit or penalize individuals for leaving the state religion.[19] This is the "exception" to secularization that is applied to many predominantly Muslim countries where freedom of and from religion does not exist. Twenty-five countries around the world have laws restricting whether someone can leave the dominant religion;[20] eleven countries punish religious exiting with extensive prison sentences or death.[21] For some of these countries, there is no specific legal code that mandates death as a punishment for leaving Islam but instead leaves the punishment up to Shariʿa courts. However, some of these countries have written punishments for leaving Islam into their legal code, like Mauritania:

> Any Muslim guilty of the crime of apostasy, either by word or by apparent or obvious action, will be asked to repent within three days. If he does not repent within this time, he is condemned to death as an apostate, and his property will be confiscated for the benefit of the Treasury.[22]

Saudi Arabia took a slightly different approach when it classified atheism as a form of terrorism in an Interior Ministry Regulation issued on March 7, 2014. The passage states that the following can be considered terrorism and will be punished as such: "calling for atheist thought in any form, or calling into question the fundamentals of the Islamic religion on which this country is based."[23] The governments in these countries are not alone in advocating death for leaving Islam. Research into attitudes in many predominantly Muslim countries suggests varied levels of support for killing those who leave religion, ranging from a high of more than 75 percent of the population supporting death for those who leave Islam in Pakistan to a low of less than 5 percent in Albania and Azerbaijan.[24]

When leaving the state religion can lead to lengthy prison sentences or death, that can provide a compelling reason to retain a religious identity, curtailing most outward indicators of secularization.[25] However, to argue that these countries are exceptions to secularization when there is literally no differentiation between religion and government makes very little sense. For many of these countries, the linkage between religion and government is explicit either in the name of the country (e.g., the Islamic Republic of Iran, the Islamic Republic of Mauritania, the Islamic Emirate of Afghanistan, etc.) or in the constitutions. For instance, Article 2 of the 2014 Egyptian Constitution reads, "Islam is the religion of the state and Arabic is its official language. The principles of Islamic Sharia are the principal source of legislation."[26]

Countries that do not allow freedom of religion are actually excellent illustrations of secularization theory because they exhibit very little differentiation between religion and other aspects of social life. As a result, secularization theory would propose that secularization would *not* be widespread regardless of the country's level of economic development, just as seen in chapter 2. We refer to the situation in these countries as one of "artificial religiosity," a descriptor that makes the situation more apparent; the high levels of religiosity are artificially inflated due to the penalties in place for those who leave the dominant religion. Predominantly Muslim countries with minimal or no differentiation between Islam and the secular government are not exceptions to secularization. They fall squarely within the proposition we detailed earlier: *The greater the differentiation at the societal, institutional, or individual levels, the more likely secularization is to occur.*

Intriguingly, the lack of differentiation in these contexts appears to be insufficient to curtail the effects of development and rationalization on the religiosity of the citizens depending on how religiosity is measured. There is growing evidence that even in these countries there are indications of religious decline. For example, as seen in chapter 2, the countries with high development and low differentiation were somewhat more secular than countries with low development. It may be the case that many people are quite secular, but that they will only admit as much in anonymous surveys or when posting anonymously online in order to not be punished. One such study of literate adult Iranians found that 22 percent of the population were nonreligious, that 60 percent do not pray regularly, 68 percent want separation between government and religion, 35 percent drink alcohol (which is prohibited in Islam), and 72 percent do not want the hijab to be compulsory.[27] The Arab Barometer surveys found that the majority of fifteen- to twenty-nine-year-olds in eleven Middle Eastern and North African countries were not religious:

58 percent in Iraq, 64 percent in Egypt, 67 percent in Yemen, 68 percent in Sudan, 72 percent in Palestine, 76 percent in Morocco, 77 percent in Lebanon, 78 percent in Jordan, 82 percent in Libya, 84 percent in Tunisia, and 85 percent in Algeria.[28] Despite the lack of differentiation in many of these countries, results from anonymous surveys suggest that secularization has begun.

Forced/Artificial Secularization

In 1956 in what was then Kuibyshev (now Samara), Russia, a fabulous story was born. Zoia Karnaukhova, a young woman, was attending a party at 84 Chkalov Street. The other attendees were dancing, but Zoia was waiting for her partner, Nikolai. When Nikolai didn't show up, Zoia told everyone that she was going to dance with the icon of Nikolai the Miracle Worker that was hanging in the corner of the house instead. As she pulled down the framed icon and began to dance with it, lightning struck and Zoia was turned to stone for her blasphemy.[29] This fabulation of divine retribution for blasphemy spread far and wide in the Soviet Union and was even discussed among the communist leaders. We encourage readers to note the year: 1956. This is deep into the Soviet era when Russians were supposed to all be "godless communists." Yet thousands of believers traveled to Kuibyshev to see where Zoia was turned to stone, and the story functioned as a pillar to bolster the sacred canopies of millions of Orthodox Russians whose religion was under attack by the communist government.

The third and last exception that we want to examine in this chapter is the recently observed increase in religiosity in former Soviet countries. Following the writings of Karl Marx, the Communist Party saw religion as an impediment to class consciousness.[30] The Marxist-Leninist government of the Soviet Union tried to force secularization in most of Russia and in many parts of the wider Soviet Union and the Eastern Bloc; the intentional efforts of the Marxist-Leninist government to weaken and destroy religion are well-documented.[31] Forced secularization included closing and destroying churches, closing holy sites, filling in holy wells with concrete, imprisoning and killing clergy, persecuting religious individuals, and concerted efforts to spread atheism and secular rituals as replacements for religion. These efforts began shortly after the Bolshevik Revolution in 1917 and were broadened after World War II as the Union of Soviet Socialist Republics (USSR) expanded.[32] The severity of the persecution of religion waxed and waned over the duration of the Soviet experiment depending on contextual factors (e.g., WWII) and the leader in power.[33]

Some scholars have insinuated that these efforts were broadly successful at secularizing the citizens of the USSR and the Eastern Bloc.[34] What then might make these countries an exception to secularization is that, after the collapse of the Soviet Union, some of them have seen an increase on some measures of religiosity. The following countries are the ones we noted in chapter 2 that have experienced an increase on all three measures of religiosity: Armenia, Bulgaria, Kazakhstan, Latvia, Moldova, North Macedonia, Russia, and Ukraine.

In chapter 1, we described scenarios in which secularization can be reversed. We argued that there are such scenarios, but they are relatively rare. This raises the question of whether the countries just mentioned fit those criteria: was there either a de-differentiation of religion from other aspects of society and/or a de-rationalization?

To examine this question, we are going to focus on one country in particular: Russia. We are focusing on Russia for two reasons. First, there are many published studies and more English source material on Russia than the other countries, making Russia more accessible for those, like us, who are not native language speakers. Second, and more importantly, we believe Russia is generally illustrative of what happened in the other countries.[35] Figure 6.3 illustrates the increase in religiosity in Russia over the last thirty years.

Our question for this section is, then: Is twenty-first century Russia an exception to secularization?

The short answer is no.

The long answer involves two components. Part of the explanation is de-differentiation, which we will explore in detail below, but there is also a twist: while the Marxist-Leninist government of Russia was explicitly atheist and attempted to suppress religion, the efforts were never particularly successful.[36] Despite the suggestion by some scholars that an atheist government undertaking religious persecution and atheist propaganda efforts effectively secularized the citizens of Russia,[37] forced secularization did not eradicate personal religious belief or private religious practice.

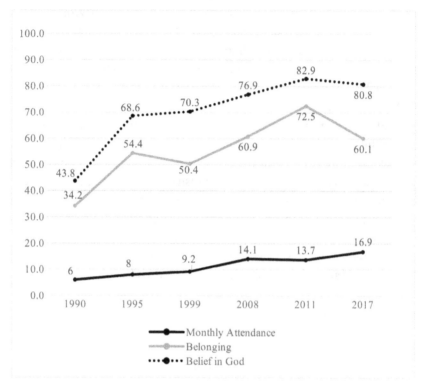

Figure 6.3: Religious Change in Russia, 1990–2017 (Percent). Data from the European Values Study and the World Values Survey.

Forced secularization as attempted in Russia drove down people's participation in public religious services, and for many, their stated religious affiliation (i.e., belonging). This was done primarily by cutting off the supply of religion by closing churches, killing clergy, and destroying religious literature.[38] Before the Bolshevik Revolution of 1917, there were an estimated 50,000 functioning Orthodox churches in Russia. While the history of the Orthodox Church in Russia is complicated,[39] the vast majority of Russians identified as Orthodox before the 1917 revolution.[40] During the first roughly twenty years following the revolution, around 80,000 Orthodox priests and clergy were killed and the total number of open and functioning Orthodox churches had fallen to somewhere between 200 and 300 by 1939.[41] During the Soviet era, almost all monasteries were closed and priests who attempted to perform religious rites outside the confines of their churches could lose their ability to function as clergy provided by the Council on Religious Affairs.[42]

The harsh persecution of religion following the 1917 revolution fluctuated, with periods of greater and lesser persecution. In particular, persecution was tempered during and following World War II.[43] The communist government recognized that it would be challenging to unify its citizens to fight an external threat while one of the most cherished aspects of Russian culture—the Russian Orthodox Church—was under attack.[44] Likewise, following WWII, millions of active Christians in countries like Lithuania, Bulgaria, and Poland were annexed by the Soviet Union. As a result, there was, at least for a time, a lessening of persecution of religion during and after WWII. The reduction in persecution of religion was quickly apparent in how the Russian Orthodox Church responded. By January 1946, the Russian Orthodox Church had registered 10,504 parishes, and that number continued to increase.[45] The detente between the Soviet government and the Russian Orthodox Church came at the cost of the Russian Orthodox Church committing to support the regime, which occurred in 1927 when Metropolitan Sergii made it clear that the Russian Orthodox Church's loyalty was to the communist government.[46] This capitulation to communism resulted in internal division within the Russian Orthodox Church as well as several breakaway religions, though many were relatively short-lived.[47]

With fewer open churches, a reduction in the number of clergy, and explicit opposition to religion by the totalitarian government, it made sense for many citizens to both stop attending religious services and to stop identifying as religious. It's obviously hard to attend religious services that are not being performed. It also would invite persecution to continue to outwardly manifest religious devotion when there is open and explicit persecution of the religious by the government.[48] Young people who regularly attended religious services were tracked by the KGB and parents who baptized children ran the risk of being fired from their jobs.[49] As noted above in our discussion of predominantly Muslim countries, most people will avoid engaging in behavior that invites punishment, particularly when that punishment can be as severe as death[50] or institutionalization in a mental hospital, as was often done in the Soviet Union for individuals who were openly and devoutly religious.[51] The result of government persecution of all religions results in "artificial secularization."

Despite the very intentional efforts of the Marxist-Leninist government to destroy religion, there is evidence that the efforts were only partially successful.[52] In 1937, the Soviet government fielded a census in which a question about religious affiliation was included; 56 percent of the citizens identified as religious.[53] Certainly that is a decline from what was likely more than 90 percent before the revolution. But the majority of Soviet citizens continued to identify as religious despite efforts to destroy religion. After the 1937 census, no other censuses included questions about religious affiliation. Some estimates from the 1980s put the number of religious adherents in the USSR at somewhere between 30 and 60 million, which would be anywhere from 12 percent to 20 percent of the population.[54] But there were no high quality, reliable surveys of religiosity in the USSR until after the collapse of the Soviet Union. In other words, we don't actually know how successful religious persecution by Marxist-Leninist governments was at driving down religiosity. What little data we do have suggests that a substantial portion of the citizens remained religious and credulous, continuing to venerate icons, pray, and believe in God and/or other supernatural phenomena, even if their religiosity was isolated to their homes.[55] Despite committing substantial resources and dedicating a number of social scientists to understand how to convert people to atheism, Soviet efforts were never particularly effective.[56] One social scientist studying rural religiosity in Russia found that more than 90 percent of farm workers had icons in their homes and 87 percent took part in religious rituals.[57] The Marxist-Leninist government's persecution resulted in artificial secularization.

In writing about the status of the Orthodox Church after the collapse of the Soviet Union, Zoe Knox argued that forced secularization in the Soviet Union was not effective:

> An additional factor influencing religiosity in the postcommunist period derived from the specific historic experiences of religion in the region, and particularly in Russia. In the West in the mid- to late nineteenth century the process of secularisation of knowledge began, and a scientific, rational, and logical worldview came to predominate. There was a reappraisal of religious doctrine in the light of scientific progress. Russia did not experience an identical process due to its isolation from the West, its comparative backwardness and the persistence of the intimate

link between the autocrat and the Orthodox Church . . . [I]n the early
twentieth century there were social and political conditions conducive to
the emergence of civil society. The movement for Church reform called
for the Church's independence from the state and the democratization of
Church life. It is likely that the process of secularisation which developed
in the West would have taken place organically had it not been for the Soviet experiment, which halted the organic spread of anti-clericalism and
replaced it with state-sanctioned anti-religious and atheist propaganda.[58]

We don't mean to suggest here that no one became an atheist as a
result of the intentional efforts at secularization by the Marxist-Leninist
government. Certainly, many millions moved away from religion. But
forced secularization in Russia did not wipe out all aspects of religiosity.
What resulted was artificial secularization. Russian citizens appeared to
have secularized because they were reluctant to admit to being religious
out of fear of persecution. This is arguably the inverse of the situation we
described in predominantly Muslim countries above. In predominantly
Muslim countries that lack differentiation, religiosity is artificially inflated
(aka "artificial religiosity"). In Marxist-Leninist countries during the soviet years, religiosity was artificially deflated out of fear of persecution.[59]

The secularization efforts of the Marxist-Leninist government were
problematic for multiple reasons, including: they did not reach many of
those who were believers; logical arguments were not particularly effective at undermining faith;[60] the anti-religious propagandists were not
passionate about their message but rather were employees of the state
and lacked charisma; anti-religious propagandists were also not particularly competent; much of the propaganda was irrelevant to believers; and
despite efforts to curtail religious services, religious persecution did not
reach into the homes of believers where religiosity continued and was
passed on to children.[61] It is only among those with training in logic and
philosophy that consistency in beliefs matters. Many Russians during
the Soviet era were both atheists and Muslims,[62] or atheists and baptized
their children in the Russian Orthodox Church.[63] Logical consistency is
a rare attribute in humans. Efforts to force secularization resulted in a
perception of widespread secularity or artificial secularization, but many
citizens of the USSR were privately and discreetly more devout than the
government suggested.[64]

Our first point, then, is that the intentional efforts to destroy, undermine, and weaken religion in the USSR were only marginally effective. We are tempted to offer another proposition here that formalizes the idea that forced secularization will most likely result in artificial secularization but are reluctant to do so given that there are so few examples of forced secularization. Even so, we think it is accurate to state that the decline of religion results from modernization. We do not believe the inverse is true: modernization *does not* result from the decline of religion, and, in particular, from forced or violent secularization. Forcing people to claim they are not religious does not modernize them. As Karl Marx put it, "We know that violent measures against religion are nonsense; but this is an opinion: as socialism grows, religion will disappear."[65] In the case of Russia, efforts to destroy religion did not result in a completely secular, atheistic, non-believing citizenry. A large percentage of the population remained religious throughout the Soviet era.[66]

The second component to the explanation is what occurred toward the end of the Soviet era and gained steam after the collapse of the USSR: ethnonationalism.[67] In order to unify support for communism and diminish support for pre-Soviet nation-states, the government of the USSR institutionalized ethnicities by creating new territorial boundaries that were based on ethnic divides.[68] For instance, Ukrainians and Georgians were both formalized into their own Republics that were named after them. Within Russia, certain territories were assigned to different ethnicities, like that of the Tatars and Kalmyks.[69] It was believed that emphasizing ethnicity within geographic units would help unify different groups in favor of communism. It was believed that dividing regions based on ethnicity—such that a single ethnic group made up the majority of the population in many political units—would reduce internal ethnic tensions. That may have been the case early on, but these ethnic divides eventually contributed to the collapse of the Soviet Union.

As problems with the Soviet experiment began to appear in the 1970s and 1980s, the generally unified ethnicity-based units turned inward for identity and support instead of to the Soviet movement. When the Soviet Union finally collapsed in the late 1980s and early 1990s, there was widespread disillusionment among the former citizens of the USSR and a realization that they had been deceived about the success of the Soviet movement.[70] The plausibility structure underlying their communist sacred canopy had been destroyed.[71] In order to rebuild their world-view, many individuals turned to their ethnic identity that had been reinforced during the Soviet era.[72]

In rebuilding a sense of identity, people in the formerly Soviet territories began to look backward in time to elements of their ethnicity that pre-dated the Soviet experiment.[73] Grounding an identity on long-standing tradition or something perceived to be ancient or historical seems to add legitimacy and gravitas to identities, making them more tangible and compelling.[74] For many, that meant turning to religion. Ethnicity is, of course, linked with religion, though which religion varies. For most ethnic Russians, that meant the Russian Orthodox Church.[75] In Poland, this was Catholicism, as noted above.[76] For ethnic Tatars, that meant Islam.[77]

In combination with the need for new identities, there were many attempts at ethnonationalism that arose out of the ashes of the Soviet Union. Nationalism is an idea or movement that supports identification with and advocacy for the interests of one's nation, typically prioritizing the interests of the nation over those of other nations. Ethnonationalism links ethnicity (i.e., shared culture) with nationalism, rooting national identity in specific cultural elements, like a shared language and, par-ticularly in the case of former Soviet countries, in a shared religion. Eth-nonationalism can produce solidarity among the specific ethnic group by heightening fears of outgroups.[78] Nationalism in Russia is somewhat unique in that it often centers on the "Russian Idea," namely that Rus-sia is different from the West culturally, historically, and religiously.[79] Included in this Russian Idea is the notion that Moscow is a third Rome, from which the true Christianity will emanate. Both Boris Yeltsin and Vladimir Putin embraced this idea as leaders of Russia.[80]

As the Marxist-Leninist government neared collapse, a number of nationalist movements developed. Neo-Slavophilism, the All-Russia Monarchist Centre, the Union of Christian Regeneration, and Pamyat Society (aka National Patriotic Front "Memory") were movements organized around the importance of Russian identity, with Russian Orthodoxy at the center of that identity.[81] Many of these movements found allies within the Russian Orthodox Church, which, while split into various factions, included a number of ethnonationalist elements, anti-Semitism, and various nationalist organizations, like the Union of Orthodox Brotherhoods.[82]

While these extreme ethnonationalist movements did not take control of the government, they had the effect of shifting the general sentiment of political discourse toward nationalism and linked citizenship with specific religions.[83] Importantly for secularization theory, ethnonationalism is literally a de-differentiation of religion from other aspects of society. Ethnonationalists advocate for an integration of religion with national identity, which undoes attempts to separate religion from other aspects of society. As a result, ethnonationalism helped contribute to the rise of religiosity after the collapse of the Soviet Union, which we'll describe in detail below.

In addition to broader and perhaps more diffuse ethnonationalist movements, many of the politicians who were either elected or assumed power during and following the collapse of the Soviet Union saw an opportunity to use religion to increase social solidarity and support for their government. In 1988, in celebration of the one-thousand-year anniversary of the arrival and adoption of Christianity in Russia, Mikhail Gorbachev met with Patriarch Pimen of the Russian Orthodox Church. This was the first time a Soviet leader had met with the leaders of the Russian Orthodox Church since 1943, when Stalin had enlisted their help.[84] Gorbachev was trying to reform the communist government through his policy of *glasnost* and needed the help of the Russian Orthodox Church. In his speech celebrating the occasion, he linked Orthodoxy with Russian statehood and identity.[85] Gorbachev's government shifted official policy toward embracing believers and the Russian Orthodox Church. While these efforts may have been self-serving and politically minded given the broader societal changes taking place in the Soviet Union, the effect was a change in Soviet policy toward religion; Orthodox believers would no longer be persecuted but rather embraced.

These reforms continued under Boris Yeltsin's government, which returned religious property to the Russian Orthodox Church with a 1993 decree and, under substantial pressure from a conservative Duma and the Russian Orthodox Church signed the 1997 law "On Freedom of Conscience and Religious Associations."[86] This law formalized substantial privileges for the Russian Orthodox Church and restricted the rights of minority religions in Russia.[87] In addition to the legal relationship between the Russian Orthodox Church and the Russian government, the Russian Orthodox Church has also signed agreements of cooperation with the Russian army, border guards, and the Ministries of Defense, Education, Health, and Taxation, formalizing a privileged relationship between the Russian Orthodox Church and all of these branches of the Russian government.[88] These reforms and the realignment of the relationship between the Russian government and the Russian Orthodox Church have arguably resulted in an establishment of religion in Russia, or as one scholar put it, "Orthodoxy is thus declared the Russian national religion."[89] A formal alignment between the Russian Orthodox Church and the Russian government is precisely the scenario we described in chapter 1 that could lead to a reversal of secularization: de-differentiation.

One clear illustration of the new relationship between the Russian Orthodox Church and the Russian government was the reconstruction of the Cathedral of Christ the Saviour in Moscow. The Church was destroyed during Stalin's administration and, while it was intended to be turned into a monument to the Soviet government, it was eventually turned into a public swimming pool. The Mayor of Moscow in 1993, Iurii Luzhkov, led the initiative to reconstruct the Cathedral. His political connections resulted in much of the cost of the reconstruction, estimated to be close to $500 million USD, being paid by the Russian federal government.[90] The rebuilt Cathedral was where Boris Yeltsin laid in state when he died in 2007[91] and was the location for the Pussy Riot protest in 2012 against the Russian Orthodox Church's support for Vladimir Putin.[92]

A number of studies found a rapid increase in self-reported religious affiliation in former Soviet countries in the 1990s.[93] Of note is that the first measure of religiosity to increase was affiliation, not belief or attendance. Over time, belief and attendance have also increased (see Figure 6.3), but there is still evidence that attendance in many former Soviet countries is quite low, and knowledge of religion is extremely low. Some scholars have suggested that the Soviet era repression resulted in Russians not being able to distinguish between religious and pseudo-religious teachings, leading to widespread acceptance of reincarnation and astrology, in addition to eclectic religious teachings.[94] One Russian Orthodox priest noted that, at least in Russia, the continued insistence on performing religious services in medieval Slavonic, a language almost no one but clergy understands, has resulted in an extremely ignorant and ill-informed laity. As a result, he argued that those who are attending services do so for the ritualistic elements—to kiss an icon, anoint themselves with oil, acquire holy water, or feel the mystery of God—not to learn the finer points of Orthodox doctrine.[95]

Regardless of the motivations Russians have for attending religious services, the increase in religiosity raises one final question we want to address in this section: Has the increase in religiosity in Russia following the collapse of the USSR resulted in levels of religiosity that are higher than would be expected given Russia's level of modernization? Given that secularization relies upon modernization and that more modernized countries would be expected to have lower levels of religiosity, this means that we can estimate how religious a country should be given its level of development.

As noted in chapter 2, we aggregated a dataset of weighted measures of religiosity using data from the World Values Survey and the European Values Study. We also supplemented this data with statistics from the World Bank on measures of urbanization and economic development. To estimate where Russia should fall on the three measures of religiosity included in our dataset—percent of the population that believes in God, percent attending services monthly, and percent who report a religious affiliation—we limited the dataset to single observations of every country that had data after 2009 to ensure that the data were recent. This left us with 95 countries with observations ranging from 2010 (just one country) to 2020 (13 countries), with most coming from 2018 (39 countries). We then removed Russia from the dataset (2017 data), as it was Russian religiosity that we wanted to estimate.

We created a relatively simple model to estimate each dimension of religiosity separately:

a) Percent attend monthly = log of GDP per capita + log of percent of population urban + percent of population employed full time
b) Percent believe in God = log of GDP per capita + log of percent of population urban + percent of population employed full time
c) Percent report religious affiliation = log of GDP per capita + log of percent of population urban + percent of population employed full time

These relatively simple models were actually quite powerful predictors of religiosity. Our models accounted for 37 percent of the variance in monthly attendance across countries, 44 percent of the variation in belief in God, and 30 percent of the variance in religious affiliation.

We then used the resulting model coefficients with the values from Russia to estimate how religious Russians *should* be given the level of development in the country. Our model estimated that 31.3 percent of Russians should be attending monthly based on the level of development in the country; just 16.9 percent attended monthly in 2017. Likewise, our model estimated that 72 percent of Russians should report a religious affiliation; just 61 percent of Russians did in 2017. Finally, our model estimated that 77.9 percent should report believing in God; 80.8 percent reported believing in God in 2017. On two out of three measures, religious affiliation and weekly attendance, Russians are less religious than we would expect given the level of development of the country. On one measure, belief in God, Russians are almost exactly where our model predicts they should be.

What does this tell us about Russia and, more importantly, about exceptions to secularization? Religiosity in Russia was artificially deflated during the Soviet experiment—people were more religious than they reported. Russia illustrates that artificial secularization results when religiosity is suppressed by authoritarian governments. In reality, many Russians remained quite credulous and religious throughout the Soviet experiment. Once the USSR collapsed, there was a transition period during which Russian religiosity shifted such that it came much closer in line with where we expect it to be given the level of modernization. It is possible that, without ethnonationalist movements in Russia, levels of religiosity may have remained below expected values. Even so, Russia is no more religious today than we would expect given its level of modernization. Russia is not an exception to secularization theory. To the contrary, it is a clear illustration of the theory.

Conclusion

In this chapter, we have examined three possible exceptions to secularization: countries where religiosity is used to generate solidarity among the citizens in defense of an external threat, countries that restrict people's ability to leave religion, and countries that try to force secularization all have low levels of differentiation. Careful scrutiny of these possible exceptions has illustrated that these situations are not actually exceptions but rather that they all fall cleanly in line with our formulation of secularization theory.

What might an actual exception of secularization theory look like? As we argued in chapter 1, such an exception would require a country with high levels of *both* differentiation and rationalization that is also extremely religious. We are unaware of any such countries.

Reality is, of course, complicated. We showed in chapter 2 with our cluster analysis of nearly one hundred countries that they fall into four clusters along two dimensions: low to high in differentiation and low to high in development. The bulk of this chapter has focused on countries that were low in differentiation, precluding secularization, or, in the case of Russia and some former Soviet bloc countries, slightly reversing artificial secularization now that there is greater freedom of religion and religion has become a component of national identity.

There are other countries that are even more complicated in 2021. The most obvious one is China, where the communist government is explicitly atheist. In China, there is substantial government regulation of religion. But the aim is not to prop up religion artificially like in Saudi Arabia or Iran. It is more akin to Russia, where the ruling Communist Party is atheist and the leaders would prefer for Chinese citizens to likewise be atheists. However, perhaps recognizing the problems with Russia's approach, the Chinese government has, instead, allowed a limited number of religions to exist, with substantial restrictions on what those religions can and cannot do. As was the case with the Soviet Union, it's possible that these restrictions have artificially secularized China. The problem, of course, is that, unlike former Soviet bloc countries where, at least in some of them (e.g., Poland, Hungary, Estonia, Latvia, Romania, etc.), citizens are now likely to be honest in survey responses, it is not entirely clear if the same is true in China. It's possible that there is much higher religious demand in China than we are aware of. Or, the Chinese communist government may have been more successful at forced secularization than was the Russian communist government, in part due to different approaches but also potentially because of the non-Christian historical context in China. In short, while China is home to a large number of secular people, we are reluctant to use China as a clear example of secularization or to consider it an exception given the challenges of understanding the dynamics in situations where there is substantial government regulation and severe limitations on the free flow of accurate information. As the adage goes, "the jury is still out" on China, meaning we are unsure what is happening or will happen in China in the future. Even so, if China continues to modernize, it is unlikely that there will be a dramatic reversal of secularization in the future.

Conclusion

Beyond Doubt

For many individuals who abandon religion and subsequently go on to live a secular life, that personal transition often starts with various forms of doubt.

For example, in his analysis of Muslim apostates, Simon Cottee explained that "this is how it begins: with the feeling that something 'isn't right,' 'doesn't make sense' or 'doesn't add up.' All respondents felt it: the stab of doubt."[1] There was Omar, who started to doubt the existence of God; Masood, who couldn't understand why an all-powerful, all-just god would allow so much unnecessary suffering in the world; Azhar, who couldn't believe in the existence of hell; Amir, who doubted certain stories about Muhammad; Yasmin, who couldn't figure out why the religion she happened to be born into was any more likely to be true than the many other religions out there in the world, or why there was such unequal treatment of women within Islam; Luqman, whose learning about the evidence for evolution caused him to question the Islamic account of creation; and so forth.[2]

Numerous other studies of religious exiting[3] have found the same thing: doubt is often the initial seedling that eventually blossoms into full-blown secularity. Given that doubt is a personal, inner experience, and given that religious exiting is an individual journey of disaffiliation, neither constitutes a societal phenomenon, per se. It is only when numerous individuals within a society begin to experience similar doubts, and those doubts lead to a measurable loss of faith and religious beliefs, and/or to a significant diminishing of religious behaviors and practices, and/or to a demonstrable level of decreased identification with religion—losses that are evident over generations—that we have a societal phenomenon known as secularization.

As we have shown in this book, that is exactly what has occurred: in most modern societies around the world today, people are less religious than their parents, grandparents, or great-grandparents were in the past. Taking the best available evidence into account, there's simply no doubt about it—secularization is happening. Of course, again, this specifically refers to modernized societies. In less developed nations, birth rates tend to be much higher. And since such nations tend to be relatively more religious—as traditional secularization theory explains—this has led some to project that religiosity will increase globally, strictly based on fertility.[4]

As we look back over the past 150 years of scholarship on this topic, we see the following: the early founders of sociology, such as Durkheim and Weber, had a sense that religion was waning. They predicted religion's diminishment, if not demise. Their early viewpoint became the foundation for classical secularization theory. However, these early articulations of the theory were rather inchoate: the definitions vague, the causal arguments underdeveloped, and sound evidence was sorely lacking.

Over the course of the twentieth century, theoretical and empirical advances in the understanding and analysis of secularization were put forth by many, such as Bryan Wilson, David Martin, Peter Berger, Karel Dobbelaere, and Steve Bruce. Yet, despite such progress, a formidable amalgam of scholars emerged who were brazenly critical of the whole notion that religion was fading in the wake of modernity. Starting in the 1970s and gaining momentum in the 1980s and 1990s, the body of scholarship that was critical of secularization theory was impressive: theoretically rigorous, definitionally precise, and often backed by empirical findings. As such, many leading sociologists of religion (primarily in the US), and many of their students, became convinced that secularization had not—in fact, *cannot*—occur.

As mid-career sociologists of religion, we are fascinated—if not a little troubled—that the leading North American scholars in our field could have been so mistaken about the reality of secularization for so long. It is especially noteworthy that most of these individuals strove to be deeply empiricist in their claims, insisting that they were motivated not by ideology, but rather, a clear-eyed analysis of the facts. Back in the 1990s—in but one typical example—Rodney Stark and Laurence

Iannaccone[5] dismissed secularization theory as "unscientific philosophizing," insisting that the very term "secularization" be dropped from usage because it was merely "ideological and polemical" in nature, lacking any evidentiary support; in contrast, their position that secularization had not and could not occur was, in their view, based solely on propositions sustained by "a variety of pertinent cases" and "quantitative analysis." In other words, the scholars who argued that secularization could, and sometimes did, occur were believed to be driven by unscientific motives, while the social scientists who argued that secularization had not and could not occur were actually the ones doing sound empirical sociological work. Given our assessment of the state of declining religiosity evident in the world today, we are almost tempted to propose that just the opposite may be the case: perhaps those who sought to debunk secularization were the ones who were ideologically motivated.[6]

Despite the provocative protestations, interesting theoretical assertions, and presumably sound empiricism of so many sociologists of religion—Rodney Stark, Roger Finke, Andrew Greeley, Robert Bellah, among others—religion has in fact weakened and faded over the course of the past century, just as the classical theorists of secularization expected it would. Whether we are talking about religious faith and belief, participation and behavior, or identification and belonging, the best available data show that where modernization advances, religiosity retreats.

The wonderful and frustrating nature of social science is that scholars will and should argue and disagree over what is going on in the world and why. Amidst such debate, we should all try to wed theory with data as parsimoniously as possible and accept that ongoing interpretation, misinterpretation, and re-interpretation of social phenomena are unavoidable. Ideally, we all strive for the "best truth for now," always ready and willing to revise our conclusions based on new and better data.

Currently, secularization is a reality; Stark and his colleagues were wrong.

Implications

In this book we have provided an overview of secularization theory—its meanings, definitions, and main components. We have provided the best available evidence showing that, in many societies around the world, religion has diminished; that key components of modernity, such as differentiation, rationalization, religious pluralism, autonomy in child-rearing, and improved existential well-being, are responsible for this diminishing of religion; that life lived without religion is not some aberrant, unnatural mutation, but a fully possible, natural, and increasingly common reality; that secular life contains its own values, contours, characteristics, and rhythms; and that even some apparent exceptions to secularization theory—nations that have not experienced a loss of religion, but rather, an uptick in recent decades—can actually be fairly understood and best explained by drawing upon the secularization framework. We have laid all of this out in order to provide a theoretically sound, empirically rigorous analysis of the state of religion in the world today: it is fading.

Will religion continue to fade? Will more and more people continue to live in increasingly secular societies?

Yes, so long as the relevant forces of modernity continue to be experienced by an ever-widening circle of humanity. And yes, given that more and more secular people are raising their children without religion.

However, we don't expect religion to disappear. Religion meets so many deep human needs: it provides psychological comfort in the face of uncertainty, ambiguity, misery, and suffering; it offers comforting hope to the painful reality of death; it provides powerful symbols, institutions, and identities that link generations and transcend demographic divisions; it enhances national and ethnic identity; it offers rituals that make life's transitions meaningful; it provides community; it tells compelling stories; it inspires great works of art. All of these aspects of religion help explain why it has been so pervasive throughout human history, and why we don't expect it to disappear. It will, however, become less prevalent, less potent, less hegemonic, and less taken-for-granted.

And as we've laid out in the chapters of this book, the best truth for now is that secularization is occurring throughout much of the world. Even nations that were long regarded as resistant to secularization are secularizing.

Limitations

As with any scholarly work, there are some obvious limitations in this volume as well. As chapter 2 makes clear, we are missing data on more than a third of the countries around the world. Additionally, the variables that we have to capture different processes of modernization are satisfactory but probably not ideal. More thought needs to be given to how to operationalize modernization, including differentiation and rationalization. We strongly encourage scholars to consider better measures of these concepts.

Another limitation of our volume is that we did not cover every country for which we have data in as much detail as we covered the four countries that are the focus of chapter 3. By digging deeply into the secularization trends in the US, South Korea, Chile, and Norway, it should be clear to readers that secularization plays out differently in different countries. Future research should do as we did with those four countries and illustrate the differences and nuances of secularization within countries. This would make for a very nice, albeit quite large, edited volume. We would, however, discourage the use of terms or phrases like "multiple secularities" or "many secularisms."[7] As noted, such language is not used to describe democracy even though democracy looks very different in South Korea, Chile, the US, and Norway. We don't call it "multiple democracies" or "many democracies." It's just different manifestations of democracy. Likewise, what we see in Norway, Chile, South Korea, and the US is still secularization, just playing out in subtly different ways given the historical and cultural context of each country.

Future Directions

We do not see this book as the final work on secularization. As Stolz recently noted, a lot of progress has been made in testing various aspects of secularization.[8] However, he also noted that not much has occurred in the last twenty years in further developing the theory of secularization. Our hope is that, by formalizing secularization theory and by adding to the substantial empirical evidence for the theory, our book will serve as motivation for future work on secularization theory. Looking forward, there are a number of ways that secularization theory can be advanced.

The most obvious one is by putting greater thought into ways to operationalize modernization, differentiation, and rationalization. As noted, some progress has been made in these areas over the last twenty years.[9] Even so, scholars need to spend far more time and energy wrestling with what modernization, differentiation, and rationalization are and how best to measure them.

Additionally, as we noted in chapter 1, secularization occurs at three levels: macro, meso, and micro. Most attempts to measure secularization—including our own—are actually aggregate measures of micro secularization. Scholars look to see how often people attend religious services, what percentage reports an affiliation with a religion, and what percentage believes in some supernatural phenomenon. They then tally those numbers up for a country and assign those aggregated micro measures as an indicator of macro secularization. That approach seems less than ideal to us. What is needed are cohesive and clear measures of secularization at all three levels. There should be a standard micro or individual-level measure of secularization that can be employed easily and universally.[10] Likewise, there should be a scale or index that captures secularization for countries in a single indicator. Almost completely ignored in this volume and in almost all of the research on secularization is meso-level secularization. There should also be a clear and coherent measure of how secular any given organization or institution is that can be applied universally. We're rather disappointed that, over a century after scholars suggested the idea of secularization, we are effectively using yardsticks to measure distances between countries and ignoring the presence of cities altogether. We need better measures of secularization at all three levels.

With better measures, we could then do a better job of developing clear and robust tests of secularization theory. How much of the decline of religion is accounted for by differentiation versus rationalization? And which aspects of differentiation and rationalization account for religious decline? Scholars should consider examining these questions moving forward.

Final Thoughts

We have attempted in this volume to provide a simplified, coherent, and testable version of secularization theory. We have also shown that there is substantial evidence supporting our version of secularization theory. We hope that we have opened a path forward for other scholars to continue to refine and develop the theory. There is much to do, as we have detailed above.

We also want to reiterate that challenges to secularization at this point—specifically the religious supply and religious economies models—should be sidelined. They were always problematic challenges to secularization theory, but the evidence we have mustered in this volume should make it clear that some of the core assumptions of these approaches—particularly the ideas that religion is cyclical, that state churches just need to be freed from regulation to excel, that competition results in higher levels of religiosity, and that demand for religiosity is constant—are rooted more in wishful thinking than reality. There is plenty of work to be done understanding secularization and no more need to consider challenges from the religious supply and religious economies models.

The evidence for secularization is clear. Secularization is happening. Secularization is real. It's beyond doubt.

APPENDIX

Detailed Tables

TABLE A.1: Attendance at Religious Services (At Least Monthly). Y1/Y2 = First and most current year that the country participated in the EVS/WVS; No change = change of < +/- 2.5 percentage points between Y1 and Y2

Country	Year 2	% Y2	Year 1	% Y1	Direction
Albania	2018	14.9	1998	35.3	Decrease
Algeria	2013	53.5	2002	50.1	Increase
Andorra	2018	16.1	2005	11.8	Increase
Argentina	2017	36.0	1984	55.8	Decrease
Armenia	2018	43.7	1997	29.5	Increase
Australia	2018	17.6	1981	39.8	Decrease
Austria	2018	26.9	1990	43.9	Decrease
Azerbaijan	2018	14.3	1997	14.0	No Change
Bahrain	-	-	2014	85.8	-
Bangladesh	2018	54.3	1996	90.0	Decrease
Belarus	2018	20.2	1990	5.9	Increase
Belgium	2009	18.8	1981	38.3	Decrease
Bolivia	-	-	2017	65.1	-
Bosnia & Herzegovina	2019	44.1	1998	48.5	Decrease
Brazil	2018	60.2	1991	50.3	Increase
Bulgaria	2018	17.5	1991	9.1	Increase
Burkina Faso	-	-	2007	76.9	-
Canada	2006	34.2	1982	46.5	Decrease
Chile	2018	31.2	1990	46.4	Decrease
China	2018	2.8	1990	0.8	No Change
Colombia	2018	58.2	1997	66.7	Decrease
Croatia	2017	33.9	1996	36.2	No Change
Cyprus	2019	51.7	2006	33.8	Increase
Czech Republic	2017	9.0	1991	11.5	Decrease
Denmark	2017	6.5	1981	12.8	Decrease
Dominican Republic	-	-	1996	55.3	-

(continued)

TABLE A.1: (cont.)

Country	Year 2	% Y2	Year 1	% Y1	Direction
Ecuador	2018	61.5	2013	69.3	Decrease
Egypt	2018	58.9	2001	44.7	Increase
El Salvador	-	-	1998	68.8	-
Estonia	2018	8.0	1996	8.6	No Change
Ethiopia	2020	93.0	2007	86.9	Increase
Finland	2017	11.2	1981	13.1	No Change
France	2018	12.4	1981	17.9	Decrease
Georgia	2018	33.7	1996	27.4	Increase
Germany	2018	19.1	1990	30.4	Decrease
Ghana	2012	83.8	2007	88.9	Decrease
Great Britain	2018	16.7	1981	22.2	Decrease
Greece	2018	44.9	1999	33.6	Increase
Guatemala	2020	63.6	2004	87.4	Decrease
Hong Kong	2018	16.2	2005	10.1	Increase
Hungary	2018	17.4	1982	33.5	Decrease
Iceland	2017	8.5	1984	10.6	No Change
India	2014	49.2	1990	70.7	Decrease
Indonesia	2018	77.9	2001	75.5	No Change
Iran	2020	43.4	2000	46.5	Decrease
Iraq	2018	45.1	2004	35.9	Increase
Ireland	2008	53.7	1981	88.0	Decrease
Italy	2018	41.6	1981	51.7	Decrease
Japan	2019	12.4	1981	14.7	No Change
Jordan	2018	56.7	2001	46.8	Increase
Kazakhstan	2018	34.7	2011	19.6	Increase
Kosovo	-	-	2008	49.8	-
Kyrgyzstan	2020	39.4	2003	24.4	Increase
Latvia	2008	16.4	1990	8.7	Increase
Lebanon	2018	53.6	2013	61.6	Decrease
Libya	-	-	2014	52.7	-
Lithuania	2018	30.3	1997	30.8	No Change
Luxembourg	2008	22.9	1999	31.8	Decrease
Macau SAR	-	-	2020	9.5	-
Malaysia	2018	60.3	2006	79.9	Decrease
Mali	-	-	2007	74.2	-
Malta	2008	81.6	1983	94.1	Decrease
Mexico	2018	60.7	1981	80.9	Decrease
Moldova	2008	29.4	1996	22.7	Increase
Montenegro	2019	37.3	1996	10.4	Increase

TABLE A.1: (cont.)

Country	Year 2	% Y2	Year 1	% Y1	Direction
Morocco	2007	92.3	2001	50.0	Increase
Myanmar	-	-	2020	43.5	-
Netherlands	2017	16.4	1981	39.8	Decrease
New Zealand	2020	16.8	1998	22.1	Decrease
Nicaragua	-	-	2020	54.2	-
Nigeria	2018	90.4	1990	88.2	No Change
North Macedonia	2019	41.2	1998	17.7	Increase
Northern Ireland	2008	49.9	1981	67.9	Decrease
Norway	2018	11.9	1982	15.4	Decrease
Pakistan	2018	61.7	2001	91.2	Decrease
Palestine	-	-	2013	58.6	-
Peru	2018	57.3	1996	64.1	Decrease
Philippines	2018	81.8	1996	89.9	Decrease
Poland	2017	65.0	1990	83.6	Decrease
Portugal	2020	29.9	1990	41.3	Decrease
Puerto Rico	2018	54.2	1995	65.1	Decrease
Romania	2018	46.3	1993	30.6	Increase
Russia	2017	16.9	1990	6.0	Increase
Rwanda	2012	78.2	2007	95.6	Decrease
Saudi Arabia	-	-	2003	44.2	-
Serbia	2018	20.9	1996	14.6	Increase
Singapore	2012	44.7	2002	44.1	No Change
Slovakia	2017	36.3	1990	40.2	Decrease
Slovenia	2017	23.9	1992	35.1	Decrease
South Africa	2013	73.2	1982	68.2	Increase
South Korea	2018	22.8	1982	44.6	Decrease
Spain	2017	23.2	1981	53.6	Decrease
Sweden	2017	9.7	1982	14.4	Decrease
Switzerland	2017	16.3	1989	42.5	Decrease
Taiwan	2019	21.7	1994	14.5	Increase
Tajikistan	-	-	2020	40.7	-
Tanzania	-	-	2001	86.6	-
Thailand	2018	38.1	2007	87.5	Decrease
Trinidad & Tobago	2011	57.8	2006	60.1	No Change
Tunisia	2019	43.9	2013	45.5	No Change
Turkey	2018	42.1	1990	38.2	Increase
Uganda	-	-	2001	88.3	-

(continued)

TABLE A.1: (cont.)

Country	Year 2	% Y2	Year 1	% Y1	Direction
Ukraine	2020	34.8	1996	17.6	Increase
United States	2017	39.1	1982	60.0	Decrease
Uruguay	2011	18.4	1996	23.6	Decrease
Uzbekistan	-	-	2011	9.6	-
Venezuela	2000	47.9	1996	49.3	No Change
Vietnam	2020	17.2	2001	12.8	Increase
Yemen	-	-	2014	53.2	-
Zambia	-	-	2007	80.9	-
Zimbabwe	2020	84.8	2001	81.0	Increase

TABLE A.2: Religious Belonging. Y1/Y2 = First and most current year that the country participated in the EVS/WVS; No change = change of < +/− 2.5 percentage points between Y1 and Y2

Country	Year 2	% Y2	Year 1	% Y1	Direction
Albania	2018	94.0	1998	98.8	Decrease
Algeria	2013	100.0	2002	100.0	No change
Andorra	2018	69.9	2005	59.4	Increase
Argentina	2017	82.7	1984	87.1	Decrease
Armenia	2018	90.4	1997	86.5	Increase
Australia	2018	46.9	1995	81.1	Decrease
Austria	2018	73.3	1990	85.1	Decrease
Azerbaijan	2018	94.5	1997	94.0	No change
Bangladesh	2018	100.0	1996	99.6	No change
Belarus	2018	65.2	1996	64.7	No change
Belgium	2009	57.5	1981	83.8	Decrease
Bolivia	-	-	2017	84.7	-
Bosnia & Herzegovina	2019	96.7	1997	60.7	Increase
Brazil	2018	82.6	1991	86.9	Decrease
Bulgaria	2018	74.0	1991	33.4	Increase
Burkina Faso	-	-	2007	98.9	-
Canada	2006	67.4	1982	89.4	Decrease
Chile	2018	73.0	1990	82.7	Decrease
China	2018	13.0	1990	3.2	Increase
Colombia	2018	53.5	1997	90.3	Decrease
Croatia	2017	81.0	1996	87.5	Decrease
Cyprus	2019	98.5	2006	96.4	No change
Czech Republic	2017	23.3	1991	40.7	Decrease

TABLE A.2: *(cont.)*

Country	Year 2	% Y2	Year 1	% Y1	Direction
Denmark	2017	81.5	1981	94.4	Decrease
Dominican Republic	–	–	1996	76.0	–
Ecuador	2018	64.0	2013	76.5	Decrease
Egypt	2018	100.0	2001	100.0	No change
El Salvador	–	–	1999	84.1	–
Estonia	2018	18.9	1990	12.7	Increase
Ethiopia	2020	99.8	2007	86.9	Increase
Finland	2017	73.1	1981	88.4	Decrease
France	2018	41.8	1981	73.8	Decrease
Georgia	2018	94.3	1996	93.8	No change
Germany	2018	64.9	1990	79.0	Decrease
Ghana	2012	95.2	2007	100.0	Decrease
Great Britain	2018	38.5	1981	90.6	Decrease
Greece	2018	96.1	1999	96.0	No change
Guatemala	2020	87.3	2004	91.0	Decrease
Hong Kong	2018	28.5	2005	27.1	No change
Hungary	2018	44.1	1982	98.3	Decrease
Iceland	2017	81.8	1984	98.7	Decrease
India	2014	100.0	1990	98.9	No change
Indonesia	2018	100.0	2001	100.0	No change
Iran	2020	97.8	2000	98.9	No change
Iraq	2018	100.0	2004	100.0	No change
Ireland	2008	85.4	1981	98.7	Decrease
Israel	–	–	2001	100.0	–
Italy	2018	77.4	1981	93.5	Decrease
Japan	2019	33.9	1981	96.2	Decrease
Jordan	2018	100.0	2001	100.0	No change
Kazakhstan	2018	91.3	2011	79.0	Increase
Kosovo	–	–	2008	91.2	–
Kyrgyzstan	2020	93.9	2003	85.1	Increase
Latvia	2008	65.89	1990	36.1	Increase
Lebanon	2018	100.0	2013	100.0	No change
Libya	–	–	2014	100.0	–
Lithuania	2018	85.9	1990	63.0	Increase
Luxembourg	2008	73.3	1999	71.8	No change
Macau SAR	–	–	2020	32.1	–
Malaysia	2018	98.0	2006	98.5	No change

(continued)

TABLE A.2: *(cont.)*

Country	Year 2	% Y2	Year 1	% Y1	Direction
Mali	-	-	2007	99.7	-
Malta	2008	97.87	1983	100.0	No change
Mexico	2018	87.3	1981	96.2	Decrease
Moldova	2008	93.3	1996	84.7	Increase
Montenegro	2019	71.9	1996	94.5	Decrease
Morocco	2007	100.0	2001	100.0	No change
Myanmar	-	-	2020	92.6	-
Netherlands	2017	37.6	1981	63.5	Decrease
New Zealand	2020	51.7	1998	83.2	Decrease
Nicaragua	-	-	2020	81.1	-
Nigeria	2018	99.8	1990	94.7	Increase
North Macedonia	2019	91.9	1998	72.1	Increase
Northern Ireland	2008	80.3	1981	96.8	Decrease
Norway	2018	64.0	1982	95.9	Decrease
Pakistan	2018	100.0	1997	98.0	No change
Peru	2018	97.2	1996	93.0	Increase
Philippines	2018	97.2	1996	99.9	Decrease
Poland	2017	91.7	1990	96.3	Decrease
Portugal	2020	75.3	1990	72.4	Increase
Puerto Rico	2018	79.0	1995	81.3	No change
Romania	2018	96.2	1993	94.1	No change
Russia	2017	60.1	1990	34.2	Increase
Rwanda	2012	88.8	2007	98.0	Decrease
Saudi Arabia	-	-	2003	99.8	-
Serbia	2018	61.4	1996	81.4	Decrease
Singapore	2012	82.3	2002	80.3	No change
Slovakia	2017	70.4	1990	79.0	Decrease
Slovenia	2017	64.2	1992	73.5	Decrease
South Africa	2013	81.41	1982	80.5	No change
South Korea	2018	36.0	1982	53.3	Decrease
Spain	2017	62.5	1981	91.1	Decrease
Sweden	2017	61.5	1982	93.1	Decrease
Switzerland	2017	70.0	1989	92.3	Decrease
Taiwan	2019	78.3	1994	79.1	No change
Tajikistan	-	-	2020	96.5	-
Tanzania	-	-	2001	98.3	-
Thailand	2018	100.0	2007	99.9	No change

TABLE A.2: (*cont.*)

Country	Year 2	% Y2	Year 1	% Y1	Direction
Trinidad & Tobago	2011	92.9	2006	93.4	No change
Tunisia	2019	98.9	2013	100.0	No change
Turkey	2018	98.8	1999	100.0	No change
Uganda	-	-	2001	99.1	-
Ukraine	2020	97.0	1991	66.1	Increase
United States	2017	57.0	1982	93.9	Decrease
Uruguay	2011	38.9	1996	52.1	Decrease
Uzbekistan	-	-	2011	99.4	-
Venezuela	2000	72.9	1996	92.3	Decrease
Vietnam	2020	27.9	2001	53.7	Decrease
Yemen	-	-	2014	100.0	-
Zambia	-	-	2007	94.5	-
Zimbabwe	2020	88.1	2001	85.8	No change

TABLE A.3: Belief in God. Y1/Y2 = First and most current year that the country participated in the EVS/WVS; No change = change of < +/− 2.5 percentage points between Y1 and Y2

Country	Year 2	% Y2	Year 1	% Y1	Direction
Albania	2018	97.0	1998	93.7	Increase
Algeria	2013	100.0	2002	99.8	No Change
Andorra	-	-	2011	64.1	-
Argentina	2017	93.4	1984	88.9	Increase
Armenia	2018	92.0	1997	85.6	Increase
Australia	2018	56.8	1981	84.6	Decrease
Austria	2018	73.7	1990	85.7	Decrease
Azerbaijan	2018	98.5	1997	97.8	No Change
Bangladesh	2018	99.8	1996	98.6	No Change
Belarus	2018	80.6	1990	42.7	Increase
Belgium	2009	61.4	1981	86.7	Decrease
Bolivia	-	-	2017	97.8	-
Bosnia & Herzegovina	2019	96.0	1998	89.1	Increase
Brazil	2018	97.5	1991	98.6	No Change
Bulgaria	2018	79.4	1991	40.3	Increase
Canada	2000	89.2	1982	93.5	Decrease

(*continued*)

TABLE A.3: (cont.)

Country	Year 2	% Y2	Year 1	% Y1	Direction
Chile	2018	86.3	1990	94.9	Decrease
China	2018	17.0	2012	19.0	No Change
Colombia	2018	96.4	1998	99.1	Decrease
Croatia	2017	85.3	1996	80.8	Increase
Cyprus	2019	95.6	2007	97.7	No Change
Czech Republic	2017	38.4	1991	35.4	Increase
Denmark	2017	50.8	1981	68.3	Decrease
Dominican Republic	–	–	1996	92.7	–
Ecuador	2018	97.9	2013	97.3	No Change
Egypt	–	–	2001	100.0	–
El Salvador	–	–	1999	99.4	–
Estonia	2018	45.7	1996	51.8	Decrease
Ethiopia	–	–	2020	99.9	–
Finland	2017	56.7	1990	75.9	Decrease
France	2018	53.7	1981	58.0	Decrease
Georgia	2018	98.7	1996	93.2	Increase
Germany	2018	59.3	1990	69.1	Decrease
Ghana	–	–	2012	99.7	–
Great Britain	2018	48.4	1981	82.1	Decrease
Greece	2018	93.7	1999	91.0	Increase
Guatemala	–	–	2020	96.3	–
Hong Kong	2018	53.0	2013	58.4	Decrease
Hungary	2018	71.1	1982	57.3	Increase
Iceland	2017	61.2	1984	81.3	Decrease
India	2014	78.4	1990	93.6	Decrease
Indonesia	2018	97.0	2001	99.9	Decrease
Iran	2020	99.3	2000	99.4	No Change
Iraq	2012	99.1	2004	99.8	No Change
Ireland	2008	89.9	1981	97.1	Decrease
Italy	2018	84.4	1981	89.5	Decrease
Japan	2019	54.8	1981	62.5	Decrease
Jordan	2018	99.7	2001	99.8	No Change
Kazakhstan	2018	94.4	2011	89.3	Increase
Kosovo	–	–	2008	99.6	–
Kyrgyzstan	2020	97.2	2013	95.0	No Change
Latvia	2008	76.6	1990	58.3	Increase
Lebanon	2018	99.6	2013	98.8	No Change
Lithuania	2018	84.8	1997	86.0	No Change

TABLE A.3: (cont.)

Country	Year 2	% Y2	Year 1	% Y1	Direction
Luxembourg	2008	69.8	1999	73.2	Decrease
Macau	–	–	2020	41.6	–
Malaysia	2018	95.2	2012	98.4	Decrease
Malta	2008	98.6	1983	100.0	No Change
Mexico	2018	95.9	1981	98.0	No Change
Moldova	2008	97.8	1986	90.6	Increase
Montenegro	2019	96.1	1996	65.1	Increase
Morocco	–	–	2011	99.9	–
Myanmar	–	–	2020	98.9	–
Netherlands	2017	43.7	1981	72.2	Decrease
New Zealand	2020	56.6	1998	79.3	Decrease
Nicaragua	–	–	2020	92.2	–
Nigeria	2018	98.9	1990	100.0	No Change
North Macedonia	2019	92.5	1998	83.8	Increase
Northern Ireland	2008	91.5	1981	96.6	Decrease
Norway	2018	47.3	1982	75.5	Decrease
Pakistan	2018	98.6	1997	100.0	No Change
Peru	2018	98.2	1996	98.6	No Change
Philippines	2018	99.7	1996	99.7	No Change
Poland	2017	93.4	1990	97.5	Decrease
Portugal	2020	84.9	1990	85.7	No Change
Puerto Rico	2018	96.9	1995	99.3	No Change
Romania	2018	96.5	1993	93.7	Increase
Russia	2017	80.7	1990	43.8	Increase
Rwanda	–	–	2012	97.9	–
Saudi Arabia	–	–	2003	99.9	–
Serbia	2018	84.1	1996	69.2	Increase
Singapore	2012	82.8	2002	87.1	Decrease
Slovakia	2017	72.8	1991	73.2	No Change
Slovenia	2017	60.5	1997	62.7	No Change
South Africa	2013	98.3	1982	98.1	No Change
South Korea	2018	40.6	1982	60.4	Decrease
Spain	2017	68.0	1981	91.9	Decrease
Sweden	2017	36.1	1982	60.4	Decrease
Switzerland	2017	67.2	1996	83.6	Decrease
Taiwan	2019	82.4	1994	76.4	Increase

(continued)

TABLE A.3: (cont.)

Country	Year 2	% Y2	Year 1	% Y1	Direction
Tajikistan	–	–	2020	99.9	–
Tanzania	–	–	2001	99.3	–
Thailand	2018	46.0	2013	32.7	Increase
Trinidad & Tobago	–	–	2011	99.3	–
Tunisia	–	–	2019	99.8	–
Turkey	2019	95.3	1996	98.0	Decrease
Uganda	–	–	2001	99.4	–
Ukraine	2020	84.1	1996	76.5	Increase
United States	2017	77.8	1982	97.9	Decrease
Uruguay	2011	82.6	1996	86.7	Decrease
Uzbekistan	–	–	2011	98.7	–
Venezuela	–	–	1996	99.1	–
Vietnam	2020	48.5	2001	18.8	Increase
Zimbabwe	2020	99.8	2001	99.4	No Change

NOTES

INTRODUCTION

1 Davie, Grace. 2003. "The Evolution of the Sociology of Religion," in *Handbook of the Sociology of Religion*, edited by Michele Dillon, pp. 61–75. Cambridge: Cambridge University Press.

2 Gorski, Philip. 2003. "Historicizing the Secularization Debate," in *Handbook of the Sociology of Religion*. Pp. 110–122.

3 Guyau, Jean-Marie. 1897. *The Non-Religion of the Future: A Sociological Study*. New York: Henry Holt and Company. Weber, Max. 1946. "Science as Vocation," in *From Max Weber: Essays in Sociology*. New York: Oxford University Press. Pp. 129–56. Original lecture was given in 1917.

4 Durkheim, Emile. 1995. *The Elementary Forms of Religious Life*. New York: Free Press. Pg. 475.

5 Durkheim, Emile. 1997. *The Division of Labor in Society*. New York: The Free Press. Pg. 120.

6 Mills, C. Wright. 1959. *The Sociological Imagination*. Oxford: Oxford University Press. Pp. 32–33.

7 Wilson, Bryan R. 1966. *Religion in Secular Society*. Penguin. Pg. xi.

8 Wilson. *Religion in Secular Society*. Pg. 232.

9 Hammond, Philip, ed. 1985. *The Sacred in a Secular Age*. Berkeley: University of California Press. Pp. 14–15.

10 Stark, Rodney and Laurence R. Iannaccone. 1994. "A Supply-Side Reinterpretation of the 'Secularization' of Europe," *Journal for the Scientific Study of Religion* 33(3): 230–52. Pg. 249.

11 Stark, Rodney. 1996. "Bringing Theory Back In," in *Rational Choice Theories of Religion*, edited by Lawrence Young. London: Routledge.

12 Stark and Iannaccone. "A Supply-Side Reinterpretation." Pg. 249.

13 Stark, Rodney. 1999. "Secularization, R.I.P.," *Sociology of Religion* 60: 249–73. Pg. 72.

14 Greeley, Andrew, 1972. *Unsecular Man*. New York: Schocken Books. Pg. 5.

15 Greeley. *Unsecular Man*. Pg. 1.

16 Bellah, Robert. 1970. *Beyond Belief*. Berkeley: University of California Press. Pg. 246.

17 Hadden, Jeffrey K. 1987. "Toward Desacralizing Secular Theory," *Social Forces* 65(3): 587–611.

18 Warner, Stephen. 1993. "Work in Progress toward a New Paradigm for the So-
    ciological Study of Religion in the United States," *American Journal of Sociology*
    98(5): 1044–93.
19 Berger, Peter. 1992. *A Far Glory*. Anchor. Pg. 15.
20 Berger, Peter. 1999. "The Desecularization of the World: A Global Overview," in
    The Desecularization of the World, edited by Peter Berger. Grand Rapids, MI: Wil-
    liam B. Eerdmans Publishing. Pg 2.
21 Gorski, Philip S. and Ates Altinordu. 2008. "After Secularization?" *Annual Review
    of Sociology* 34(1): 55–85.
22 Christiano, Kevin, William Swatos, and Peter Kivisto 2002. *Sociology of Religion*.
    Walnut Creek, CA: AltaMira Press.
23 Stark, Rodney and William Sims Bainbridge. 1985. *The Future of Religion*. Berke-
    ley: University of California Press. Pg. 3.
24 Stark and Bainbridge. *The Future of Religion*. Pg. 431.
25 Stark and Bainbridge. *The Future of Religion*. Pg. 8.
26 Finke, Roger and Rodney Stark. 1992. *The Churching of America*. New Brunswick,
    NJ: Rutgers University Press. Pg. 43.
27 Stark and Bainbridge. *The Future of Religion*. Pp. 429–30.
28 Stark and Bainbridge. *The Future of Religion*. Pg. 2.
29 Stark and Bainbridge. *The Future of Religion*. Pg. 3.
30 Stark, Rodney and Roger Finke. 2003. "The Dynamics of Religious Economies," in
    Handbook of the Sociology of Religion. Pp. 96–109.
31 Stark, Rodney and Roger Finke. 2000. *Acts of Faith*. Berkeley: University of Cali-
    fornia Press. Pg. 193.
32 Stark and Finke. *Acts of Faith*.
33 Stark and Finke. "The Dynamics of Religious Economies." Pg. 99.
34 Stark and Finke. 2000. *Acts of Faith*. Pg. 63.
35 Finke and Stark. *The Churching of America*.
36 Stark and Finke. *Acts of Faith*. Pg. 62.
37 Rodney Stark, Eva Hamberg, and Alan S. Miller. 2005. "Exploring Spirituality and
    Unchurched Religions in America, Sweden, and Japan," *Journal of Contemporary
    Religion*, 20:(1): 3–23. Pg. 17.
38 Stark and Finke. *Acts of Faith*. Pg. 78.
39 Stark and Finke. *Acts of Faith*. Pg. 77.
40 Stark, Rodney. 2015. *The Triumph of Faith: Why the World Is More Religious than
    Ever*. Wilmington, DE: Intercollegiate Studies Institute. Pg. 9.
41 Stark. *The Triumph of Faith*. Pg. 9.
42 Smith, Christian. 2007. "Why Christianity Works," *Sociology of Religion* 68(2):
    165–78. Pg. 177.
43 Leonhardt, David. 2015. "The Rise of Young Americans Who Don't Believe in
    God." *New York Times*, May 12. (www.nytimes.com).
44 Grossman, Cathy Lynn. 2015. "Christians Drop, 'Nones' Soar in New Religion
    Portrait." *USA TODAY*, May 12. (www.usatoday.com).

45 Stetzer, Ed. 2015. "Nominal Christians Are Becoming More Secular, and That's Creating a Startling Change for the U.S." *Washington Post*, November 4. (www .washingtonpost.com).

46 Bullard, Gabe. 2016. "The World's Newest Major Religion: No Religion." *Culture*, April 22. (www.nationalgeographic.com).

47 Grundy, Trevor. 2016. "A Majority of People in Scotland Have No Religion." *Religion News Service*, April 5. (https://religionnews.com).

48 Leins, Casey. 2017. "Americans Are Becoming Less Religious." *US News & World Report*, April 11. (www.usnews.com).

49 Berlinger, Joshua. 2017. "Australians Ditch Religion at Rapid Rate, Becoming More Diverse." *CNN*, June 27. (www.cnn.com).

50 Borowiec, Steven. 2017. "Why Young South Koreans Are Turning away from Religion." May 28. (www.aljazeera.com).

51 Bulman, May. 2017. "Record Number of British People Have 'No Religion.'" *Independent*, September 4. (www.independent.co.uk).

52 Shermer, Michael. 2018. "The Number of Americans with No Religious Affiliation Is Rising." *Scientific American*, April 1. (www.scientificamerican.com).

53 Sherwood, Harriet. 2018. "'Christianity as Default Is Gone': The Rise of a Non-Christian Europe." *Guardian*, March 21. (www.theguardian.com).

54 Navia, Patricio. 2018. "Pope's Chile Trip Shows Declining Church Influence—and Does Little to Revert It." *Americas Quarterly*, January 25. (www.americasquarterly .org).

55 Monahan, Neil, and Saeed Ahmed. 2019. "There Are Now as Many Americans Who Claim No Religion as There Are Evangelicals and Catholics, a Survey Finds." *CNN*, April 13. (www.cnn.com).

56 Thompson, Derek. 2019. "Three Decades Ago, America Lost Its Religion. Why?" *Atlantic*, September 26. (www.theatlantic.com).

57 Cox, Daniel and Amelia Thomson-DeVeaux. 2019. "Millennials Are Leaving Religion and Not Coming Back." *FiveThirtyEight*, December 12. (https: //fivethirtyeight.com).

58 Allen, Bonnie. 2019. "From Sacred to Secular: Canada Set to Lose 9,000 Churches, Warns National Heritage Group." *CBC News*, March 10. (www.cbc.ca).

59 Toynbee, Polly. 2019. "Faith in Religion Is Dwindling, but When Will British Politics Reflect That?" *Guardian*, July 11. (www.theguardian.com).

60 BBC News. 2019. "The Arab World in Seven Charts: Are Arabs Turning Their Backs on Religion?" *BBC News*, June 23. (www.bbc.com).

61 Brown, Callum G. 2001. *The Death of Christian Britain: Understanding Secularisation, 1800–2000*. Psychology Press.

62 Sherkat, Darren E. 2014. *Changing Faith: The Dynamics and Consequences of Americans' Shifting Religious Identities*. New York: New York University Press.

63 Bruce, Steve. 2013. *Secularization: In Defence of an Unfashionable Theory*. Oxford: Oxford University Press.

64 Voas, David and Alasdair Crockett. 2005. "Religion in Britain: Neither Believing nor Belonging," *Sociology* 39(1), 11–28. Crockett, Alasdair and David Voas. "Generations of Decline: Religious Change in 20th-Century Britain," *Journal for the Scientific Study of Religion* 45(4): 567–84.

65 Keysar, Ariela. 2014. "Shifts along the American Religious-Secular Spectrum," *Secularism and Nonreligion* 3(1): 1–16.

66 Voas, David and Mark Chaves. 2016. "Is the United States a Counterexample to the Secularization Thesis?" *American Journal of Sociology* 121(5): 1517–56.

67 Wilkins Laflamme, Sarah. 2016. "Secularization and the Wider Gap in Values and Personal Religiosity between the Religious and Nonreligious," *Journal for the Scientific Study of Religion* 54(4): 717–36.

68 Cragun, Ryan T. 2017. "The Declining Significance of Religion: Secularization in Ireland," in *Values and Identities in Europe: Evidence from the European Social Survey, Routledge Advances in Sociology*, edited by Michael J. Breen, pp. 17–35. Oxon, UK: Routledge. Cragun, Ryan T. and Ronald Lawson. 2010. "The Secular Transition: The Worldwide Growth of Mormons, Jehovah's Witnesses, and Seventh-Day Adventists," *Sociology of Religion* 71(3): 349–73. doi: 10.1093/socrel/srq022. Kasselstrand, Isabella. 2015. "Nonbelievers in the Church: A Study of Cultural Religion in Sweden," *Sociology of Religion*, 76(3): 275–94. Kasselstrand, Isabella. 2019. "Secularity and Irreligion in Cross-National Context: A Nonlinear Approach," *Journal for the Scientific Study of Religion*, 58(3): 626–42. Kasselstrand, Isabella and Setareh Mahmoudi. 2020. "Secularization among Immigrants in Scandinavia: Religiosity across Generations and Duration of Residence," *Social Compass* 67(4): 617–36. Zuckerman, Phil. 2008. *Society Without God: What the Least Religious Nations Can Tell Us about Contentment.* New York University Press. Zuckerman, Phil. 2010. *Atheism and Secularity.* Santa Barbara, CA: Praeger.

69 Furseth, Inger and Pål Repstad. 2006. *An Introduction to the Sociology of Religion.* Burlington, VT: Ashgate. See specifically chapter 2.

70 Platvoet, Jan, and Arie Molendijk, eds. 1999. *The Pragmatics of Defining Religion: Contexts, Concepts, and Contests.* Leiden: Brill.

71 Kosmin, Barry and Ariela Keysar. 2006. *Religion in a Free Market: Religious and Non-Religious Americans.* Ithaca, NY: Paramount Market Publishing.

72 Shiner, Larry. 1967. "The Concept of Secularization in Empirical Research," *Journal for the Scientific Study of Religion* 6(2): 207–220. Dobbelaere, Karel. 2002. *Secularization: An Analysis at Three Levels.* New York: Peter Lang. Tschannen, Olivier. 1991. "The Secularization Paradigm: A Systematization," *Journal for the Scientific Study of Religion* 30(4): 395–415. Gorski and Altinordou. "After Secularization?"

73 Hadden, Jeffrey. 1987. "Toward Desacralizing Secularization Theory."

74 Yinger, J. Milton. 1957. *Religion, Society and the Individual.* New York: Macmillan. Pg. 119.

75 Wilson, Bryan. 1966. *Religion in Secular Society.* London: C. A. Watts. Pg. xiv.

76 Wilson, Bryan. 1985. "Secularization: The Inherited Model," in *The Sacred in a Secular Age*, edited by Phillip Hammond. Berkeley: University of California Press.

77 Berger, Peter. 1967. *The Sacred Canopy*. Doubleday. Pp. 107–108.

78 Casanova, José. 2009. "The Secular and Secularism," *Social Research* 76(4): 1049–1066. Pg. 1050.

79 Casanova, José. 2006. "Rethinking Secularization: A Global Comparative Perspective," *Hedgehog Review*. Spring and Summer. Pp. 7–22.

80 Chaves, Mark. 1994. "Secularization as Declining Religious Authority," *Social Forces*, 72(3): 749–74.

81 Dobbelaere, Karel. 2007. "Testing Secularization Theory in Comparative Perspective," *Nordic Journal of Religion and Society* 2(20): 137–47.

82 Bruce. *Secularization*. Pg. 2.

83 Barker, Eileen, James A. Beckford, and Karel Dobbelaere. 1993. *Secularization, Rationalism, and Sectarianism: Essays in Honour of Bryan R. Wilson*. Oxford: Clarendon Press. Snape, Michael and Callum G. Brown. 2010. *Secularisation in the Christian World*. London: Routledge.

84 Chaves, Mark. 1994. "Secularization as Declining Religious Authority." Dobbelaere, Karel. 1999. "Towards an Integrated Perspective of the Processes Related to the Descriptive Concept of Secularization," *Sociology of Religion* 60(3): 229–47.

85 Kay, William K. 1997. "Belief in God in Great Britain 1945–1996: Moving the Scenery Behind Classroom RE," *British Journal of Religious Education* 20(1): 28–41.

86 Kay. "Belief in God in Great Britain."

87 Jordan, William. 2015. "A Third of British Adults Don't Believe in a Higher Power." *YouGov*. Retrieved March 4, 2022 (https://yougov.co.uk).

88 Jordan. "A Third of British Adults."

89 Swerling, Gabriella. 2019. "Atheism and Islam on the Rise in the UK as Christianity Suffers 'Dramatic Decline.'" *Telegraph*, July 11. (www.telegraph.co.uk).

90 Reader, Ian. 2012. "Secularisation, R.I.P.? Nonsense! The 'Rush Hour away from the Gods' and the Decline of Religion in Contemporary Japan," *Journal of Religion in Japan* 1(1): 7–36. See also Ishii, Kenji. 2007. *Dētabukku: Gendai nihon no shūkyō*. Tokyo: Shinyōsha.

91 Saad, Lydia. 2017. "Record Few Americans Believe Bible Is Literal Word of God." *Gallup.Com*. Retrieved March 4, 2022 (https://news.gallup.com).

92 Higgins, Scott J. 2017. "The Decline of Religion in Australia." *Scottjhiggins.com*. Retrieved March 4, 2022 (https://scottjhiggins.com).

93 Kasselstrand, Isabella. 2014. *Tell the Minister Not to Talk about God: A Comparative Study of Secularisation in Protestant Europe*. PhD diss., University of Edinburgh. Pg. 235. Svenska Kyrkan. 2022. "Svenska kyrkan i siffror." Retrieved August 16, 2022 (www.svenskakyrkan.se).

94 Congostrina, Alfonso L. and Julio Núñez. 2019. "Losing Their Religion? New Report Shows Spaniards Are Turning Their Backs on Faith." *El Pais*. Retrieved March 4, 2022 (https://english.elpais.com).

95 Stats NZ. 2019. "Losing Our Religion." *Stats NZ*. Retrieved March 4, 2022 (www .stats.govt.nz).

96 Pew Research Center. 2019. *In U.S., Decline of Christianity Continues at Rapid Pace: An Update on America's Changing Religious Landscape*. Washington, DC: Pew Research Center. (www.pewforum.org).

97 Jones, Jeffrey M. 2021. "U.S. Church Membership Falls Below Majority for First Time." *Gallup.com*. Retrieved March 4, 2022 (https://news.gallup.com).

98 BBC News. 2019. "The Arab World in Seven Charts: Are Arabs Turning Their Backs on Religion?" *BBC News*, June 23. (www.bbc.com).

99 Inglehart, Ronald F. 2020. *Religion's Sudden Decline: What's Causing It, and What Comes Next?* New York: Oxford University Press. Norris, Pippa and Ronald Inglehart. 2004. *Sacred and Secular: Religion and Politics Worldwide*. Cambridge: Cambridge University Press. Kosmin, Barry A., and Ariela Keysar, eds. 2007. *Secularism and Secularity: Contemporary International Perspectives*. Hartford, CT: Institute for the Study of Secularism in Society and Culture.

100 Wilkins-Laflamme, Sarah. 2021. "A Tale of Decline or Change? Working Toward a Complementary Understanding of Secular Transition and Individual Spiri- tualization Theories, " *Journal for the Scientific Study of Religion* 60(3): 516–39. Pollack, Detlef and Gert Pickel. 2007. "Religious Individualization or Seculariza- tion? Testing Hypotheses of Religious Change—The Case of Eastern and Western Germany," *British Journal of Sociology* 58(4): 603–32.

101 Kasselstrand, Isabella. 2022. "Secularization or Alternative Faith? Trends and Conceptions of Spirituality in Northern Europe," *Journal of Religion in Europe*. https://doi.org/10.1163/18748929-bja10049.

102 Gervais, Will M., Dimitris Xygalatas, Ryan T. McKay, Michiel van Elk, Emma E. Buchtel, Mark Aveyard, Sarah R. Schiavone, Ilan Dar-Nimrod, Annika M. Svedholm-Häkkinen, Tapani Riekki, Eva Kundtová Klocová, Jonathan E. Ramsay, and Joseph Bulbulia. 2017. "Global Evidence of Extreme Intuitive Moral Preju- dice against Atheists," *Nature Human Behaviour* 1(8): 1–6. https://doi.org/10.1038 /s41562-017-0151.

103 For examples of qualitative work on secularizing societies, see Jerome Baggett on atheism in America; Callum Brown regarding secularization in Britain; Johannes Quack regarding secularism in India; Phil Zuckerman and Isabella Kasselstrand on the waning of religion in Scandinavia, etc. Baggett, Jerome. 2019. *The Varieties of Nonreligious Experience: Atheism in American Culture*. New York: New York University Press. Brown, Callum. 2001. *The Death of Christian Britain*. London: Routledge. Quack, Johannes. 2012. *Disenchanting India: Organized Rationalism and Criticism of Religion in India*. New York: Oxford University Press. Zuckerman, Phil. 2020. *Society without God*. Second edition. New York: New York University Press. Kasselstrand, Isabella. 2016. "Lived Secularity: Atheism, Indifference, and the Social Significance of Religion," in *Beyond Religion*, edited by Phil Zuckerman, pp. 37–52. Macmillan.

1. SECULARIZATION THEORY

1 Brown, Evan Nicole. 2018. "How a St. Louis Church Became a Skate Park." *Atlas Obscura*. Retrieved March 5, 2022 (www.atlasobscura.com).

2 Our source for somewhere between 6,000 and 10,000 religious congregations closing each year is Merritt, Jonathan. 2018. "America's Epidemic of Empty Churches." *Atlantic*, November 25. (www.theatlantic.com).

   A separate study estimated that close to 3,000 Protestant churches open each year in the US: Earls, Aaron. 2021. "Protestant Church Closures Outpace Openings in U.S. Lifeway Research." (https://research.lifeway.com). We were unable to find an estimate for the total number of religious congregations that open each year. Even so, what the numbers suggest is that there are many more congregations closing than opening.

3 Lipka, Michael. 2014. "U.S. Nuns Face Shrinking Numbers and Tensions with the Vatican." *Pew Research Center*. Retrieved March 5, 2022 (www.pewresearch.org).

4 Barna, George. 2021. "American Worldview Inventory 2021; Release #3: The Seismic Generational Shift in Worldview: Millennials Seek a Nation without God, Bible and Churches." May 12. (www.arizonachristian.edu).

5 Chaves, Mark. 1994. "Secularization as Declining Religious Authority," *Social Forces* 72(3): 749–74.

6 Sommerville, C. John. 2002. "Stark's Age of Faith Argument and the Secularization of Things: A Commentary," *Sociology of Religion* 63(3): 361–72. doi: 10.2307/3712474.

7 Gorski, Philip S. 2000. "Historicizing the Secularization Debate: Church, State, and Society in Late Medieval and Early Modern Europe, ca. 1300 to 1700," *American Sociological Review* 65(1): 138–67.

8 Bruce, Steve. 2002. *God Is Dead: Secularization in the West*. London: Blackwell Publishers. Pg. 2.

9 Tschannen argues that prior theorists have distinguished between three—differentiation, rationalization, and worldliness. However, worldliness is just turning one's focus to the secular and away from the religious, which is secularization. It makes little sense to argue that secularization is a process that underlies secularization. Thus, we argue that there are really two broad social processes that underlie secularization: differentiation and rationalization. See Tschannen, Olivier. 1991. "The Secularization Paradigm: A Systematization," *Journal for the Scientific Study of Religion* 30(4): 395–415.

10 In some instances, it may be more accurate to describe this process as the "creation" or "invention" of religion. See Josephson, Jason Ānanda. 2012. *The Invention of Religion in Japan*. Chicago and London: The University of Chicago Press.

11 Sharer, Robert J. and Loa P. Traxler. 2006. *The Ancient Maya*. Stanford, CA: Stanford University Press.

12 Galbraith, Kate. 2011. "Governor Declares Days of Prayer for Rain." *Texas Tribune*, April 21.

13 Cravey, Beth Reese. 2021. "Jacksonville-Based Goodwill Brings Back 'Friend-Raising' Fashion Show to Support Employment Programs." *Florida Times-Union*, July 7.

14 Bellah, Robert N. 1970. "Civil Religion in America," in *Beyond Belief: Essays on Religion in a Post-Traditional World*, edited by Robert N. Bellah, pp. 168–89. Berkeley: University of California Press. Luckmann, Thomas. 1967. *The Invisible Religion: The Problem of Religion in Modern Society*. MacmMillan Publishing Company.

15 Siebold, Sabine and Ingrid Melander. 2021. "EU Companies Can Ban Headscarves under Certain Conditions, Court Says." *Reuters*, July 15.

16 Sommerville, C. J. 1998. "Secular Society Religious Population: Our Tacit Rules for Using the Term 'Secularization,'" *Journal for the Scientific Study of Religion* 37(2): 249–53.

17 Ståhl, Tomas, Maarten P. Zaal, and Linda J. Skitka. 2016. "Moralized Rationality: Relying on Logic and Evidence in the Formation and Evaluation of Belief Can Be Seen as a Moral Issue," *PLOS ONE* 11(11):e0166332. doi: 10.1371/journal.pone.0166332.

18 Wilson, Bryan R. 1985. "Morality in the Evolution of the Modern Social System," *British Journal of Sociology* 36(3): 315–32. doi: 10.2307/590455.

19 BBC News. 2004. "Pope Canonises Pro-Life Heroine." *BBC News*, May 16.

20 Dobbelaere, Karel. 2002. *Secularization: An Analysis at Three Levels*. New York: Peter Lang.

21 Lenski, Gerhard. 1966. *Power and Privilege: A Theory of Social Stratification*. New York: McGraw-Hill.

22 Pun intended. :)

23 Guyau, Jean-Marie. 1897. *The Non-Religion of the Future: A Sociological Study*. New York: Henry Holt and Company.

24 Comte, Auguste. 1891. *The Catechism of Positive Religion: Or Summary Exposition of the Universal Religion in Thirteen Systematic Conversations between a Woman and a Priest of Humanity*. London: Savill and Edwards. Originally published in 1883.

25 Comte. *The Catechism of Positive Religion*. Pg. 9.

26 Kalberg, Stephen. 1980. "Max Weber's Types of Rationality: Cornerstones for the Analysis of Rationalization Processes in History," *American Journal of Sociology* 85(5): 1145–79.

27 Weber, Max. 1946. "Science as Vocation," in *From Max Weber: Essays in Sociology*. New York: Oxford University Press. Pp. 129–56. Original lecture was given in 1917.

28 Durkheim, E. 1997. *The Division of Labor in Society*. New York: The Free Press. Originally published in 1893. Durkheim, Emile. 1995. *The Elementary Forms of Religious Life*. New York: Free Press.

29 Durkheim. *The Division of Labor in Society*. New York: The Free Press, p. 169.

30 By "mechanism" we mean a specific social process that causes secularization directly. An example unrelated to religion may help. Imagine that someone wants to remove the seat from a bicycle, and what is holding the seat in place is a bolt that

can be loosened with an Allen wrench. The seat has the potential to be removed, but it is only with the application of a mechanism—the Allen wrench—that the seat can and will be removed. In the context of religion and secularization, by mechanism we are referring to social processes, events, or phenomena that can directly lead to secularization.

31 Berger, Peter L. and Thomas Luckmann. 1967. *The Social Construction of Reality: A Treatise in the Sociology of Knowledge.* New York: Anchor.

32 Berger, Peter L. 1967. *The Social Reality of Religion.* New York: Faber and Faber. Berger, Peter L. 1990. *The Sacred Canopy: Elements of a Sociological Theory of Religion.* New York: Anchor.

33 Parsons, Talcott. 1991. *The Social System.* Routledge. Originally published in 1951.

34 Hammarberg, Melvyn. 2013. *The Mormon Quest for Glory: The Religious World of the Latter-Day Saints.* New York: Oxford University Press.

35 Cragun, Ryan T. and J. E. Sumerau. 2015. "God May Save Your Life, but You Have to Find Your Own Keys: Religious Attributions, Secular Attributions, and Religious Priming," *Archive for the Psychology of Religion* 37(3): 321–42. doi: 10.1163/15736121-12341307.

36 Cragun, Ryan, Kevin McCaffree, Ivan Puga-Gonzalez, Wesley Wildman, and F. LeRon Shults. 2021. "Religious Exiting and Social Networks: Computer Simulations of Religious/Secular Pluralism," *Secularism and Nonreligion* 10(1): 2. doi: 10.5334/snr.129.

37 McPherson, Miller, Lynn Smith-Lovin, and James M. Cook. 2001. "Birds of a Feather: Homophily in Social Networks," *Annual Review of Sociology* 27: 415–44.

38 Stark, Rodney, and Roger Finke. 2000. *Acts of Faith: Explaining the Human Side of Religion.* Berkeley: University of California Press.

39 Voas, David, Daniel V. A. Olson, and Alasdair Crockett. 2002. "Religious Pluralism and Participation: Why Previous Research Is Wrong," *American Sociological Review* 67: 212–30.

40 Olson, Daniel, Joey Marshall, Jong Hyun Jung, and David Voas. 2020. "Sacred Canopies or Religious Markets? The Effect of County-Level Religious Diversity on Later Changes in Religious Involvement," *Journal for the Scientific Study of Religion* 59(2): 227–46. doi: 10.1111/jssr.12651.

41 Baker, Joseph O. and Buster G. Smith. 2015. *American Secularism: Cultural Contours of Nonreligious Belief Systems.* New York: New York University Press.

42 Berger, Peter L., ed. 1999. *The Desecularization of the World: Resurgent Religion and World Politics.* Washington, DC: Grand Rapids, MI: Wm. B. Eerdmans Publishing Co.

43 Inglehart, Ronald F. 2021. *Religion's Sudden Decline: What's Causing It, and What Comes Next?* New York: Oxford University Press.

44 Norris, Pippa and Ronald Inglehart. 2004. *Sacred and Secular: Religion and Politics Worldwide.* Cambridge: Cambridge University Press. Pg. 4.

45 Stolz, Jörg, Judith Könemann, Mallory Schneuwly Purdie, Thomas Englberger, and Michael Krüggeler. 2016. *(Un-)Believing in Modern Society: Religion, Spirituality, and Religious-Secular Competition.* London: Routledge.

46 Baker-Sperry, Lori. 2001. "Passing on the Faith: The Father's Role in Religious Transmission," *Sociological Focus* 34(2): 185–98. Hoge, Dean R., Gregory H. Petrillo, and Ella I. Smith. 1982. "Transmission of Religious and Social Values from Parents to Teenage Children," *Journal of Marriage and the Family* 44(3): 569–80. Kelley, Jonathan and Nan Dirk De Graaf. 1997. "National Context, Parental Socialization, and Religious Belief: Results from 15 Nations," *American Sociological Review* 62(4): 639–59. Martin, Todd F., James M. White, and Daniel Perlman. 2003. "Religious Socialization: A Test of the Channeling Hypothesis of Parental Influence on Adolescent Faith Maturity," *Journal of Adolescent Research* 18(2): 169–87.

47 Brown, Callum G. 2012. *Religion and the Demographic Revolution: Women and Secularisation in Canada, Ireland, UK and USA since the 1960s*. Woodbridge: The Boydell Press.

48 Stolz et al. *(Un-)Believing in Modern Society*.

49 Denton, Melinda Lundquist, Richard Flory, and Christian Smith. 2020. *Back-Pocket God: Religion and Spirituality in the Lives of Emerging Adults*. New York: Oxford University Press.

50 Crockett, Alasdair and David Voas. 2006. "Generations of Decline: Religious Change in Twentieth-Century Britain," *Journal for the Scientific Study of Religion* 45(4): 567–84. Voas, David, and Mark Chaves. 2018. "Even Intense Religiosity Is Declining in the United States: Comment," *Sociological Science* 5: 694–710. doi: 10.15195/v5.a29.

51 One of the anonymous reviewers of this book noted the similarity between Figure 1.2 and the work of Wildman et al. that arrived at very similar conclusions: Wildman, Wesley J., F. LeRon Shults, Saikou Y. Diallo, Ross Gore, and Justin Lane. 2020. "Post-Supernatural Cultures: There and Back Again," *Secularism and Nonreligion* 9(0): 6. doi: 10.5334/snr.121. We were unaware of the similarity before the reviewer noted it. Even so, we can only conclude that the well-worn adage is appropriate here: Great minds think alike!

52 Bruce, Steve. 2002. *God Is Dead: Secularization in the West*. London: Blackwell Publishers; Bruce, Steve. 2011. *Secularization: In Defence of an Unfashionable Theory*. Oxford: Oxford University Press.

53 Kelley, Dean M. 1986. *Why Conservative Churches Are Growing: A Study in Sociology of Religion with a New Preface for the Rose Edition*. Macon, GA: Mercer University Press.

54 Warner, R. Stephen. 1993. "Work in Progress toward a New Paradigm for the Sociological Study of Religion in the United States," *American Journal of Sociology* 98(5): 1044–93.

55 Stark and Finke. *Acts of Faith*.

56 Proposition 74: "Our model of religious economies holds that the demise of religious monopolies and the deregulation of religious economies will result in a general increase in individual religious commitment as more firms (and more motivated firms) gain free access to the market." Stark and Finke. *Acts of Faith*. Pg. 200.

57 Jelen, Ted G., ed. 2002. *Sacred Markets, Sacred Canopies: Essays on Religious Markets and Religious Pluralism*. Rowman & Littlefield Publishers.

58 Stark and Finke. *Acts of Faith*.

59 Stark, Rodney. 1999. "Secularization, R.I.P.," *Sociology of Religion* 60(3): 249–73.

60 Finke, Roger and Rodney Stark. 1993. *The Churching of America, 1776–1990: Winners and Losers in Our Religious Economy*. New Brunswick, NJ: Rutgers University Press.

61 Bruce, Steve. 1997. "The Pervasive World-View: Religion in Pre-Modern Britain," *British Journal of Sociology* 48(4): 667–80. doi: 10.2307/591602.

62 Levack, Brian P. 2006. *The Witch-Hunt in Early Modern Europe*. 3rd edition. Harlow, England; New York: Routledge.

63 Bruce. "The Pervasive World-View." 667.

64 Luckmann. *The Invisible Religion*.

65 Davie, Grace. 2015. *Religion in Britain: A Persistent Paradox*. Second edition. London: Wiley-Blackwell.

66 Day, Abby. 2011. *Believing in Belonging: Belief and Social Identity in the Modern World*. Oxford; New York: Oxford University Press.

67 Ammerman, Nancy T. 2021. *Studying Lived Religion: Contexts and Practices*. New York University Press. Ammerman, Nancy T., ed. 2007. *Everyday Religion: Observing Modern Religious Lives*. Oxford: Oxford University Press; Ammerman, Nancy Tatom. 2013. *Sacred Stories, Spiritual Tribes: Finding Religion in Everyday Life*. Oxford; New York: Oxford University Press. McGuire, Meredith B. 2008. *Lived Religion: Faith and Practice in Everyday Life*. Oxford University Press.

68 Heelas, Paul, Linda Woodhead, Benjamin Seel, Bronislaw Szerszynski, and Karin Tusting. 2005. *The Spiritual Revolution: Why Religion Is Giving Way to Spirituality*. Malden, MA: Wiley-Blackwell.

69 de Jager Meezenbroek, Eltica, Bert Garssen, Machteld van den Berg, Dirk van Dierendonck, Adriaan Visser, and Wilmar B. Schaufeli. 2012. "Measuring Spirituality as a Universal Human Experience: A Review of Spirituality Questionnaires," *Journal of Religion and Health* 51(2): 336–54. doi: 10.1007/s10943-010-9376-1. Cragun, Ryan T., Joseph H. Hammer, and Michael Nielsen. 2015. "The Nonreligious-Nonspiritual Scale (NRNSS): Measuring Everyone from Atheists to Zionists," *Science, Religion, and Culture* 2(3): 36–53. http://dx.doi.org/10.17582/journal.src/2015/2.3.36.53.

70 Ecklund, Elaine Howard. 2010. *Science vs. Religion: What Scientists Really Think*. Oxford: Oxford University Press.

71 The argument that spirituality is a symptom of secularization is also presented in an article by one of the authors: Kasselstrand, Isabella. 2022. "Secularization or Alternative Faith? Trends and Conceptions of Spirituality in Northern Europe," *Journal of Religion in Europe*. https://doi.org/10.1163/18748929-bja10049.

72 McGuire. *Lived Religion*. Pg. 7.

73 This is simple logic. If religion is "everything" then what is "irreligion" or "nonreligion"? Such terms cease to be meaningful. It is the same argument that can be applied to how Stark and Finke in *Acts of Faith* use "rational." They argue that

what is rational is subjective, making every action by every person rational. As a result, there is no such thing as an "irrational" action. If all action is rational, there is no reason to call it "rational" as it simply becomes "action."

74 Durkheim, E. 1997. *Suicide: A Study in Sociology*. Free Press. Pg. 66.

75 Warren, Rich. 2017. "More than Half of Iceland Believes in Elves." *National Geographic*, December 1.

76 Voas, David. 2020. "Is the Secularization Research Programme Progressing? Debate on Jörg Stolz's Article on Secularization Theories in the 21st Century: Ideas, Evidence, and Problems," *Social Compass* 67(2): 323–29.

77 Bruce, Steve. 2018. *Secular Beats Spiritual: The Westernization of the Easternization of the West*. New York: Oxford University Press.

78 Kasselstrand. "Secularization or Alternative Faith?"

79 Bruce, Steve. 2002. *God Is Dead: Secularization in the West*. London: Blackwell Publishers. Voas, David. 2007. "The Continuing Secular Transition," in *The Role of Religion in Modern Societies*, edited by Detlef Pollack and Daniel V. A. Olson, pp. 25–48. Routledge.

80 Stanley, J. 2020. *How Fascism Works: The Politics of Us and Them* (Reprint edition). Random House Trade Paperbacks.

81 We return to this possibility in chapter 6.

82 This may be our favorite sentence of the whole book. We got to include a zombie apocalypse in our volume in a serious way. Well, half-serious.

83 Cragun, Ryan T. and Ronald Lawson. 2010. "The Secular Transition: The Worldwide Growth of Mormons, Jehovah's Witnesses, and Seventh-Day Adventists," *Sociology of Religion*, 71(3), 349–373. https://doi.org/10.1093/socrel/srq022. Voas, David. 2007. "The Continuing Secular Transition," in *The Role of Religion in Modern Societies*, edited by Detlef Pollack and Daniel V. A. Olson, pp. 25–48. Routledge.

84 Guyau. *The Non-Religion of the Future*.

85 Hurd, E. S. 2015. *Beyond Religious Freedom: The New Global Politics of Religion*. Oxford: Oxford University Press.

2. THE EVIDENCE, PART I

1 Graham, Michael. 2013. *The Blasphemies of Thomas Aikenhead*. Edinburgh: Edinburgh University Press.

2 Bruce, Steve. 2014. "The Secularisation of Scotland," *International Journal for the Study of the Christian Church*, 14(2): 193–206. doi: 10.1080/1474225X.2014.931183. Williams, Teri. 2017. "Secularisation and Religious Decline in 21st-Century Scotland." (https://euppublishingblog.com). Chaves, Mark. 1994. "Secularization as Declining Religious Authority," *Social Forces* 72(3): 749–74.

3 The Guardian. 2015. "Pipe Down! Bagpiper Drowns out Anti-Gay 'Preacher.'" *Guardian*, September 21. (www.theguardian.com).

4 Scotland's Census. 2021. "Scotland's Census at a Glance: Religion." *Scotland's Census*. Retrieved March 5, 2022 (www.scotlandscensus.gov.uk).

5   Clements, Ben. 2017. "Religious Change and Secularisation in Scotland: An Analysis of Affiliation and Attendance," *Scottish Affairs* 26(2): 133–62. Bruce, Steve. 2014. *Scottish Gods: Religion in Modern Scotland 1900–2012*. Edinburgh: Edinburgh University Press.

6   This is a decline of nearly 10 percent of congregations, from 4,100 to 3,700. Alexander, Michael. 2018. "Faith No More: Are Scotland's Churches Facing a Crisis of Christianity?" *Courier*, April 27. (www.thecourier.co.uk).

7   BBC News. 2017. "Dramatic Drop in Church Attendance in Scotland." *BBC News*, April 16. (www.bbc.com).

8   Farley, Harry. 2018. "Membership Decline Means Church of Scotland's 'Very Existence' under Threat, Report Warns." *Christianity Today*, May 21.

9   Brown, Craig. 2014. "Church of Scotland 'Struggling to Stay Alive.'" April 29. (www.scotsman.com).

10 Kasselstrand, Isabella. 2018. "'We Still Wanted That Sense of Occasion': Traditions and Meaning-Making in Scottish Humanist Marriage Ceremonies," *Scottish Affairs*, 27(3): 273–93.

11 BBC News. 2017. "Majority of Scots Say They Are 'Not Religious.'" *BBC News*, September 16. (www.bbc.com).

12 Goodwin, Karin. 2018. "Secular Scotland: Losing Our Religion?" *Herald*, April 1. (www.heraldscotland.com).

13 Collins, Charles. 2018. "Survey Finds Scotland Is More Secular, but Catholics Are Keeping Faith." *Crux*. Retrieved March 5, 2022 (https://cruxnow.com).

14 Bruce, Steve. 2018. *Secular Beats Spiritual*. Oxford: Oxford University Press.

15 Data sets are accessed from the World Values Survey (www.worldvaluessurvey.org) and the European Values Study (https://europeanvaluesstudy.eu). With survey questions replicated in both the WVS and the EVS, these data sets were combined for a larger sample of countries.

16 World Values Survey. 2022. "What We Do." Retrieved August 16, 2022 (www.worldvaluessurvey.org).

17 Acock, Alan C. and Vern L. Bengtson. 1978. "On the Relative Influence of Mothers and Fathers: A Covariance Analysis of Political and Religious Socialization," *Journal of Marriage and the Family* 40(3): 519–30. Bao, Wan-Ning, Les B. Whitbeck, Danny R. Hoyt, and Rand D. Conger. 1999. "Perceived Parental Acceptance as a Moderator of Religious Transmission among Adolescent Boys and Girls," *Journal of Marriage and the Family* 61(2): 362–74. Hoge, Dean R., Gregory H. Petrillo, and Ella I. Smith. 1982. "Transmission of Religious and Social Values from Parents to Teenage Children," *Journal of Marriage and the Family* 44(3): 569–80. Thiessen, Joel. 2016. "Kids, You Make the Choice: Religious and Secular Socialization among Marginal Affiliates and Nonreligious Individuals," *Secularism and Nonreligion* 5(1). doi: 10.5334/snr.60. Kasselstrand, Isabella and Setareh Mahmoudi. 2020. "Secularization among Immigrants in Scandinavia: Religiosity across Generations and Duration of Residence," *Social Compass* 67(4): 617–36.

18 Bengtson, Vern L., with Norella M. Putney and Susan Harris. 2013. *Families and Faith: How Religion Is Passed Down across Generations.* New York: Oxford University Press.

19 Bruce, Steve. 2002. *God Is Dead.* Oxford, England: Blackwell Publishing.

20 Keysar, Ariela. 2014. "Shifts along the American Religious-Secular Spectrum," *Secularism and Nonreligion* 3(1): 1–16.

21 Voas, David and Mark Chaves. 2016. "Is the United States a Counterexample to the Secularization Thesis?" *American Journal of Sociology* 121(5): 1517–56. doi: 10.1086/684202.

22 Molteni, Francesco and Ferruccio Biolcati. 2018. "Shifts in Religiosity across Cohorts in Europe: A Multilevel and Multidimensional Analysis Based on the European Values Study," *Social Compass* 65(3): 413–32. doi: 10.1177/0037768618772969. Monnot, Christophe and Jörg Stolz, eds. 2018. *Congregations in Europe.* Cham, Switzerland: Springer. Tromp, Paul, Anna Pless, and Dick Houtman. 2020. "'Believing Without Belonging' in Twenty European Countries (1981–2008): De-Institutionalization of Christianity or Spiritualization of Religion?" *Review of Religious Research* 62(4): 509–31. doi: 10.1007/s13644-020-00432-z. Voas, David. 2009. "The Rise and Fall of Fuzzy Fidelity in Europe," *European Sociological Review* 25(2): 155–68. doi: 10.1093/esr/jcn044.

23 As students of religion will be quick to note, some of these countries were, historically, predominantly Buddhist and regular service attendance does not provide the same indicator of religiosity in those countries as it does in countries that are/were predominantly Christian, Jewish, or Muslim (see Brenner, Philip. 2016. "Cross-National Trends in Religious Service Attendance," *Public Opinion Quarterly* 80(2): 563–83). We note these countries here both because they are part of the dataset but also because we believe it is important to use consistent measures across countries. We do recognize the limitations of such an approach. We are not trying to suggest that, in these countries, religious attendance used to be substantially higher—only that religious service attendance today is quite low, even if that is an imperfect measure.

24 Brenner. "Cross-National Trends."

25 Gez, Yonatan N., Nadia Beider, and Helga Dickow. 2021. "African and Not Religious: The State of Research on Sub-Saharan Religious Nones and New Scholarly Horizons," *Africa Spectrum.* doi: 10.1177/00020397211052567.

26 Gachau, James. 2016. "Communicating Difference through Social Media: The Case of a Kenyan Facebook Group," *African Journalism Studies,* 37(4): 62–80. Yirenkyi, Kwasi and Baffour K. Takiy. 2010. "Atheism and Secularity in Ghana." In *Atheism and Secularity: Global Expressions (Volume 2),* edited by Phil Zuckerman, pp. 73–89. Santa Barbara, CA: Praeger.

27 However, due to social norms and expectations, the phenomenon of over-reporting religious service attendance is present in a number of Muslim-majority countries. Brenner, Philip. 2014. "Testing the Veracity of Self-Reported Religious Behavior in the Muslim World," *Social Forces* 92: 1009–1037.

28 Berger, Peter, Grace Davie, and Effie Fokas. 2008. *Religious America, Secular Europe?* Aldershot, England: Ashgate. Davie, Grace. 2002. *Europe: The Exceptional Case: Parameters of Faith in the Modern World.* London, England: Darton, Longman, and Todd. Schnabel, Landon, and Sean Bock. 2018. "The Continuing Persistence of Intense Religion in the United States: Rejoinder," *Sociological Science* 5: 711–21. doi: 10.15195/v5.a30.

29 Hadaway, C. Kirk, Penny Long Marler, and Mark Chaves. 1993. "What the Polls Don't Show: A Closer Look at U.S. Church Attendance," *American Sociological Review* 58(6): 741–52.

30 In the 1992 data from the ISSP, 52 percent of Americans attended church monthly. In 2008, this figure was 45 percent.

31 Pew Research Center. 2019. *In U.S., Decline of Christianity Continues at Rapid Pace: An Update on America's Changing Religious Landscape.* Washington, DC: Pew Research Center.

32 Voas, David and Mark Chaves. 2016. "Is the United States a Counterexample to the Secularization Thesis?" *American Journal of Sociology* 121(5):1517–56. doi: 10.1086/684202.

33 Kasselstrand, Isabella. 2019 "Secularity and Irreligion in Cross-National Context: A Nonlinear Approach." *Journal for the Scientific Study of Religion*, 58(3): 626–42. Titarenko, Larissa. 2008. "On the Shifting Nature of Religion during the Ongoing Post-Communist Transformation in Russia, Belarus and Ukraine," *Social Compass* 55(2): 237–54.

34 Rieffer, Barbara-Ann J. 2003. "Religion and Nationalism: Understanding the Consequences of a Complex Relationship," *Ethnicities* 3(2): 215–42.

35 Lim, Chaeyoon, Carol Ann MacGregor, and Robert D. Putnam. 2010. "Secular and Liminal: Discovering Heterogeneity Among Religious Nones," *Journal for the Scientific Study of Religion* 49(4): 596–618. Storm, Ingrid. 2009. "Halfway to Heaven: Four Types of Fuzzy Fidelity in Europe," *Journal for the Scientific Study of Religion* 48(4): 702–18. doi: 10.1111/j.1468-5906.2009.01474.x. Voas, David. 2009. "The Rise and Fall of Fuzzy Fidelity in Europe," *European Sociological Review* 25(2): 155–68. doi: 10.1093/esr/jcn044.

36 Demerath, Nicholas Jay. 2000. "The Rise of 'Cultural Religion' in European Christianity: Learning from Poland, Northern Ireland, and Sweden," *Social Compass* 47(1): 127–39. Kasselstrand, Isabella, Phil Zuckerman, Robert Little, and Donald A. Westbrook. 2018. "Nonfirmands: Danish youth who choose not to have a Lutheran confirmation," *Journal of Contemporary Religion* 33(1): 87–105. Kasselstrand, Isabella. 2015. "Nonbelievers in the Church: A Study of Cultural Religion in Sweden," *Sociology of Religion* 76(3): 275–94. Zuckerman, Phil. 2020. *Society without God.* Second edition. New York: New York University Press.

37 Stark, Rodney and Roger Finke. 2000. *Acts of Faith: Explaining the Human Side of Religion.* Berkeley: University of California Press.

38 It is important to note that the particular measure of belief discussed here is a binary question of yes and no on belief in God. There are limitations to such a

measure of religiosity—or secularity for that matter. Additional measures of religious beliefs are discussed in the next chapter, where case studies of secularizing countries are explored.

39 Davie, Grace. 1994. *Religion in Britain Since 1945: Believing without Belonging*. First edition. Hoboken, NJ: Wiley-Blackwell. Stark, Rodney. 1999. "Secularization RIP," *Sociology of Religion*, 60(2): 249–73. Stark and Finke. *Acts of Faith*. Stark, Rodney, Eva Hamberg, and Alan Miller. 2005. "Exploring Spirituality and Unchurched Religions in America, Sweden, and Japan," *Journal of Contemporary Religion*, 20(1): 3–23.

40 Berger et al. *Religious America, Secular Europe?* Davie. *Europe: The Exceptional Case.*

41 www.thearda.com

42 Government Regulation of Religion is an index created by Grim and Finke (2006). Government regulation of religion is made up of "any laws, policies, or administrative actions that impinge on the practice, profession, or selection of religion" (Grim and Finke, 2006: 9). This index consists of six questions that address the restriction of missionary work; proselytizing, preaching, or conversion; an individual's right to worship; and respect for and contribution to freedom of religion. For this analysis, China and Vietnam were excluded. Grim, Brian J., and Roger Finke. 2006. "International Religion Indexes: Government Regulation, Government Favoritism, and Social Regulation of Religion," *Interdisciplinary Journal of Research on Religion* 2: 1–40.

43 K-means cluster analysis was performed to create the clusters. This is a technique that uses an algorithm to group together cases based on their similarities on certain characteristics—in this case development and government regulation of religion.

44 Berger et al. *Religious America, Secular Europe?* Davie, Grace. *Europe: The Exceptional Case.* Finke, Roger. 1992. "An Unsecular America," in *Religion and Modernization: Sociologists and Historians Debate the Secularization Thesis*, edited by Steve Bruce, pp. 145–69. Oxford: Oxford University Press.

3. THE EVIDENCE, PART II

1 Egge, Julie Haugen. 2012. "Snart slutt for statskirken i Norge." *NRK*. May 15. (www.nrk.no).

2 This trend follows similar patterns elsewhere, particularly with their Scandinavian neighbors of Sweden and Finland, the former which disestablished its own state church in 2000.

3 Stark, Rodney and Roger Finke. 2000. *Acts of Faith: Explaining the Human Side of Religion*. Berkeley: University of California Press

4 Stark, Rodney and Laurence R. Iannaccone. 1994. "A Supply-Side Reinterpretation of the 'Secularization' of Europe," *Journal for the Scientific Study of Religion* 33(3): 230–52.

5 Furseth, I., L. Ahlin, K. Ketola, A. Leis-Peters, and B. R. Sigurvinsson. 2018. "Changing Religious Landscapes in the Nordic Countries," in *Religious Complex-*

ity in the Public Sphere: Comparing Nordic Countries, edited by Inger Furseth, pp. 31–80. Cham: Palgrave Macmillan.

6 Davie, Grace. 2002. *Europe: The Exceptional Case: Parameters of Faith in the Modern World*. London: Darton, Longman, and Todd. Heelas, Paul and Linda Woodhead. *The Spiritual Revolution: Why Religion Is Giving Way to Spirituality*. Oxford: Blackwell Publishing, 2005. Stark, Rodney, Eva Hamberg, and Alan Miller. 2005. "Exploring Spirituality and Unchurched Religions in America, Sweden, and Japan," *Journal of Contemporary Religion*, 20(1): 3–23.

7 By atheist we mean individuals who report not believing in a God. By agnostic we mean either those who are unsure if there is a God or do not believe there is a way to find out if there is a God.

8 Bruce, Steve. 2002. *God Is Dead: Secularization in the West*. London: Blackwell Publishers. Kasselstrand, Isabella. 2016. "Lived Secularity: Atheism, Indifference, and the Social Significance of Religion," in *Beyond Religion*, edited by Phil Zuckerman, pp. 37–52. MacMillan. Kasselstrand, Isabella. 2019 "Secularity and Irreligion in Cross-National Context: A Nonlinear Approach," *Journal for the Scientific Study of Religion*, 58(3): 626–64. Zuckerman, Phil. 2020. *Society Without God*. Second edition. New York: New York University Press.

9 https://human.no

10 Human Development Report 2020: http://hdr.undp.org.

11 Erickson, Amanda. 2018. "In Trip to Chile, Pope Francis Asks for Forgiveness amid Protests and Death Threats over Clergy Sex Abuse." *Washington Post*, January 16. (www.washingtonpost.com).

12 Winfield, Nicole and Eva Vergara. 2018. "In Chile, Pope Francis Met with Protests, Passion and Skepticism." *Denver Post*, January 15. (www.denverpost.com).

13 Navia, Patricio. 2018. "Pope's Chile Trip Shows Declining Church Influence—and Does Little to Revert It." *Americas Quarterly*, January 25. (www.americasquarterly.org).

14 Ontiveros, Eva. 2018. "Why Pope Francis's Trip to Chile Poses a Challenge." *BBC News*, January 16. (www.bbc.com).

15 Navia, "Pope's Chile Trip."

16 Pew Research Center. 2014. *Religion in Latin America*. Washington, DC: Pew Research Center. (www.pewforum.org).

17 Navia, "Pope's Chile Trip."

18 Raymond, Christopher. 2021. "Dealigned or Still Salient? Religious-Secular Divisions in Chilean Presidential Elections," *Bulletin of Latin American Research* 40(1): 100–116. (https://onlinelibrary.wiley.com/doi/epdf/10.1111/blar.13111).

19 "GDP per Capita." Worldometer. (www.worldometers.info).

20 Kasselstrand, Isabella. 2019. "Secularity and Irreligion in Cross-National Context: A Nonlinear Approach," *Journal for the Scientific Study of Religion*, 58(3): 626–64.

21 Voas, David and Mark Chaves. 2016. "Is the United States a Counterexample to the Secularization Thesis?" *American Journal of Sociology*, 121(5): 1517–56. doi: 10.1086/684202.

22 Stark and Finke. *Acts of Faith*.

23 Choi, Hyaeweol. 2020. "The Sacred and the Secular: Protestant Christianity as Lived Experience in Modern Korea: An Introduction," *Journal of Korean Studies* 25(2): 279–89. https://doi.org/10.1215/07311613-8551979.

24 Bell, Matthew. 2017. "The Biggest Megachurch on Earth and South Korea's 'Crisis of Evangelism.'" *The World from PRX*. Retrieved March 5, 2022 (https://theworld .org).

25 Choi. "The Sacred and the Secular."

26 Baker, Don. 2013. "Korea's Path of Secularisation," in *Making Sense of the Secular: Critical Perspective from Europe to Asia*, edited by Ranjan Ghosh, pp. 182–94. New York: Routledge. Baar, Jemima. 2021. "The Secularisation Thesis Recast: Christianity in Modern China and South Korea," *International Journal of Asian Christianity*, 4(1), 5–27. Stark, Rodney. 2015. *The Triumph of Faith: Why the World Is More Religious than Ever*. Wilmington, DE: Intercollegiate Studies Institute.

27 Baar. "The Secularisation Thesis Recast."

28 Park, S. Nathan. 2021. "'Minari' Is about Korean American Faith as Well as Family." *Foreign Policy*. Retrieved March 5, 2022 (https://foreignpolicy.com).

29 Choi. "The Sacred and the Secular."

30 Baar. "The Secularisation Thesis Recast."

31 The corresponding figure in the ISSP is 48.2 percent. The trend of disaffiliation is confirmed by other sources. Citing figures from Statistics Korea, Steven Borowiec demonstrates an increase in the proportion of religious nones in South Korea, stating that 56 percent were unaffiliated in 2015. Borowiec, Steven. 2017. "Why Young South Koreans Are Turning Away from Religion." *Al Jazeera*, May 28. (www.aljazeera.com).

32 In the ISSP, a similar level, 50.9 percent of the respondents, "never" attend religious services.

33 Here, she argues that stability and security is a more convincing cause for secularization than urbanization and industrialization. Baar. "The Secularisation Thesis Recast."

34 Pew Research Center. 2021. *How COVID-19 Has Strengthened Religious Faith*. Washington, DC: Pew Research Center. (www.pewforum.org).

35 Borowiec. "Why Young South Koreans Are Turning Away."

36 Bell. "The Biggest Megachurch on Earth."

37 Park, Seong Won. 2009. "The Present and Future of Americanization in South Korea," *Journal of Futures Studies* 14(1): 51–66.

38 Choi. 2020. "The Sacred and the Secular."

39 Stark. *The Triumph of Faith*. Pp. 170–171.

40 Cragun, Ryan T. and Ronald Lawson. 2010. "The Secular Transition: The Worldwide Growth of Mormons, Jehovah's Witnesses, and Seventh-Day Adventists," *Sociology of Religion* 71(3): 349–73. doi: 10.1093/socrel/srq022.

41 Berger, Peter, Grace Davie, and Effie Fokas. 2008. *Religious America, Secular Europe? A Theme and Variations*. Burlington, VT: Ashgate. Pg. 141

42 Gorski, Philip S. and Ates Altinordu. 2008. "After Secularization?" *Annual Review of Sociology* 34: 55–85.

43 Kosmin, Barry A., Ariela Keysar, Ryan T. Cragun, and Juhem Navarro-Rivera. 2009. *American Nones: The Profile of the No Religion Population*. Hartford, CT: Institute for the Study of Secularism in Society and Culture.

44 Note we wrote "hard to deny," not impossible. Rodney Stark, of course, denied the evidence.

45 Voas and Chaves, "Is the United States a Counterexample?"

46 Cox, Daniel, and Amelia Thomson-DeVeaux. 2019. "Millennials Are Leaving Religion and Not Coming Back." *FiveThirtyEight*, December 12. (https://fivethirtyeight.com). Smith, Gregory A. 2021. *About Three-in-Ten U.S. Adults Are Now Religiously Unaffiliated*. Washington, DC: Pew Research Center. (www.pewforum.org).

47 Inglehart, Ronald F. 2021. *Religion's Sudden Decline: What's Causing It, and What Comes Next?* New York: Oxford University Press. Pg. 83.

48 Mehta, Hemant. 2021. "Congratulations, Atheists: Church Attendance in America Is at an All-Time Low." *Friendly Atheist*. Retrieved March 5, 2022 (https://friendlyatheist.patheos.com).

49 PRRI. 2021. *The 2020 Census of American Religion*. Washington, DC: PRRI.

50 Downey, Allen. 2017. "College Freshmen Are Less Religious than Ever." *Scientific American Blog Network*. Retrieved March 5, 2022 (https://blogs.scientificamerican.com).

51 Cox, Daniel A. 2019. *The Decline of Religion in American Family Life*. Washington, DC: American Enterprise Institute. (www.aei.org).

52 Cox. *The Decline of Religion*.

53 Lupfer, Jacob. 2018. "Fewer Couples Are Marrying in Churches. Does It Matter?" *Religion News Service*. Retrieved March 5, 2022 (https://religionnews.com).

54 "Share of Americans Who Feel a Religious Component in a Funeral of a Loved One Is Very Important from 2012 to 2019." (www.statista.com).

55 Hadaway, C. Kirk, Penny Long Marler, and Mark Chaves. 1993. "What the Polls Don't Show: A Closer Look at U.S. Church Attendance," *American Sociological Review* 58(6): 741–52. Hadaway, C. Kirk, Penny Long Marler, and Mark Chaves. 1998. "Overreporting Church Attendance in America: Evidence That Demands the Same Verdict," *American Sociological Review* 63(1): 122–30. Rossi, Maurizio and Ettore Scappini. 2014. "Church Attendance, Problems of Measurement, and Interpreting Indicators: A Study of Religious Practice in the United States, 1975–2010," *Journal for the Scientific Study of Religion* 53(2): 249–67. doi: 10.1111/jssr.12115.

56 Brenner, Philip S. 2011. "Identity Importance and the Overreporting of Religious Service Attendance: Multiple Imputation of Religious Attendance Using the American Time Use Study and the General Social Survey," *Journal for the Scientific Study of Religion* 50(1): 103–15.

57 Schnabel, Landon and Sean Bock. 2018. "The Continuing Persistence of Intense Religion in the United States: Rejoinder," *Sociological Science* 5: 711–21. doi:

10.15195/v5.a30. Smith, Christian, Michael O. Emerson, Sally K. Gallagher, P. Kennedy, and David Sikkink. 1998. *American Evangelicals: Embattled and Thriving*. Chicago: University of Chicago Press. Smith, Christian and Melinda Lundquist Denton. 2005. *Soul Searching: The Religious and Spiritual Lives of American Teenagers*. Oxford: Oxford University Press.

58 Merritt, Jonathan. 2018. "America's Epidemic of Empty Churches." *Atlantic*. Retrieved March 5, 2022 (www.theatlantic.com).

59 Shimron, Yonat. 2021. "Study: More Churches Closing than Opening." *Religion News Service*. Retrieved March 5, 2022 (https://religionnews.com).

60 Inglehart. *Religion's Sudden Decline*. Pg. 89, citing the General Social Survey.

61 Barna, George. 2021. "American Worldview Inventory 2021; Release #3: The Seismic Generational Shift in Worldview: Millennials Seek a Nation without God, Bible and Churches." May 12. (www.arizonachristian.edu).

62 Cox. *The Decline of Religion*. (www.aei.org).

63 Cragun, Ryan T. 2017. "The Declining Significance of Religion: Secularization in Ireland," in *Values and Identities in Europe: Evidence from the European Social Survey, Routledge Advances in Sociology*, edited by Michael J. Breen, pp. 17–35. Oxon, UK: Routledge.

64 Philanthropy News Digest. 2021. "Fewer than 50 Percent of Americans Indicate Religion Is Very Important." *Philanthropy News Digest (PND)*. Retrieved March 5, 2022 (https://philanthropynewsdigest.org).

65 Earls, Aaron. 2019. "Losing Our Religion: Less than Half of Americans Say Religion Can Answer Today's Problems." *Lifeway Research*. Retrieved March 5, 2022 (https://research.lifeway.com).

66 Berger et al. *Religious America, Secular Europe?* Davie. *Europe: The Exceptional Case*.

67 Stark and Finke. *Acts of Faith*. Stark and Iannaccone. "A Supply-Side Reinterpretation."

4. IS BEING SECULAR UNNATURAL?

1 Barrett, Justin L. 2012. *Born Believers: The Science of Children's Religious Belief*. New York: Simon and Schuster.

2 Benedict, Ruth. 2019. *Patterns of Culture*. London: Routledge. Berger, Peter L. 2011. *Invitation to Sociology: A Humanistic Perspective*. New York: Open Road Media.

3 Antweiler, Christopher. 2016. *Our Common Denominator: Human Universals Revisited*. New York: Berghan Books. Barash, David. 2012. *Homo Mysterious: Evolutionary Puzzles of Human Nature*. New York: Oxford University Press.

4 Wade, Nicholas. 2009. *The Faith Instinct: How Religion Evolved and Why It Endures*. New York: Penguin.

5 Wade. *The Faith Instinct*. Pg. 3.

6 Wade. *The Faith Instinct*. Pg. 5.

7 Wade. *The Faith Instinct*. Pg. 3.

8   Bloom, Paul. 2007. "Religion Is Natural," *Developmental Science* 10(1): 147–51.
    Hinde, Robert. 1999. *Why Gods Persist*. New York: Routledge. Boyer, Pascal. 2001.
    Religion Explained. New York: Basic Books. Wilson, David Sloan. 2002. *Darwin's
    Cathedral*. Chicago: University of Chicago Press. Guthrie, Stewart. 1993. *Faces in
    the Clouds: A New Theory of Religion*. New York: Oxford University Press. Shermer,
    Michael. 2010. "Why Belief in God Is Innate," *Wall Street Journal*, April 10.

9   Friedman, Jack and Timothy Samuel Shah. 2018. "Introduction," in *Homo Religio-
    sus? Exploring the Roots of Religion and Religious Freedom in Human Experience*,
    edited by Jack Friedman and Timothy Samuel Shah, pg. 2. New York: Cambridge
    University Press.

10 Smith, Christian. 2018. "Are Human Beings Naturally Religious?" in *Homo
    Religiosus? Exploring the Roots of Religion and Religious Freedom in Human
    Experience*, edited by Jack Friedman and Timothy Samuel Shah, pg. 39. New York:
    Cambridge University Press.

11 Smith. "Are Human Beings Naturally Religious?" Pg. 45.

12 Smith. "Are Human Beings Naturally Religious?" Pp. 50–51.

13 Smith. "Are Human Beings Naturally Religious?" Pg. 51. Ironically, it is religious
    people who are prone to flagellation!

14 Smith. "Are Human Beings Naturally Religious?" Pg. 51.

15 Smith. "Are Human Beings Naturally Religious?" Pg. 52.

16 Greeley, Andrew. 1972. *Unsecular Man*. New York: Delta Books. Pg. 16.

17 Greeley. *Unsecular Man*. Pp. 261–262.

18 Greeley. *Unsecular Man*. Pg. 262.

19 Berger, Peter. 1999. "The Desecularization of the World: A Global Overview," in
    The Desecularization of the World: Resurgent Religion and World Politics, edited by
    Peter Berger, pg. 13. Grand Rapids, MI: William Eerdmans.

20 Berger. "The Desecularization of the World." Pg. 13.

21 McCauley, Robert. 2011. *Why Religion Is Natural and Science Is Not*. New York:
    Oxford University Press.

22 Barrett, Justin. 2010. "The Relative Unnaturalness of Atheism: On Why Geertz
    and Markússon are Both Right and Wrong," *Religion* 40(3): 169–72.

23 Barrett, Justin. 2004. *Why Would Anyone Believe in God?* Lanham, MD: AltaMira
    Press.

24 Barrett. *Why Would Anyone Believe in God?* Pg. 118.

25 Iannaconne, Laurence. 2020. "Smart and Spiritual: The Coevolution of Religion
    and Rationality," in *Religion and Human Flourishing*, edited by Adam B. Cohen.
    Waco, TX: Baylor University Press. Pg. 177.

26 Szocik, Konrad and Philip Walden. 2015. "Why Atheism Is More Natural than
    Religion," *Studia Reliologica* 48(4): 313–26; Mercier, Brett, Stephanie Kramer, and
    Azximn Shariff. 2018. "Belief in God: Why People Believe, and Why They Don't,"
    Current Directions in Psychological Science 27(4): 263–68.

27 Geertz, Armin and G. I. Markusson, 2010. "Religion Is Natural, Atheism Is Not:
    On Why Everybody Is Both Wrong and Right," *Religion* 40: 152–65.

28 Norenzayan, Ara and Will Gervais. 2013. "The Origins of Religious Disbelief." *Trends in Cognitive Science* 17(1): 20–25.
29 Whitmarsh, Tim. 2015. *Battling the Gods*. London: Faber & Faber. Pp. 5–6.
30 Hecht, Jennifer M. 2004. *Doubt: A History*. New York: HarperOne. pp. 96, 98. See also chapter 5 in Quack, Johannes. 2012. *Disenchanting India: Organized Rationalism and Criticism of Religion in India*. New York: Oxford University Press.
31 Whitmarsh. *Battling the Gods*.
32 Hecht. *Doubt: A History. New York*: HarperOne. Esolen, Anthony M., ed. and trans. 1995. *Lucretius. On the Nature of Things*. Baltimore: Johns Hopkins University Press. Thrower, James. 2000. *Western Atheism: A Short History*. Amherst, NY: Prometheus. Couprie, Dirk L., Robert Hahn, and Gerard Naddaf. 2003. *Anaximander in Context: New Studies in the Origins of Greek Philosophy*. Albany: State University of New York Press.
33 Malkin, Yaakov. 2007. *Epicurus and Apikorsim: The Influence of the Greek Epicurus and Jewish Apikorsim on Judaism*. Detroit: Milan Press.
34 Warraq, Ibn. 2003. *Leaving Islam: Apostates Speak Out*. Amherst, NY: Prometheus Books.
35 Quote in Van Doren, Carl. 2007 [1926]. "Why I Am an Unbeliever." In *The Portable Atheist*, edited by Christopher Hitchens. Philadelphia: Da Capo.
36 Hecht. *Doubt: A History*. Thrower. *Western Atheism*.
37 Pew Research Center. 2015. *The Future of World Religions: Population Growth Projections, 2010–2050*. Washington, DC: Pew Research Center.
38 Alper, Becka A. 2018. "Why America's 'Nones' Don't Identify with a Religion." Pew Research Center. Retrieved January 7, 2022 (www.pewresearch.org). Pew Forum on Religion. 2012. *"Nones" on the Rise: One-in-Five Adults Have No Religious Affiliation*. Washington, DC: The Pew Forum on Religion & Public Life. (www.pewforum.org).
39 Albert, Eleanor and Lindsay Maizland. 2020. "The State of Religion in China." *Council on Foreign Relations*. Retrieved March 5, 2022 (www.cfr.org).
40 Office of International Religious Freedom. 2019. "2019 Report on International Religious Freedom: Taiwan." United States Department of State. Retrieved March 5, 2022 (www.state.gov).
41 Roemer, Michael. 2009. "Religious Affiliation in Contemporary Japan: Untangling the Enigma," *Review of Religious Research* 50(3): 298–320. Iwai, Noriko. 2017. "Measuring Religion in Japan: ISM, NHK and JGSS Survey Research and the Study of Religion in East Asia." October 11. Pew Research Center. (www.pewresearch.org).
42 Evans, Jonathan. 2017. "Unlike Their Central and Eastern European Neighbors, Most Czechs Don't Believe in God." Pew Research Center. Retrieved March 5, 2022 (www.pewresearch.org).
43 Statista Research Department. 2022. "Netherlands: Population, by Religion 2010–2018." *Statista*. Retrieved March 5, 2022 (www.statista.com). CBS Staff. 2018. "Over Half of the Dutch Population Are Not Religious." *Statistics Netherlands*. Retrieved

March 5, 2022 (www.cbs.nl). NL Times Staff. 2016. "Atheism Rises in Netherlands: Half of Dutch People Do Not Believe in Deities." *NL Times*. Retrieved March 5, 2022. (https://nltimes.nl). Dutch News Staff. 2016. "Two-Thirds of People in Netherlands Have No Religious Faith." *DutchNews.Nl*. Retrieved March 5, 2022 (www .dutchnews.nl).

44 Statista Research Department. 2021. "Belief in God France 2019." Statista. Retrieved March 5, 2022 (www.statista.com). Pew Forum on Religion. 2018. *Being Christian in Western Europe*. Washington, DC: Pew Research Center. (www .pewforum.org).

45 Australian Bureau of Statistics. 2018. "Census Reveals Australia's Religious Diversity on World Religion Day." *Australian Bureau of Statistics*. Retrieved March 5, 2022 (www.abs.gov.au).

46 Bargsted Matías, Somma Nicolás M., and Valenzuela Eduardo. 2019. "Atheism and Nonreligion in Latin America, Geography," in *Encyclopedia of Latin American Religions*, edited by Henri Gooren. Springer, Cham. https://doi.org/10.1007/978-3 -319-27078-4_558.

47 BBC News. 2019. "The Arab World in Seven Charts: Are Arabs Turning Their Backs on Religion?" *BBC News*. June 23. (www.bbc.com).

48 Whitaker, Brian. 2015. "The Rise of Arab Atheism." *New Humanist*. Retrieved March 5, 2022 (https://newhumanist.org.uk).

49 Lipka, Michael. 2016. "Religion and Politics in Israel: 7 Key Findings." *Pew Research Center*. Retrieved March 5, 2022 (www.pewresearch.org).

50 Manglos, Nicolette D. and Alexander A. Weinreb. 2013. "Religion and Interest in Politics in Sub-Saharan Africa," *Social Forces* 92(1): 195–219. https://doi.org/10 .1093/sf/sot070.

51 Schoeman, Willem J. 2017. 'South African Religious Demography: The 2013 General Household Survey," *HTS Teologiese Studies / Theological Studies* 73(2): a3837. https://doi.org/10.4102/hts.v73i2.3837.

52 Barrett. *Why Would Anyone Believe in God?* Pg. 118.

53 See Appendix.

54 ScotCen. 2017. "Scots with No Religion at Record Level." *ScotCen*. Retrieved March 5, 2022 (www.scotcen.org.uk).

55 BBC News. 2017. "Majority of Scots Say They Are 'Not Religious.'" *BBC News*, September 16. (www.bbc.com).

56 Remmel, Atko. 2017. "Religion, Interrupted? Observations on Religious Indifference in Estonia," in *Religious Indifference*, edited by Johannes Quack and Cora Schuh. Springer, Cham. https://doi.org/10.1007/978-3-319-48476-1_7.

57 Remmel. "Religion, Interrupted?"

58 Remmel. "Religion, Interrupted?"

59 Sultanova, Shahla. 2013. "Azerbaijan: Islam Comes with a Secular Face." *Eurasianet*. Retrieved March 5, 2022 (https://eurasianet.org).

60 Nuruzade, Shahla. 2016. "Religious Views in Modern Azerbaijan." *Journal of Socialomics* 5(4). doi: 10.41 72/2167-0358.1000187.

61 Sultanova. "Azerbaijan: Islam Comes with a Secular Face."

62 Pals, Daniel. 2006. *Eight Theories of Religion*. New York: Oxford University Press. Guthrie, Stewart. 1993. *Faces in the Clouds*. New York: Oxford University Press. Thrower, James. 1999. *Religion: The Classical Theories*. Washington, DC: Georgetown University Press.

63 Sherkat, Darren. 2003. "Religious Socialization: Sources of Influence and Influences of Agency," in *Handbook of the Sociology of Religion*, edited by Michele Dillon, pp. 61–75. Cambridge: Cambridge University Press.

64 "Helt ikke sandt" means "totally not true" in Danish.

65 Pew Research Center. 2016. *One-In-Five U.S. Adults Were Raised in Interfaith Homes*. Washington, DC: Pew Research Center. (www.pewforum.org).

66 Stark, Rodney and Roger Finke. 2000. *Acts of Faith: Explaining the Human Side of Religion*. Berkeley: University of California Press. Pg. 119.

67 Myers, Scott. 1996. "An Interactive Model of Religiosity Inheritance: The Importance of Family Context," *American Sociological Review* 61(5): 858–66. Pg. 864.

68 Sherkat. "Religious Socialization." See also Argyle, Michael. 2000. *Psychology and Religion: An Introduction*. New York: Routledge, 2000. Vern L. Bengtson, with Norella M. Putney and Susan Harris. 2013. *Families and Faith: How Religion Is Passed Down across Generations*. Oxford: Oxford University Press. Bader, Christopher D. and Scott A. Desmond. 2006. "Do as I Say and as I Do: The Effects of Consistent Parental Beliefs and Behaviors upon Religious Transmission," *Sociology of Religion* 67(3): 313–29.

Braswell, Gregory S., Karl S. Rosengren, and Howard Berenbaum. 2012. "Gravity, God and Ghosts? Parents' Beliefs in Science, Religion, and the Paranormal and the Encouragement of Beliefs in their Children," *International Journal of Behavioral Development* 36(2): 99–106. Wink, Paul, Lucia Ciciolla, Michele Dillon, and Allison Tracy. "Religiousness, Spiritual Seeking, and Personality: Findings from a Longitudinal Study," *Journal of Personality* 75(5): 1051–70.

69 Merino, Stephen M. 2011. "Irreligious Socialization? The Adult Religious Preferences of Individuals Raised with No Religion," *Secularism and Nonreligion* 1(0): 1–16. Pg. 12.

70 Nelsen, Hart M. 1990. "The Religious Identification of Children from Interfaith Marriages." *Review of Religious Research* 32(2): 122–34.

71 Bruce, Steve and Tony Glendinning. 2003. "Religious Beliefs and Differences," in *Devolution—Scottish Answers to Scottish Questions*, edited by Catherine Bromley, John Curtice, Kerstin Hinds, and Alison Park, pp. 86–115. Edinburgh: Edinburgh University Press.

72 "Scottish Social Attitudes." NatCen. (https://natcen.ac.uk).

73 Bengtson et al. *Families and Faith*. Pg. 152.

74 Pew Research Center. *One-In-Five U.S. Adults*.

75 Evans, Geoffrey and Ksenia Northmore-Ball. 2012. "The Limits of Secularization? The Resurgence of Orthodoxy in Post-Soviet Russia," *Journal for the Scientific Study of Religion* 51(4): 795–808.

76 Froese, Paul. 2008. *The Plot to Kill God: Findings from the Soviet Experiment in Secularization*. Berkeley: University of California Press. Pg. 184.

77 Froese. *The Plot to Kill God*. Pg. 186.

78 Peris, Daniel. 1998. *Storming the Heavens: The Soviet League of the Militant Godless*. Ithaca: Cornell University Press.

5. WHAT SECULARITY LOOKS LIKE

1 CIA. 2022. "Hong Kong." *The World Factbook*. (www.cia.gov).

2 Davie, Grace. 1994. *Religion in Britain since 1945: Believing Without Belonging*. Oxford: Blackwell. Stark, Rodney and Roger Finke. 2000. *Acts of Faith: Explaining the Human Side of Religion*. Berkeley: University of California Press. Heelas, Paul. 1996. *The New Age Movement: The Celebration of the Self and the Sacralization of Modernity*. Oxford; Cambridge, MA: Blackwell Publishers. Stark, Rodney. 2015. *The Triumph of Faith: Why the World Is More Religious than Ever*. Wilmington, DE: Intercollegiate Studies Institute.

3 Kasselstrand, Isabella. 2016. "Lived Secularity: Atheism, Indifference, and the Social Significance of Religion," in *Beyond Religion*, edited by Phil Zuckerman, pp. 37–52. Macmillan. Zuckerman, Phil. 2020. *Society without God*. Second edition. New York: New York University Press.

4 Bruce, Steve. 2002. *God Is Dead: Secularization in the West*. London: Blackwell Publishers. Kasselstrand, Isabella. 2019. "Secularity and Irreligion in Cross-National Context: A Nonlinear Approach," *Journal for the Scientific Study of Religion* 58(3): 626–64.

5 Smolkin, Victoria. 2018. *A Sacred Space Is Never Empty: A History of Soviet Atheism*. Princeton, NJ: Princeton University Press.

6 Shook, John R. *The God Debates: A 21st Century Guide for Atheists and Believers (and Everyone in Between)*. Hoboken, NJ: Wiley-Blackwell, 2010.

7 Zuckerman. *Society without God*. Kasselstrand, Isabella. 2016. "Lived Secularity."

8 Remmel, Atko. 2017. "Religion, Interrupted? Observations on Religious Indifference in Estonia," in *Religious Indifference: New Perspectives From Studies on Secularization and Nonreligion*, edited by Johannes Quack and Cora Schuh, pg. 130. New York: Springer, Cham. https://doi.org/10.1007/978-3-319-48476-1_7. Pg. 130.

9 Quack and Schuh, eds. *Religious Indifference*. Pg. 5.

10 On this note, Johannes Quack and Cora Schuh state, "Religious indifference labels populations for whom religion in various of its aspects have become unimportant and peripheral to their lives. In contrast to e.g. anti-religious positions, this does not include a negative perception of religion." *Religious Indifference*. pg. 10.

11 Nash. "Genealogies of Indifference?" Pg. 39.

12 Cotter, Chris. 2017. "A Discursive Approach to 'Religious Indifference:' Critical Reflections from Edinburgh's Southside," in *Religious Indifference*.

13 Kasselstrand, Isabella. 2016. "Lived Secularity."

14 Bullivant, Stephen. 2012. "Not So Indifferent after All? Self-Conscious Atheism and the Secularisation Thesis," *Approaching Religion* 2(1): 100–106. Pg. 100.

15 Vern L. Bengtson, with Norella M. Putney and Susan Harris. 2013. *Families and Faith: How Religion is Passed Down across Generations*. Oxford: Oxford University Press. Pg. 163.

16 Zuckerman, Phil, Luke W. Galen, and Frank L. Pasquale. 2016. *The Nonreligious: Understanding Secular People and Societies*. Oxford: Oxford University Press. Zuckerman, Phil. 2019. *What It Means to Be Moral: Why Religion Is Not Necessary for Living an Ethical Life*. Catapult. Cragun, Ryan T. 2014. *What You Don't Know about Religion (But Should)*. Durham, NC: Pitchstone Publishing.

17 Gervais, Will M. 2014. "Everything Is Permitted? People Intuitively Judge Immorality as Representative of Atheists," *PLoS ONE* 9(4). doi: 10.1371/journal. pone.0092302. Gervais, Will M., Dimitris Xygalatas, Ryan T. McKay, Michiel van Elk, Emma E. Buchtel, Mark Aveyard, Sarah R. Schiavone, Ilan Dar-Nimrod, Annika M. Svedholm-Häkkinen, Tapani Riekki, Eva Kundtová Klocová, Jonathan E. Ramsay, and Joseph Bulbulia. 2017. "Global Evidence of Extreme Intuitive Moral Prejudice against Atheists," *Nature Human Behaviour* 1(8): 1–6. doi: 10.1038/s41562-017-0151. Thiessen, Joel, and Sarah Wilkins-Laflamme. 2020. *None of the Above: Nonreligious Identity in the US and Canada*. New York: New York University Press.

18 Zuckerman, Phil. 2014. *Living the Secular Life: New Answers to Old Questions*. New York: Penguin Press.

19 Chalabi, Mona. 2015. "Are Prisoners Less Likely to Be Atheists?" *FiveThirtyEight*. Retrieved March 5, 2022 (https://fivethirtyeight.com).

20 Zuckerman, Phil. 2020. *Society without God: What the Least Religious Nations Can Tell Us About Contentment*. Second edition. New York University Press. Paul, Gregory S. 2005. "Cross-National Correlations of Quantifiable Societal Health with Popular Religiosity and Secularism in the Prosperous Democracies," *Journal of Religion and Society* 7: 1–17. Zuckerman, Phil. 2013. "Atheism and Societal Health," in *The Oxford Handbook of Atheism*, edited by Stephen Bullivant and Michael Ruse. Oxford: Oxford University Press.

21 Saslow, Laura R., Robb Willer, Matthew Feinberg, Paul K. Piff, Katharine Clark, Dacher Keltner, and Sarina R. Saturn. 2013. "My Brother's Keeper? Compassion Predicts Generosity More among Less Religious Individuals," *Social Psychological and Personality Science* 4(1): 31–38. doi: 10.1177/1948550612444137.

22 Saslow et al. "My Brother's Keeper?"

23 Piazza, Jared. 2012. "'If You Love Me Keep My Commandments': Religiosity Increases Preference for Rule-Based Moral Arguments," *International Journal for the Psychology of Religion* 22(4): 285–302.

24 Cragun, Ryan T. 2013. *What You Don't Know About Religion*. Pg. 87

25 Zuckerman, Phil. 2021. "Staunch Atheists Show Higher Morals than the Proudly Pious, from the Pandemic to Climate Change." *Salon*. Retrieved March 5, 2022 (www.salon.com).

26 Bump, Philip. 2018. "The Group Least Likely to Think the U.S. Has a Responsibility to Accept Refugees? Evangelicals." *Washington Post*, May 24. (www.washingtonpost.com).

27 Franz, Berkeley and R. Khari Brown. 2020. "Race, Religion and Support for the Affordable Care Act," *Review of Religious Research* 62(1): 101–20. doi: 10.1007/s13644-020-00396-0.

28 PRRI Staff. 2019. "Fractured Nation: Widening Partisan Polarization and Key Issues in 2020 Presidential Elections." *PRRI*. Retrieved March 5, 2022 (www.prri.org).

29 Masci, David. 2018. "American Religious Groups Vary Widely in Their Views of Abortion." Pew Research Center. Retrieved March 5, 2022 (www.pewresearch.org).

30 Hall, Deborah L., David C. Matz, and Wendy Wood. 2010. "Why Don't We Practice What We Preach? A Meta-Analytic Review of Religious Racism," *Personality and Social Psychology Review* 14(1):126–39. doi: 10.1177/1088868309352179.

31 Connaughton, Aidan. 2020. "Religiously Unaffiliated People More Likely than Those with a Religion to Lean Left, Accept Homosexuality." Pew Research Center. Retrieved March 5, 2022 (www.pewresearch.org).

32 Smith, Gregory A. 2017. "Views of Transgender Issues Divide along Religious Lines." Pew Research Center. Retrieved March 5, 2022 (www.pewresearch.org).

33 Sharp, Shane. 2019. "Belief in Life after Death and Attitudes toward Voluntary Euthanasia," *OMEGA—Journal of Death and Dying* 79(1): 72–89. doi: 10.1177/0030222817715755.

34 Aebersold, Cassandra, Luke Galen, Victoria Stanton, and Jamie DeLeeuw. 2007. "Support for Animal Rights as a Function of Belief in Evolution, Religious Fundamentalism, and Religious Denomination," *Society & Animals* 15(4): 353–63. doi: 10.1163/156853007X235528.

35 Thiessen and Wilkins-Laflamme. *None of the Above.*

36 Baggett, Jerome. 2019. *The Varieties of Nonreligious Experience.* New York: New York University Press.

37 Caldwell-Harris, Catherine L., Angela L. Wilson, Elizabeth LoTempio, and Benjamin Beit-Hallahmi. 2010. "Exploring the Atheist Personality: Well-Being, Awe, and Magical Thinking in Atheists, Buddhists, and Christians," *Mental Health, Religion & Culture.* doi: 10.1080/13674676.2010.509847. Lindeman, Marjaana, Annika M. Svedholm-Häkkinen, and Jari Lipsanen. 2015. "Ontological Confusions but Not Mentalizing Abilities Predict Religious Belief, Paranormal Belief, and Belief in Supernatural Purpose," *Cognition* 134:63–76. doi: 10.1016/j.cognition.2014.09.008.

38 Zuckerman. *Living the Secular Life.*

39 Pepper, Miriam, Tim Jackson, and David Uzzell. 2010. "A Study of Multidimensional Religion Constructs and Values in the United Kingdom," *Journal for the Scientific Study of Religion* 49(1): 127–46. doi: 10.1111/j.1468-5906.2009.01496.x. Zuckerman, Phil. 2009. "Atheism, Secularity, and Well-Being: How the Findings of Social Science Counter Negative Stereotypes and Assumptions," *Sociology Compass* 3(6): 949–71. Reiss, Steven. 2000. "Why People Turn to Religion: A Motivational Analysis," *Journal for the Scientific Study of Religion* 39(1): 47–52. Beit-Hallahmi, Benjamin. 2006. "Atheists: A Psychological Profile," in *The Cambridge Companion*

to Atheism, edited by Michael Martin, pp. 300–318. Cambridge: Cambridge University Press. Altemeyer, Bob. 2010. "Atheism and Secularity in North America," in *Atheism and Secularity: Volume 2—Global Expressions*, edited by Phil Zuckerman, pp. 1–22. Santa Barbara, CA: Praeger.; Hunsberger, Bruce. 2006. *Atheists: A Groundbreaking Study of America's Nonbelievers*. Amherst, N.Y.: Prometheus Books.; Greeley, Andrew and Michael Hout. 2006. *The Truth about Conservative Christians*. Chicago: University of Chicago Press.; Smidt, Corwin. 2005. "Religion and American Attitudes Toward Islam and an Invasion of Iraq," *Sociology of Religion* 66(3): 243–61.; Pew Research Center. 2018. "Being Christian in Western Europe." Pew Research Center's Religion & Public Life Project. Retrieved March 5, 2022 (www.pewforum.org).

40 Funk, Cary and John Gramlich. 2021. "10 Facts about Americans and Coronavirus Vaccines." Pew Research Center. Retrieved March 5, 2022 (www.pewresearch.org).

41 Speed, David, Caitlin Barry, and Ryan Cragun. 2020. "With a Little Help from My (Canadian) Friends: Health Differences between Minimal and Maximal Religiosity/Spirituality Are Partially Mediated by Social Support," *Social Science & Medicine* 265: 1–9. doi: 10.1016/j.socscimed.2020.113387.

42 Tajfel, H. 1982. "Social Psychology of Intergroup Relations," *Annual Review of Psychology* 33(1): 1–39. doi: 10.1146/annurev.ps.33.020182.000245.

43 Fothergill, Kate E., Margaret E. Ensminger, Judy Robertson, Kerry M. Green, Roland J. Thorpe, and Hee-Soon Juon. 2011. "Effects of Social Integration on Health: A Prospective Study of Community Engagement among African American Women," *Social Science & Medicine* 72(2): 291–98. doi: 10.1016/j.socscimed.2010.10.024.

44 Cragun, Ryan T., Christel J. Manning, and Lori L. Fazzino, eds. 2017. *Organized Secularism in the United States: New Directions in Research*. Berlin: Walter de Gruyter GmbH.

45 García, Alfredo and Joseph Blankholm. 2016. "The Social Context of Organized Nonbelief: County-Level Predictors of Nonbeliever Organizations in the United States," *Journal for the Scientific Study of Religion* 55(1): 70–90. doi: 10.1111/jssr.12250.

46 Engineer, Ashgar Ali. 2007. "Secularism in India," in *Secularism and Secularity: Contemporary International Perspectives*, edited by Barry A. Kosmin and Ariela Keysar. 149–56. Hartford, CT: Institute for the Study of Secularism in Society and Culture.

47 Gez, Yonatan N., Nadia Beider, and Helga Dickow. 2021. "African and Not Religious: The State of Research on Sub-Saharan Religious Nones and New Scholarly Horizons," *Africa Spectrum* 57 (1). doi: 10.1177/00020397211052567.

48 Galen, Luke W. and Jim Kloet. 2011. "Personality and Social Integration Factors Distinguishing Nonreligious from Religious Groups: The Importance of Controlling for Attendance and Demographics," *Archive for the Psychology of Religion / Archiv Für Religionspychologie* 33(2): 205–28. doi: 10.1163/157361211X570047.

49 Langston, Joseph A., Joseph H. Hammer, and Ryan T. Cragun. 2015. "Atheism Looking In: On the Goals and Strategies of Organized Nonbelief," *Science, Reli-*

gion, and Culture 2(3): 70–85. http://dx.doi.org/10.17582/journal.src/2015/2.3.70.85. Quack and Schuh, eds., *Religious Indifference.*

50 Nica, Andreea. 2019. "Exiters of Religious Fundamentalism: Reconstruction of Social Support and Relationships Related to Well-Being," *Mental Health, Religion & Culture* 22(5): 543–56.

51 The study was conducted by Pascal Tanner and Christophe Monnot and was reported at the 2017 meeting of the International Society for the Sociology of Religion in Lausanne, Switzerland. They found that 0.1% of Swiss citizens were affiliated with a secular group.

52 For instance, the Freedom From Religion Foundation has an entire division of attorneys that is focused on policing church and state violations. Similarly, Humanists International releases reports on freedom of thought for countries around the world annually and advocates for the nonreligious with the United Nations.

53 https://human.no

54 https://english.dnt.no

55 Rejowska, Agata. 2021. "Humanist Weddings in Poland: The Various Motivations of Couples," *Sociology of Religion* 82(3): 281–304. doi: 10.1093/socrel/sraa060. Kasselstrand, Isabella. 2018. "'We Still Wanted That Sense of Occasion': Traditions and Meaning-Making in Scottish Humanist Marriage Ceremonies," *Scottish Affairs* 27(3): 273–93. Zuckerman. *Living the Secular Life.* Pg. 185.

56 Humanists UK. 2020. "More Humanist than Christian Marriages in Scotland in 2019." *Humanists UK.* Retrieved March 5, 2022 (https://humanists.uk).

57 "Vital Events." National Records of Scotland. (www.nrscotland.gov.uk).

58 A longer excerpt from this interview is published in Zuckerman. *Living the Secular Life.* Pg. 189.

59 Rejowska. "Humanist Weddings in Poland."

60 In 2017, 37.7 percent of wedding ceremonies were nonreligious. Rejowska. "Humanist Weddings in Poland."

61 Rejowska. "Humanist Weddings in Poland." Pg. 295.

62 Kasselstrand. "'We Still Wanted That Sense of Occasion.'" Pg. 289.

63 Bell, C. 1997. *Rituals: Perspectives and Dimensions.* Oxford: Oxford University Press. Van Gennep, A. (1909/2010). *The Rites of Passage,* translated by Monika B. Vizedom and Gabrielle L. Caffee. London: Routledge.

64 Manning, Christel. 2015. *Losing Our Religion.* New York: New York University Press.

65 Starks, Brian and Robert V. Robinson. 2009. "Two Approaches to Religion and Politics: Moral Cosmology and Subcultural Identity," *Journal for the Scientific Study of Religion* 48(4): 650–69. doi: 10.1111/j.1468–5906.2009.01471.x. Ellison, Christopher G., and Darren E. Sherkat. 1993. "Obedience and Autonomy: Religion and Parental Values Reconsidered," *Journal for the Scientific Study of Religion* 32(4): 313–29.

66 Additional information from this interview is published in Zuckerman. *Living the Secular Life.*

67 Kasselstrand, Isabella, Phil Zuckerman, Robert Little, and Donald A. Westbrook. 2018. "Nonfirmands: Danish Youth Who Choose Not to Have a Lutheran Confirmation," *Journal of Contemporary Religion* 33(1): 87–105.

68 Manning, Christel A. 2016. "Secularity and Family Life," in *Beyond Religion*, edited by Zuckerman. Farmington Hills, MI: Macmillan Reference. Bengtson, Vern L., R. David Hayward, Phil Zuckerman, and Merril Silverstein. 2018. "Bringing Up Nones: Intergenerational Influences and Cohort Trends." *Journal for the Scientific Study of Religion* 57(2): 258–75. doi: 10.1111/jssr.12511.

69 Pasquale, Frank L. 2010a. "A Portrait of Secular Group Affiliates," in *Atheism and Secularity: Volume 1—Issues, Concepts, and Definitions*, edited by Phil Zuckerman, pp. 43–88. Santa Barbara, CA: Praeger.; Pasquale, Frank L. 2010b. "An Assessment of the Role of Early Parental Loss in the Adoption of Atheism or Irreligion,." *Archive for the Psychology of Religion* 32(3): 375–96. doi: 10.1163/157361210X533292.

70 Bengtson et al. *Families and Faith*. Bengtson et al. "Bringing Up Nones."

71 Zuckerman. *Living the Secular Life*.

72 Zuckerman, Phil. 2020. *Society without God*. Second edition. New York: New York University Press.

73 Lundholm, Johanna. 2021. "Därför firar vi lucia—och så blir luciafirandet 2021," *Leva & bo*. Retrieved March 5, 2022 (www.expressen.se).

74 Puskás, Tünde. 2016. "Doing Belonging in a Swedish Preschool," *Early Childhood Folio*, 20(1): 30–34.

75 Merino, Stephen M. 2011. "Irreligious Socialization? The Adult Religious Preferences of Individuals Raised with No Religion," *Secularism and Nonreligion* 1(0): 1–16. Pg. 12; Bengtson et al. "Bringing Up Nones."

76 Bengtson et al. "Bringing Up Nones."

77 Stark and Finke. *Acts of Faith*. Pg. 100.

78 Stark and Finke. *Acts of Faith*. Pg. 32.

79 Gall, T. L., R. M. de Renart, and B. Boonstra. 2000. "Religious Resources in Long-Term Adjustment to Breast Cancer," *Journal of Psychosocial Oncology* 18: 21–37. Hood, Ralph, Peter Hill, and Bernard Spilka. 2009. *The Psychology of Religion*. New York: Guilford Press. Krause, Neal, Christopher G. Ellison, Benjamin A. Shaw, John P. Marcum, and Jason D. Boardman. 2001. "Church-Based Social Support and Religious Coping," *Journal for the Scientific Study of Religion* 40(4): 637–56. Pargament, Kenneth. 1997. *The Psychology of Religion and Coping*. New York: Guilford.

80 For additional evidence that religion serves as a compensator, see: Schnabel, Landon. 2021. "Opiate of the Masses? Inequality, Religion, and Political Ideology in the United States," *Social Forces* 99(3): 979–1012. doi: 10.1093/sf/soaa027.

81 Stark, Rodney and William Sims Bainbridge. 1980. "Networks of Faith: Interpersonal Bonds and Recruitment to Cults and Sects," *American Journal of Sociology* 85(6): 1376–95.

82 Stark, Rodney and William Sims Bainbridge. 1986. *The Future of Religion: Secularization, Revival, and Cult Formation*. Berkeley: University of California Press. Pp. 121–122.

83 Of course, a simpler theory would accomplish the same, something like, "Ceteris paribus, people try to avoid dying."

84 Hwang, Karen. 2008. "Atheists with Disabilities: A Neglected Minority in Religion and Rehabilitation Research," *Journal of Religion, Disability & Health* 12(2): 186–92.

85 Hwang, Karen. 2008. "Experiences of Atheists with Spinal Cord Injury: Results of an Internet-Based Exploratory Survey," *SCI Psychosocial Process* 20(2): 4–28.

86 Bjorck, Jeffrey P. and John W. Thurman. 2007. "Negative Life Events, Patterns of Positive and Negative Religious Coping, and Psychological Functioning," *Journal for the Scientific Study of Religion* 46(2): 159–67.

87 Exline, Julie J., Crystal L. Park, Joshua M. Smyth, and Michael P. Carey. 2011. "Anger toward God: Social-Cognitive Predictors, Prevalence, and Links with Adjustment to Bereavement and Cancer," *Journal of Personality and Social Psychology* 100(1): 129–48. doi: 10.1037/a0021716.

88 Elhakeem, Norhan. The wave Sweden will never forget. *Local*, December 22, 2014. (www.thelocal.se).

89 Davie, Grace. 2007. "Vicarious Religion: A Methodological Challenge," in *Everyday Religion*, edited by Nancy T. Ammerman. Oxford: Oxford University Press.

90 Davie, Grace. 2015. "Studying Religion in the Nordic Countries: An External View," *Nordic Journal of Religion and Society* 28(2): 101–116. Pg. 106.

91 Svenska Kyrkan. 2022. "Svenska kyrkan i siffror." Retrieved August 16, 2022 (www.svenskakyrkan.se).

92 Another of the authors, Ryan, regularly votes in a Baptist church. It is the only building in his neighborhood that is large enough to accommodate the number of people who come to vote.

93 Davie, Grace. 2010. "Vicarious Religion: A Response," *Journal of Contemporary Religion*, 25(2): 261–66. https://www.tandfonline.com/doi/full/10.1080/1353790 1003750944.

94 Bruce, Steve and David Voas. 2010. "Vicarious Religion: An Examination and Critique," *Journal of Contemporary Religion* 25(2): 243–59.

95 Siegers, Pascal. 2017. "Religion, Interrupted? Observations on Religious Indifference in Estonia," in *Religious Indifference*, edited by Quack and Schuh.

96 Granqvist, Pehr and Jakob Moström. 2014. "There Are Plenty of Atheists in Foxholes—in Sweden," *Archive for the Psychology of Religion* 36(2): 199–213.

97 Zuckerman. *Living the Secular Life*. Pp. 137–67.

98 Zuckerman. *Living the Secular Life*. Pg. 164.

99 Herman, Judith. 1992. *Trauma and Recovery*. New York: Basic Books. Hwang, Karen. 2008. "Atheists with Disabilities: A Neglected Minority in Religion and Rehabilitation Research," *Journal of Religion, Disability & Health* 12(2):186–92. Pargament, Kenneth, Karen Ishler, Eric F. Dubow, Patti Stanik, Rebecca Rouiller, Patty Crowe, Ellen P. Cullman, Michael Albert, and Betty Royster. 1994. "Methods of Religious Coping with the Gulf War: Cross-Sectional and Longitudinal Analyses," *Journal for the Scientific Study of Religion* 33(4): 347–61. Thompson,

Martie and Paula Vardaman. 1997. "The Role of Religion in Coping with the Loss of a Family Member to Homicide," *Journal for the Scientific Study of Religion* 36(1): 44–51. Zuckerman. *Living the Secular Life.*

100 Pew Research Center. 2020. "Americans Far More Likely to Say Coronavirus Crisis Has Strengthened Their Faith, Rather than Weakened It." Pew Research Center. Retrieved March 6, 2022 (www.pewresearch.org).

101 Pew Research Center. 2021. "How COVID-19 Has Strengthened Religious Faith." Washington, DC: Pew Research Center. (www.pewforum.org).

6. EXCEPTIONS?

1 Stark, Rodney and Roger Finke. 2000. *Acts of Faith: Explaining the Human Side of Religion.* Berkeley: University of California Press.

2 Bruce, Steve. 2002. *God Is Dead: Secularization in the West.* London: Blackwell Publishers.

3 Durkheim, Emile. 1995. *The Elementary Forms of Religious Life.* New York: Free Press.

4 Bruce. *God Is Dead.*

5 Sowa, Kazimierz Z. 2006. "Dissent and Civil Society in Poland," *Journal of Interdisciplinary Studies* 18(1/2): 57–74. doi: 10.5840/jis2006181/23.

6 Sowa. "Dissent and Civil Society in Poland."

7 The Church of Ireland is part of the Anglican Communion.

8 Fleming, Michael. 2010. "The Ethno-Religious Ambitions of the Roman Catholic Church and the Ascendancy of Communism in Post-War Poland (1945–50)," *Nations & Nationalism* 16(4): 637–56. doi: 10.1111/j.1469-8129.2009.00427.x.

9 Fleming. "The Ethno-Religious Ambitions."

10 Fleming. "The Ethno-Religious Ambitions."

11 Sowa. "Dissent and Civil Society in Poland."

12 Knox, Zoe. 2004. *Russian Society and the Orthodox Church: Religion in Russia after Communism.* London: Routledge.

13 Bruce. *God Is Dead.*

14 Fleming. "The Ethno-Religious Ambitions."

15 Day, Abby. 2011. *Believing in Belonging: Belief and Social Identity in the Modern World.* Oxford; New York: Oxford University Press.

16 Cragun, Ryan T. 2017. "The Declining Significance of Religion: Secularization in Ireland," in *Values and Identities in Europe: Evidence from the European Social Survey,* edited by Michael J. Breen, pp. 17–35. Oxon, UK: Routledge.

17 Economist Intelligence Unit. 1991. ". . . And unto Poland, What Is God's." *Economist* 319(7708): 51–53.

18 Cragun "The Declining Significance of Religion."

19 Bruce. *God Is Dead.* Fox, Jonathan, and Ephraim Tabory. 2008. "Contemporary Evidence Regarding the Impact of State Regulation of Religion on Religious Participation and Belief," *Sociology of Religion* 69(3): 245–71.

20 Theodorou, Angelina E. 2016. "Which Countries Still Outlaw Apostasy and Blasphemy?" Pew Research Center. Retrieved July 20, 2021 (www.pewresearch.org).

21 Humanists International. 2020. *The Freedom of Thought Report 2020: Key Countries Edition*. London, UK: Humanists International.

22 Here is the original text in French, "Tout musulman coupable du crime d'apostasie, soit par parole, soit par action de façon apparente ou évidente, sera invité à se repentir dans un délai de trois jours.

   "S'il ne se repent pas dans ce délai, il est condamné à mort en tant qu'apostat, et ses biens seront confisqués au profit du Trésor." The translation is from Google Translate. The original source document can be found here: www.droit-afrique.com or https://acjr.org.za.

23 Emmerson, Ben. 2018. "Report of the Special Rapporteur on the Promotion and Protection of Human Rights and Fundamental Freedoms While Countering Terrorism on His Mission to Saudi Arabia." 19. (www.ohchr.org).

24 Gullickson, Aaron and Sarah Ahmed. 2021. "The Role of Education, Religiosity and Development on Support for Violent Practices among Muslims in Thirty-Five Countries," *PLOS ONE* 16(11). doi: 10.1371/journal.pone.0260429.

25 Johnson, Juliet. 2005. "Modern Identities in Russia: A New Struggle for the Soul?" in *Religion and Identity in Modern Russia: The Revival of Orthodoxy and Islam*, edited by Juliet Johnson, Marietta Stepaniants, and Benjamin Forest, pp. 135–43. Aldershot, England: Ashgate.

26 Egypt's Constitution of 2014. Retrieved August 26, 2021 (www.constituteproject.org).

27 Maleki, Ammar, and Pooyan Tamimi Arab. 2020. *Iranians' Attitudes toward Religion: A 2020 Survey Report*. Netherlands: Group for Analyzing and Measuring Attitudes in Iran.

28 Raz, Daniella. 2019. *Youth in Middle East and North Africa*. Arab Barometer. (www.arabbarometer.org).

29 Smolkin, Victoria. 2018. *A Sacred Space Is Never Empty: A History of Soviet Atheism*. Princeton, NJ: Princeton University Press.

30 Lukács, Georg. 1967. *History and Class Consciousness*. Translated by Rodney Livingstone. London: Merlin Press. Originally published in 1923.

31 Froese, Paul. 2008. *The Plot to Kill God: Findings from the Soviet Experiment in Secularization*. Berkeley: University of California Press. Peris, Daniel. 1998. *Storming the Heavens: The Soviet League of the Militant Godless*. Ithaca: Cornell University Press. Smolkin. *A Sacred Space*.

32 Peris. *Storming the Heavens*.

33 Knox. *Russian Society and the Orthodox Church*. Smolkin. *A Sacred Space Is Never Empty*.

34 Froese. *The Plot to Kill God*.

35 Hormel, Leontina M. 2010. "Atheism and Secularity in the Former Soviet Union," in *Atheism and Secularity: Volume 2—Global Expressions*, edited by Phil Zuckerman, pp. 45–72. Santa Barbara, CA: Praeger.

36 Smolkin. *A Sacred Space*.

37 Froese. *The Plot to Kill God*.

38 Chistiakov, Georgii. 2005. "In Search of the 'Russian Idea': A View from Inside the Russian Orthodox Church," in *Religion and Identity in Modern Russia: The Revival of Orthodoxy and Islam*, edited by Juliet Johnson, Marietta Stepaniants, and Benjamin Forest, pp. 53–64. Aldershot, England: Ashgate.

39 Knox. *Russian Society and the Orthodox Church*. Smolkin. *A Sacred Space*.

40 Gatagova, Liudmila. 2005. "Orthodoxy, Ethnicity, and Mass Ethnophobias in the Late Tsarist Era," in *Religion and Identity in Modern Russia*, pp. 39–52.

41 Knox. *Russian Society and the Orthodox Church*.

42 Chistiakov. "In Search of the 'Russian Idea.'"

43 Johnson, Juliet. 2005. "Religion after Communism: Belief, Identity, and the Soviet Legacy in Russia," in *Religion and Identity in Modern Russia*, pp. 1–25. Smolkin. *A Sacred Space*.

44 Smolkin. *A Sacred Space*.

45 Johnson. "Religion after Communism."

46 Knox. *Russian Society and the Orthodox Church*.

47 Knox. *Russian Society and the Orthodox Church*.

48 Johnson. "Religion after Communism."

49 Chistiakov. "In Search of the 'Russian Idea.'"

50 Johnson. "Religion after Communism."

51 Knox. *Russian Society and the Orthodox Church*.

52 Smolkin. *A Sacred Space*.

53 Knox. *Russian Society and the Orthodox Church*.

54 Knox. *Russian Society and the Orthodox Church*.

55 Smolkin. *A Sacred Space*.

56 Smolkin. *A Sacred Space*.

57 Smolkin. *A Sacred Space*.

58 Knox. *Russian Society and the Orthodox Church*. Pg. 101.

59 Johnson. "Religion after Communism."

60 Smolkin. *A Sacred Space*.

61 The first five of these points are made in: Powell, David E. *Antireligious Propaganda in the Soviet Union*. Cambridge, MA: MIT Press, 1975. The last comes from Knox. *Russian Society and the Orthodox Church*.

62 Yuzeev, Aidar. 2005. "Islam and the Emergence of Tatar National Identity," in *Religion and Identity in Modern Russia*, pp. 91–104.

63 Smolkin. *A Sacred Space*.

64 This is not uncommon in authoritarian regimes when there is a failure on some initiative to simply deny the failure and then to cover it up. The failure to secularize the populations of Soviet countries appears to be such a situation. Froese. *The Plot to Kill God*.

65 "Karl Marx: Interviews with the Corner-Stone of Modern Socialism," *Chicago Tribune*, January 5, 1879, 7. (www.marxists.org).

66 Smolkin. *A Sacred Space*.

67 Agadjanian, Alexander. 2001. "Revising Pandora's Gifts: Religious and National Identity in the Post-Soviet Societal Fabric," *Europe-Asia Studies* 53(3): 473–88. doi: 10.1080/09668130120045898.

68 Johnson. "Religion after Communism."

69 Johnson. "Religion after Communism." Yuzeev. "Islam and the Emergence of Tatar National Identity."

70 Stepaniants, Marietta. 2005. "Ethno-Religious Identity in Modern Russia: Orthodoxy and Islam Compared," in *Religion and Identity in Modern Russia*, pp. 26–38.

71 Berger, Peter L. 1990. *The Sacred Canopy: Elements of a Sociological Theory of Religion*. New York: Anchor.

72 Johnson. "Religion after Communism."

73 Johnson. "Religion after Communism."

74 Connell, Robert William. 1997. "Why Is Classical Theory Classical?" *American Journal of Sociology* 102(6):1511–57.

75 Knox. *Russian Society and the Orthodox Church.*

76 Fleming. "The Ethno-Religious Ambitions."

77 Yuzeev. "Islam and the Emergence of Tatar National Identity."

78 Gatagova, Liudmila. 2005. "Orthodoxy, Ethnicity, and Mass Ethnophobias in the Late Tsarist Era," in *Religion and Identity in Modern Russia*, pp. 39–52.

79 Knox. *Russian Society and the Orthodox Church.*

80 Knox. *Russian Society and the Orthodox Church.*

81 Knox. *Russian Society and the Orthodox Church.* Laqueur, Walter. 1994. *Black Hundred: The Rise of the Extreme Right in Russia.* New York: Perennial.

82 Chistiakov. "In Search of the 'Russian Idea.'" Johnson. "Religion after Communism." Knox. *Russian Society and the Orthodox Church.*

83 Ryzhova, Svetlana. 2005. "Tolerance and Extremism: Russian Ethnicity in the Orthodox Discourse of the 1990s," in *Religion and Identity in Modern Russia: The Revival of Orthodoxy and Islam*, pp. 65–90; Stepaniants. "Ethno-Religious Identity in Modern Russia."

84 Smolkin. *A Sacred Space.*

85 Knox. *Russian Society and the Orthodox Church.*

86 Pospielovsky, Dimitry V. 1995. "The Russian Orthodox Church in the Postcommunist CIS," in *The Politics of Religion in Russia and the New States of Eurasia*, edited by M. Bourdeaux, pp. 41–74. New York: M. E. Sharpe.

87 Knox. *Russian Society and the Orthodox Church.*

88 Johnson, Juliet. 2005. "Modern Identities in Russia: A New Struggle for the Soul?" in *Religion and Identity in Modern Russia: The Revival of Orthodoxy and Islam*, edited by J. Johnson, M. Stepaniants, and B. Forest, pp. 135–43. Aldershot, England: Ashgate.

89 Chistiakov. "In Search of the 'Russian Idea.'" Pg. 60.

90 Knox. *Russian Society and the Orthodox Church.*

91 Schwirtz, Michael. 2007. "In Pomp and Symbolism, Yeltsin Is Buried from a Cathedral." *New York Times*, A6.

92 Kishkovsky, Sophia and David M. Herszenhorn. 2012. "Punk Band's Moscow Trial Offers Platform for Orthodox Protesters." *New York Times*, A11.

93 Yemelianova, Galina. 1999. "Islam and Nation Building in Tatarstan and Dagestan of the Russian Federation," *Nationalities Papers* 27(4): 605–630. Borowik, Irina. 2002. "Between Orthodoxy and Eclecticism: On the Religious Transformations of Russia, Belarus, and Ukraine," *Social Compass* 49(4): 497–508.

94 Johnson. "Religion after Communism."

95 Chistiakov. "In Search of the 'Russian Idea.'"

CONCLUSION: BEYOND DOUBT

1 Cottee, Simon. 2014. *The Apostates: When Muslims Leave Islam*. C. Hurst & Co. Publishers. Pg. 32.

2 Cottee. *The Apostates*. Pp. 32—35.

3 Zuckerman, Phil. 2011. *Faith No More: Why People Reject Religion*. Oxford: Oxford University Press. Baggett, Jerome P. 2019. *The Varieties of Nonreligious Experience: Atheism in American Culture*. New York: New York University Press. Hunsberger, Bruce. 2006. *Atheists: A Groundbreaking Study of America's Nonbelievers*. Amherst, N.Y.: Prometheus Books.

4 Pew Research Center. 2015. *The Future of World Religions: Population Growth Projections, 2010–2050*. Washington, DC: Pew Research Center.

5 Stark, Rodney and Laurence R. Iannaccone. 1994. "A Supply-Side Reinterpretation of the 'Secularization' of Europe," *Journal for the Scientific Study of Religion* 33(3): 230–52.

6 It is worth noting that there are many social scientists who study religion who also work as consultants for religious organizations that are struggling to grow or retain members. It is much more compelling to tell such organizations that they need to change their product to increase engagement or membership than it is to tell them that demand is waning. This may also help explain why so many scholars in the 1990s and early 2000s were adamant about the importance of religious supply despite the growing evidence that interest in religion was declining.

7 Berg-Sørensen, Anders, ed. 2013. *Contesting Secularism: Comparative Perspectives*. Surrey, England: Ashgate.

8 Stolz, Jörg. 2020. "Secularization Theories in the Twenty-First Century: Ideas, Evidence, and Problems Presidential Address—Karel Dobbelaere Conference," *Social Compass* 67(2): 282–308. doi: 10.1177/0037768620917320.

9 Stolz. "Secularization Theories."

10 Perhaps something like this: Cragun, Ryan T., Joseph H. Hammer, and Michael Nielsen. 2015. "The Nonreligious-Nonspiritual Scale (NRNSS): Measuring Everyone from Atheists to Zionists," *Science, Religion, and Culture* 2(3): 36–53. http://dx.doi.org/10.17582/journal.src/2015/2.3.36.53.

INDEX

Page numbers in *italics* indicate Figures and Tables

birth cohort: older, 81; religious beliefs by, 87–88, 93; in South Korea, 86; supernatural beliefs and, 86; US religious belonging and, *81, 90*
Blankholm, Joseph, 123
blasphemy, 51
Bolshevik Revolution (1917), 149–50
born believers, 97–98, 111–12
Borowiec, Steven, 84
Boyle, Daniel, 51
Britain, 13, 66, 141
Britta (retired), 132–33
Brown, Callum, 8
Bruce, Steve, 8, 111, 164; change not decline argument and, 43; *Religion and Modernization* edited by, 15; religious orthodoxy and, 39; on Scottish spirituality, 53; on secularization, 11; *Secularization* by, 15; secularization theory by, 36–37
Buddhism, 83–85, 194n23
Bullivant, Stephen, 120
burden of proof, 45

Canada, 61, 69, 95, 122
capitalism, 83, 94
Carvaka (ancient Indians), 101
Casanova, José, 11
Cathedral of Christ the Saviour, 157
Catholic Church, 142–44; in Chile, 77–78, 82; sex abuse scandal of, 78; societies influenced by, 58
Catholicism, 41, 85, 110, 141–42
ceremonies, 52, 91, 127, 133
Chaves, Mark, 8, 11, 59
children: with heart conditions, 137; important qualities of, *129*; nonreligious people raising, 132; Norway and values of, 129; parents grant autonomy to, 36; religious faith of, 110–12, 128–32; religious socialization to, 35–36; secularization of, 109–10; secular societies raising, 130–31; socialization by, 109;

Sweden and values of, 129–30; US values of, 130
Chile, 58, 69; belief in God in, 79–80, *80*; Catholic Church in, 77–78, 82; modernization trend in, 80; religious beliefs and practices in, 77–82; religious beliefs in, *79*; religious belonging in, *78*; religious person and age in, *81*; religious person changes in, 80–81; secularization in, 78–79
China, 102, 104, 160–61
Choi, Hyaeweol, 83
Christ and Church (*Christo et Ecclesiae*), 24
Christianity, 41, 51, 82–83, 86, 198n31
Christiano, Kevin, 4
Christo et Ecclesiae (Christ and Church), 24
church attendance: believing without belonging and, 41; in countries, *55, 56–59, 57, 171–74*, 194n23; countries development and, 159; during crises, 136–37; in Europe, 54–58; in Poland, 58; religious changes influencing, 16; in South Korea, 58, 86–87; in Sweden, 134–35; in US, 59, 89, *91*, 91–92
churches: ceremonies of, 133; monopolies of, 72; Norway and belonging in, 72–73, *73*; US closings of, 21, 92, 187n2; voting in, 211n92. *See also* Catholic Church
The Churching of America (Stark), 1
Church of Norway, 72–75, *73*, 77
Church of Scotland, 52, 126
Church of Sweden, 136–37
civil ceremonies, 127, 133
classical secularization theory, 30–31
cluster analysis, 67, 160
cognitive scientists, 100
Cold War, 94
communism, 94, 141–42, 144
communities, 124–25
compassion, 121

ABOUT THE AUTHORS

Isabella Kasselstrand is Assistant Professor in the Department of Sociology at the University of Aberdeen. Using quantitative and mixed methods, her publications explore secularization and nonreligion from a cross-national and comparative perspective.

Phil Zuckerman is the author of several books, including *What It Means to be Moral* (Counterpoint, 2019), *The Nonreligious* (Oxford University Press, 2016), *Living the Secular Life* (Penguin, 2014), and *Society Without God* (New York University Press, 2008). He is an Associate Dean as well as Professor of Sociology at Pitzer College, and the founding chair of the nation's first Secular Studies Program.

Ryan T. Cragun is Professor of Sociology at the University of Tampa. His research focuses on the nonreligious and Mormonism and has been published in various scholarly journals. He is also the author of several books.